The Industrialist and the Diva

THE INDUSTRIALIST AND THE DIVA

Alexander Smith Cochran,
Founder of Yale's Elizabethan Club,
and Madame Ganna Walska

WALTER GOFFART

The Elizabethan Club of Yale University
Yale University Press, New Haven and London

Front cover: Constantin Aladjalov, detail of illustration
for cover of *The New Yorker* issued September 25, 1926

Copyedited and indexed by Brian Hotchkiss,
Wordesign Services

Designed and typeset by Rebecca Martz,
Office of the Yale University Printer

Printed by GHP in West Haven, Connecticut

Published by The Elizabethan Club of Yale University

Distributed by Yale University Press
P.O. Box 209040, New Haven, Connecticut 06520-9040
www.yalebooks.com/art

Library of Congress Control Number: 2020939825
ISBN 978-0-300-25548-5

Yale

CONTENTS

To the memory of Howard Spiro (1924–2012)

PREFACE AND ACKNOWLEDGMENTS

The Elizabethan Club has flourished for more than a century with scant memory of its founder, Alexander Smith Cochran. What Club members seemed to know about him when I joined in 2001 was that his fortune came from a carpet factory and that he had a difficult marriage with a Polish singer. The fullest early account of Cochran and the Elizabethan Club is a seven-page article by Richard Selzer, surgeon and novelist, and long an Incorporator of the Club. The article publishes the talk Selzer gave in February 1998 at the first of the annual commemorative dinners that the Club has held since then on or near Cochran's birthday (February 28). Selzer's account, lively and suited to the festive occasion when it was given, discusses selected aspects of Cochran's life, the foundation of the Club and its early financial vicissitudes, and quite a lot about his wife, Ganna Walska—a good beginning inviting development. What has mattered more to Club members than Cochran's life story has been the superb collection of books, notably the Shakespeare quartos and folios from the Huth library, that he gave to Yale University and deposited at the Club at its foundation. The Club library has been written about by several able bibliographers; Alan Bell's introduction to its catalogue is exemplary. Retracing these learned steps is superfluous, but there is room for a fuller study of Cochran's life and that of his wife. I wrote a brief account of Cochran and the foundation of the Club for the Centenary Album of 2011. That sketchy start was enlarged in talks at Club Nights, first about Ganna Walska (March 27, 2014), then about Cochran himself (September 11, 2016). The warm reception these talks received was an incentive to continuation of this project. Now, with the encouragement and financial support of the Club, for which I am deeply grateful, I have expanded the earlier sketches into biographies of the founder and his wife based on wide research.

The marriage of Ganna Walska and Alex Cochran in Paris on September 15, 1920, was not secret, but it was a quiet ceremony, known only to a few. The news did not take long to circulate, however, and it was a confirmed social event when the newlyweds landed in New York on October 9. By then, the nine-year-old Elizabethan Club was well-established. There is no record of when the Club leadership learned of its founder's marriage, but none too soon it decided to celebrate the event with a wedding present. On July 21, 1921, the Club president wrote to Cochran in London: "I have the pleasure to send you, under separate cover, the Elizabethan monogram which members of the Club had made into a [silver] seal for you as a wedding gift" (MSSA, RU36, box 3, folder 156). Alas, the union it meant to celebrate had broken down three months earlier. By April 1921, Cochran thought better of married life; he had left the conjugal Paris home, separating from Walska and pondering divorce. No one knows what became of the Club's gift.

The structure of my book departs from normal form. Because the lives of "the industrialist and the diva" were only briefly intertwined, I have cast each biography as a distinct part, each of which has its own apparatus of notes, appendixes, and bibliography. The narratives overlap only in the period of Cochran's and Walska's marriage. I have told their lives apart from each other, furnishing a context of the worlds in which they and the early Elizabethan Club existed. The birth of the Club is more particularly discussed in appendixes 1.1–1.3.

◆ ◆ ◆

It is the author's happy privilege to acknowledge and thank the many persons who have helped his project.

My first thanks go to the collateral descendants of Alexander Smith Cochran who have given me access to archives documenting his life. Gifford W. Cochran, of Bozeman, Montana, guided me to John Cochran, of Palm Beach, Florida, who possesses the only memorabilia of Alex Cochran's passion for sailing, namely autograph logbooks of six of his yachts. I am very grateful to him for the time he has given me with them and for supplying photographs.

Alex Cochran's sister Anna married Thomas Ewing II and their eldest son Thomas III was Alex Cochran's main heir. The descendants of this Ewing line who have graciously helped my project begin with Alex Cochran Ewing, Chancellor emeritus, University of North Carolina School of the Arts, now deceased, who furnished me with information about Alex Cochran's accomplishments. The richest archival trove—the Ewing Family Archives (EFA)—came to me from Alex Ewing's daughter, Caroline Ewing of New York City, Yale Class of 1987 and an Elizabethan Club member. Her son, Nathan Ewing-Crystal, Yale Class of 2019, served as intermediary and very kindly delivered these archives to me. Caroline has earned my deep gratitude for lending me these precious records for as long as I needed them. The involvement of Alex Cochran's family in my project has been enormously helpful, and I'm grateful to all concerned.

Before Ganna Walska focused her energies on the creation of the magnificent Lotusland garden in Santa Barbara, California, her adventurous life was often traduced in the press. The leaders of the nonprofit Ganna Walska Lotusland, charged with nurturing and promoting Walska's great creation, have taken pains to safeguard their founder's memory. This goal has seemed incompatible with unrestricted opening of the Lotusland archives (GWA) to detached research. Gwen Stauffer, Executive Director of Ganna Walska Lotusland, generously allowed Rose Thomas, Lotusland archivist, to assist me; Rose's kindness has been invaluable. She furnished me with a selection she made from the Lotusland archives, which has served me well. She has also earned my sincere gratitude for providing helpful answers to my questions. The full archives are voluminous; Ganna Walska threw little away. These many papers are worthy of fuller utilization than I have been able to make of them. Among the correspondence kept by Walska, which, with one exception, I have not seen, are autograph letters to her from Alex Cochran. Appendix 2.5 is a tantalizing inventory of the full Walska archives supplied by Rose Thomas. I thank her warmly for all her selfless efforts on my behalf.

Valued assistance has been given to me by my Elizabethan Club fellow members, whose names and titles are followed by a capsule description of their contributions: Basie Bales Gitlin, Director of Development, Yale University Library (the Club's first First Folio); John Stuart Gordon,

Benjamin Attmore Hewitt Associate Curator of American Decorative Arts, Yale University Art Gallery (Walpole Society); Judith Malafronte, Adjunct Lecturer in Music, Jacobs School of Music, Indiana University (advice on singing); Lawrence Manley, William R. Kenan, Jr., Professor of English (the First Folio again); Thomas Murray, Yale University Organist Emeritus (Cochran's and Walska's Rolls Royces); Stephen Parks, former Chairman of the Board of Incorporators and Librarian, Elizabethan Club (financial and other details); Judith Ann Schiff, Chief Research Archivist, Yale University Library (the Yale grading scheme in 1896); William Summers, Professor Emeritus of Therapeutic Radiology, Molecular Biophysics and Biochemistry, and History of Medicine (Walska's divorce from Bernard); David Swensen, Chief Investment Officer, Yale University (the Club endowment); and Anders Winroth, Birgit Baldwin Professor of History Emeritus and former Elizabethan Club Librarian (overall encouragement). I am thankful to all of them for their involvement.

The Yale University Department of History and Faculty of Arts and Sciences kindly named me a Senior Research Scholar when I came to New Haven, opening for me all the enormous research resources of the wonderful University Library, with its helpful staff, that have made this book possible. I owe them a debt of gratitude.

Further help has come to me from several directions: Angel Adeoye, Yale Class of 2020 (Club member); John Carland, Annenberg, Virginia; Beth Flynn, St. Paul's School; Paul Gerard Hackett, Columbia University; Patrick Raftery, Librarian, Westchester County Historical Society; Jeanne Solensky, Winterthur Library (for the Walpole Society); and Melanie Taylor, New Haven (Club member). They have helped fill out my research and earned my sincere thanks.

My special gratitude goes to those persons who have been most closely associated with bringing this manuscript to the light of day: Nadine Honigberg, Senior Administrative Assistant, Elizabethan Club, who amid her manifold activities in holding the Club's head above water found time to choose pictures and obtain permissions and much more; Brian Hotchkiss, my able editor, who inter alia brought order to my haphazard URLs; and Rebecca Martz, manager of the project, whose designing and composing have turned these pages into a thing of beauty.

My wife, Roberta Frank, Marie Boroff Professor of English Emerita, Yale University, and President of the Elizabethan Club at its centennial, sometimes reminds me of how many years I've tried her forbearance with talk of Cochran and Walska. My companion and sustainer for a half century, the part she has had in the creation of *The Industrialist and the Diva* is larger than she thinks.

My dedication commemorates Howard Spiro, a great physician and wise humanist, an exemplary member of the Elizabethan Club, and an unforgettable and beloved human being, whose friendship, too soon interrupted, stands out as a marked reward of my years in New Haven.

Walter Goffart
Professor of History Emeritus, University of Toronto
Senior Research Scholar in History, Yale University
Sometime Vice-President, Elizabethan Club

ABBREVIATIONS

ART   Ganna Walska, *Always Room at the Top* (New York: R.R. Smith, 1943)

Alex; or ASC   Alexander Smith Cochran

EFA   Ewing Family Archives

GWA   Ganna Walska Archives, Lotusland, Santa Barbara

IH   International Harvester Company

LACMA   Los Angeles County Museum of Art

MMA   Metropolitan Museum of Art, New York

MSSA   Yale University Library, Manuscripts and Archives

Parks I   Stephen Parks, ed., *The Elizabethan Club of Yale University, 1911–2011: A Centenary Album* (New Haven: [n.p.], 2011)

Parks II   ———. *The Elizabethan Club of Yale University and Its Library*; introduction by Alan Bell (New Haven: Yale UP, 1986)

Phelps Laudation   "William Lyon Phelps on a Good Rich Man" in *Hartford Courant* (August 4, 1929): F5

TCE   Théâtre des Champs-Élysées, Paris

Troxell I   Gilbert McCoy Troxell, "The Elizabethan Club of Yale University" in *The Papers of the Bibliographical Society of America,* vol. 27, no. 2 (1933): 83–88

Troxell II   ———. "The Elizabethan Club: Its Origin and Its Books" in *Yale University Library Gazette,* vol. 27, no. 1 (July 1952): 19–28

UP   University Press

PART ONE

Fig. 1.1. Yale graduation portrait of Alexander Smith Cochran, 1896.
Yale University Library, Manuscripts and Archives

ALEXANDER SMITH COCHRAN
(1874–1929)

Yale University has a society called the Elizabethan Club, with undergraduate, graduate, and faculty members. The Club, familiarly known as the Lizzie, celebrated its centenary in 2011. Not just another student organization among many, the Club has been said to have "changed the tone and atmosphere of modern Yale more decisively than any other innovation up to the founding of its residential colleges."[1]* The Lizzie gave a home to literary and artistic undergraduates, together with like-minded faculty, balancing the then-prevalent Yale craze for sports. The Club occupies a house in a central campus location, serves tea to its members and guests every afternoon in term, and holds a collection of "some of the most precious of English books."[2] Alexander Smith Cochran, class of 1896 (fig. 1.1), founded the Club. His portrait hangs near the walk-in vault housing the Club's literary treasure, which he presented as a founding gift and anchor along with the clubhouse itself and an endowment.

Cochran, whose established nickname was Alex,[3] envisaged creating an island of civilized discourse in a Yale that he evidently considered philistine. In his senior year (1895–96), he had gathered an eating group, whose members could converse freely on serious matters that interested them. He had a clear idea of the form he wished his club to have, and the Lizzie has not wholly forgotten his wishes. Yet he had an odd relationship with the Club. He collected Shakespearian and other Elizabethan-age rarities for three years, gave them to the Club, later added three purchases, then never again owned a rare book. Once the Club was operating, he had little

---

* Full bibliographic citations are in the Part 1 bibliography. Works are normally cited in the endnotes either by abbreviation (see page 15) or by author's surname and page number.

connection with it. Club leaders wrote to him telling him how successful his creation was, how its members longed to see him, and so forth. He replied politely and supplied the small sums needed to balance its budget, but virtually never visited; "It seems as though I had been there very little. But I think often of it," he wrote.[4] The Lizzie was said to resemble three arts-oriented New York clubs in miniature—the Century, Grolier, and Players Clubs—but none of them was among the 13 clubs of which Alex was a member. He seems to have created the Elizabethan Club, then moved on. It is generally known by the Club's members that Alex's fortune came from a carpet company in Yonkers, New York, and that he had had a short, expensive marriage to a Polish opera singer; but his "limited and sporadic" relationship to rare books and to the Club after its foundation has been little noticed. Alex's inspiration for collecting books and creating the Club is explored in Appendix 1.1. His life and how the Elizabethan Club fit into it deserve a closer look.

I

Alex's adult life was overhung by the sad fact of his having pulmonary tuberculosis. Sufferers of this affliction at the time often sought to conceal it because tuberculosis generally was "reckoned to be a 'socially shaming' disease associated with poverty and alcoholism." Many friends and acquaintances were unaware of his condition, even at his death.[5] Alex's illness was diagnosed in 1902, on the morrow of his years of working on the floor of the carpet factory, a setting that provided occasion for infection by this highly contagious disease. After he rested for a year at the family farm, his case went into remission, and he returned to the company's presidency, but he was not cured. He traveled in California with his mother for his health in the winter of 1908. In 1910 Alex resigned from the presidency on account of his disease, naming his brother Gifford his successor. After he had sailed his schooner *Westward* in a particularly strenuous (and victorious) racing season, doctors again sent him to California to recover. The next year, just when the Elizabethan Club was being created, Alex spent weeks at a sanitorium near Vienna.[6]

His disease had periods of calm, however. For example, he was well enough in 1915 to attend a military preparedness camp for one month and, in 1920, to marry. Contrary to the then-usual prescription of prolonged rest, Alex sought health through travel and open-air sports, such as riding and yachting, more often than by medical means. In both 1918 and 1924, Alex made extended sojourns in Colorado, and he also tried the benefits of the French Riviera and of prolonged sea cruises. In a life that could be envisaged as a continual quest for escape from the death sentence shadowing him, unfortunately little of the record of his temporary respites and relapses remains.

Against his doctors' counsel, Alex remained a heavy smoker all his life, except for a year of attempted abstinence. He enjoyed repeated periods of relief from his illness, and his ex-wife claimed, truthfully I think, that she was unaware of his condition. But these remissions could not recur indefinitely. Health forced him to curtail his very congenial service in the British Navy in 1917. Already at an advanced stage of infirmity by 1927, by which time he was unable to walk the length of his great sailboat *Vira* without being overcome by coughing, he died in 1929, age 55, after wintering in California.[7] Although battling tuberculosis must have been central to his existence, little of this struggle is knowable.

II

Alex was born into a rich and locally very prominent family. His maternal grandfather, Alexander Smith, built an outstandingly successful carpet industry in Yonkers. Helping him was Halcyon Skinner, a Yankee mechanical genius who continually improved carpetmaking machinery and oversaw the expansion of the plant, several times doubling the capacity of its machines. "The carpet weaving industry was revolutionized by looms invented in this plant by [Smith and Skinner]."[8] The business expanded dramatically. "Legend has it that the Smith carpet mill kept a steamship docked at Ellis Island to whisk newly arrived immigrants up the Hudson River into company-owned housing and to work the next day."[9] In the early decades of the twentieth century, Smith Carpets was considered to be the

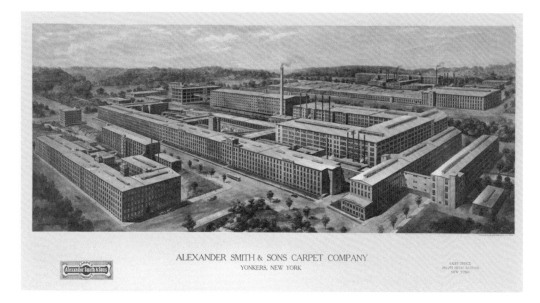

ALEXANDER SMITH & SONS CARPET COMPANY
YONKERS, NEW YORK

Fig. 1.2. At its widest, the Yonkers factory of Alexander Smith
and Sons Carpet Company occupied 19 buildings on 38 acres.
Courtesy of the Kheel Center, Cornell University

largest carpet factory in the world (fig. 1.2), employing more than 7,000
workers. A statistic from 1925 may, with allowances, give an impression of
the size of the enterprise:

> In the mills there are approximately fifteen hundred power
> looms, with a daily production of ninety thousand yards of carpet,
> made up in thirty-six different fabrics and in one hundred and
> twenty-one different sizes, which if laid flat at an average width of
> twenty-seven inches, would be fifty-one miles long.[10]

Smith carpets even found their way into the palace of the czar of Russia in
St. Petersburg.

Alexander Smith's factory and fortune passed to his two children, a son
named Warren (d. 1903) and a daughter, Eva (d. 1909; fig. 1.3), who married
William Francis Cochran (d. 1901). Eva and William, Alex's parents, had
six children, three boys and three girls. After the founder's death in 1878,

Fig. 1.3. Eva Smith Cochran, Alex's mother. Eva and her unmarried brother, Warren, were the heirs of Alexander Smith, founder of the Smith Carpet Company. She was known widely for her generosity. Her eldest son Alex's last major philanthropy—to the new Preacher's College in Washington, D.C.—was made in Eva's memory. Alex inherited both the carpet company and Warren Smith's fortune. Courtesy of Caroline Ewing

Warren Smith and William Cochran ably guided Smith Carpets for many years. "[T]he industry had gone on steadily advancing, growing as the city grew around it, dominant now in the world of carpet manufacturing."[11] Warren retired in 1894 and William three years later.[12]

From their roots in Yonkers, the children rose to a social rank commensurate with the family's fortune. All three sons prepared for college at St. Paul's School and went to Yale. The family had a house at a good address in New York City, and in 1894 the eldest daughter made a socially creditable marriage to a New York lawyer and Yonkers resident.[13] The children were well provided for in their parents' wills, each one becoming a millionaire through bequests. Alex, who shared his grandfather's name, was the eldest son and principal heir, destined to own and head the mill. He became president of Smith Carpets in 1902.

Alex was the first of his family on either side to go to college, and he did not shine at Yale academically, graduating with grades just above failing. Almost the only information in general circulation about his Yale years comes from William Phelps's "laudation" written at the time of Alex's death, and it centers on his rare book collection and the foundation of the Elizabethan Club. (It is discussed exhaustively in Appendix 1.1) Independent information is scarce and may, in fact, be limited to the following newspaper column published after Alex's death by an anonymous contemporary:

> The writer … was a poor student at Yale…. I was one of the waiters in the Yale Dining Hall and later in York Hall. So, I learned to know and admire Mr. Cochran as one of the most sincere, whole-souled and democratic men. He was one of the best sports imaginable. Much as he desired to "make" the Yale eleven, he never got much beyond the scrubs. But he played hard and took his medicine year after year, not even complaining of hard knocks when he arrived in the dining hall….
>
> He was one of the most generous, sensible and modest of all Yale's loyal supporters. [After graduation] his yacht [*Alvina*] was so frequently at the disposal of the Yale eleven, Yale nine, and Yale crew. Many the good sail, lunch and dinner Yale athletes have had through the generous ways of Alexander Smith Cochran.

[His class (1896) was famous for its gifts to Yale]; one of the best givers was the gentleman from Yonkers whom all Yale loves so much.[14]

Alex was called to the Wolf's Head secret society, and he belonged to two fraternities.[15] Sports at St. Paul's seems to have had a greater impact on him than book learning; or he may have thought that his course of study at Yale would have little relevance to his destined position as head of Smith Carpets. As intimated by the waiter-observer, he already had the sensitivity to the less privileged that led him to do well by the mill hands and to decree that the Elizabethan Club was to have no dues. Although surely well funded by his parents when at Yale, he was not then a millionaire. The family deaths that would give him a place among America's very rich men occurred well after his graduation. When he inherited from his uncle (1903) and acquired his first yacht, the good-sized steam vessel *Alvina* (1906), he shared it with Yale athletes, whom he entertained on board.

Described as being "medium height [5 foot 11 inches according to his 1914 passport], slender, strong featured with a touch of sadness in his face," he was said to share his mother's "dominant personality" and his father's quick temper. He was only superficially "shy, reserved and reticent.... He was ...intense, remarkably informed, searching."[16] His commanding role in the family business was unambiguous.

After graduating from Yale in 1896, he went at once into the family's factory and began to learn how Smith carpets were made and sold. He spent five years as an apprentice. "[A] vast plant ... was already in existence.... Acres of machinery, wools drawn from every corner of the globe, carpets and rugs sent to every quarter."[17] Alex immediately plunged into this activity.

[He] wasn't afraid to get his face or hands dirty. He pitched into the wool and learned how to spin it, to dye it, and to weave the fabric. He was popular with the workers, and his democratic demeanor inspired their confidence. He learned something from all of them. He learned all about carpets, and [after his years of apprenticeship] there wasn't a better carpet manufacturing expert in the country.[18]

He also needed a thorough introduction to the front office, which he
obtained through the guidance of executives long in the company's service
(his uncle and father having both bowed out). The company's accounting,
purchasing, and personnel were the main subjects of study. The long years
of learning demanded much of him: "his slenderness was becoming accen-
tuated, a slight sag was developing in his shoulders." His tuberculosis was
about to manifest itself. "He was moody, at times autocratic, with a hard
nugget of strength that derived from his certainty of purpose."[19]

It was a principle of Smith Carpets' management that, in the absence
of direction by a blood relative, executives who had risen from the factory
floor to positions in the front office took over for as long as needed, carrying
on the established ways. The exclusion of new blood, which continued
while Alex was a force in the company, could be a bar to new ideas and
processes. "[Alex] had come to know his men.... He was still 'shy, reserved
and reticent', but this was only the outside shell. Within the shell was a
strong, authoritarian leader, firm with himself, firm with everyone about
him—his younger brothers, the workers at the Mills, the executives."[20]
The Mills followed a long-held and unshakable directive that continued
to be honored throughout the Alexander Smith Cochran years: "Keep the
machines at full speed! At full speed! Never let them slack off! Fill the store-
houses with the rugs and carpets. Pile them high; then auction them off [at]
the big sales held ... in New York City."[21]

Alex's initiation into the company's management took place mainly
among up-from-the-ranks executives. He lived at Duncraggan (fig. 1.4), the
beautifully situated Cochran home in Yonkers, and went daily to the Mills.
In 1902, now well versed in the business, Alex became president of the firm
(fig. 1.5). His uncle, Warren Smith, died the year after in Tunisia, to which
Alex traveled to retrieve his body and bring it back to Yonkers. Warren's
death made Alex owner of Smith Carpets, which he would remain until
1919, and the heir to an enviable fortune—about $35 million (more than
$945 million in 2018). Colossal fortunes, such as that of Andrew Carnegie,
eclipsed Alex's, but there were few enough of these for Alex to stand high on
a list of rich Americans.[22]

"DUNCRAGGAN."
RESIDENCE OF WM. F. COCHRAN,
YONKERS, N. Y.

Fig. 1.4. Magnificently situated overlooking the Hudson and beautifully landscaped, Duncraggan, the family's Yonkers homestead, was built by Willian Cochran for his wife, Eva. He loved its gardens, but she preferred their New York City residence. The building was demolished when sold, and the property is now part of Yonkers's Untermyer Park. Courtesy of the Westchester Historical Society

Fig. 1.5. Cochran as the young industrialist, ca. 1905, a few years before he founded the Elizabethan Club (1911). This was about the time when he first was diagnosed with tuberculosis. Courtesy of Caroline Ewing

While president, Alex made two far-reaching changes. One had to do with the distribution of the firm's output, which till then had been handled by the New York City firm of W. and J. Sloane. In 1902, Alex withdrew from this arrangement and replaced it with periodic auctions of accumulated carpets in New York. (Years later, he reverted the company's distribution to Sloane.)[23]

The second of his initiatives was in labor policy. He lopped one hour off the working day, made the summer-Saturday half-holiday effective throughout the year, and built a large cafeteria that served meals at cost. Alex also eliminated the two-week post-injury delay for workmen's compensation to start and established a pension system.

> None of these measures was instituted because of workers' pressure. The interest of Mr. Cochran in the employees at the mill began soon after his entrance into work at the plant, and the close association he maintained at all times with the employees was the result of long hours spent in conversation with them at their daily tasks.[24]

What was instituted was, in essence, "a bonus [i.e., profit-sharing] system which nets each man, woman and child [!] who has been a worker there for one year or more a share of the profits distributed every six months."[25] The scheme was foreshadowed by the practice of the second generation of Smith Carpets owners, whose members arranged in their wills to distribute $1,000 to each 20-year employee; Alex followed this custom as well. With equal benevolence, at the end of his victorious sailing season of 1910, Alex added up all the expenses he incurred in this sport, including those of his three-month holiday, and distributed an equal sum among the members of his workforce.[26] From the start of profit sharing in 1911—with the enlargement of the plant and work force—until 1925, $5,308,000 were paid out.[27]

> His labor policy ... would be one of the brightest spots in the history of the mill: a plan whereby the extension of the [Smith-Cochran] clan, as represented by the mill-hands, would profit from the huge proceeds of the business: shares of profits being built on

the principle of long service in the mills: family loyalty rewarded by family loyalty: father to children … high wages; high bonuses: hard work.[28]

These generous measures were not philanthropy. Smith Carpets had weathered a multi-month strike in the 1880s, which the management at the time—Warren Smith and William Cochran—had met with a lockout. The striking workers suffered much. It would be prudent to avert a repeat of this damaging struggle: "[Alex] has his own idea of what's really good for his 'industrial army'…. Labor unions aren't. He is not much in favor of unions."[29] In 1925, a journalist observed that "the employees have no organization among themselves, but there is a strong tie between them and the company."[30] Smith Carpets enjoyed labor peace throughout the Alexander Cochran years. Its workers as well as the citizens of Yonkers applauded the generosity of the whole Cochran family, father and mother as well as Alex, and mourned his passing.

The start of Alex's presidency was marked by his first tubercular crisis. A relapse in 1910 caused doctors to call a halt to his yachting and send him to winter in California. This coincided with his resignation from the presidency and the naming of his brother Gifford as his successor. (Gifford was president for only three years.) Alex remained owner of the firm until after the World War, when he distributed his shares among one brother, ten nephews, and his classmate, lawyer, and friend Maitland Griggs. These measures mask his uninterrupted relationship to Smith Carpets.[31] Mainly resident outside Yonkers and often abroad, Alex nevertheless kept control of the firm "by periodic descents, swift orders to the able personnel he had built up below him. The Mills seemed not to be suffering from this absentee ownership."[32] According to the Yale *'96 Half-way Book,* published in 1915, Alex was "still the real boss." However long he was absent and otherwise occupied, and regardless of the pro tempore officers, Alex continued to be the boss to his last years.

Alex was intimate with Robert P. Perkins (1862–1924), who, since 1901, had been president of the Bigelow-Hartford Carpet Company, Smith Carpets' chief competitor and its rival for title of largest carpetmaker in the world. (If nowhere else, Alex and Perkins may have come to know each other in New York clubs.) According to Alex's wife, they were inseparable. Perkins was often on Alex's sailboats and acquired the steam yacht *Mohican* from him when Alex moved on to the much larger *Warrior*. As far back as the previous century, their companies' competition had not precluded mutual support, but there is no information about how the close friendship of Alex and Perkins affected their business lives.[33]

During the First World War, Smith Carpets took on the simpler task of weaving blankets, tent cloth, and duck for uniforms. After the war's end, the factory was reconverted to making carpets again. Although some thought the established ways of the company needed shaking up, "the boss" did not share that opinion.

> Alexander Cochran [whom the war had aged] might be ill, ... restless and uneasy, but when he descended upon the Mills in one of his unannounced visits, it was as though the whirlwind had arrived.... Fifteen minutes after his arrival in the plant the remotest department was aware of his presence.... People were still afraid of him, and in his quick conferences with his executives, his true strength was manifest; the shrewd, expert manufacturer, the wise autocrat....
>
> For weeks after one of these descents the Mills would be in a whirl, adapting itself to the changes he had decreed. Between his visits things went slack. The tendency had grown up among those in responsible posts to postpone action and decision until the Mill Master returned, lest they find themselves suddenly reversed and reprimanded.[34]

A spirit of improvement was lacking. Thomas Ewing III, Alex's nephew and heir and eventually vice president of the firm, loyally remained a true believer. In his opinion, Alex was "a titan in his time who had the keenest mind, the highest standards, and the most generous spirit of any man [Thomas] had ever encountered."[35] Alex continued to be much appreciated:

The dynamic, intellectual, generous, dominating, reserved genius ...
swooping down on his executives with brilliant decisive plans,
turning the Mill world upside down with his suddenness, but
leaving behind him, when he dashed off to some new quarter of
the globe, the foundation for a new mechanism certain to carry the
organization on to new records, the works to new planes of loyalty
and contentment.[36]

Tom's brother Bill, who had been taken into the firm, ventured limited
suggestions for improvements; Alex rejected them, and Bill left.[37] In the
1920s, while orders for Smith carpets remained strong, no provisions were
made for renewal of the machines or for investigating new processes, and
the gloomy business offices exuded Victorian mustiness. As the decade
progressed, deterioration at the Mills became so pronounced that even
Alex grew worried. He was mostly away, however, nursing his health. The
plant labored "more than ever under the immobility deriving from absentee
ownership."[38] But not even far-sighted and energetic management could
have averted the catastrophic reversal experienced by the company in scant
months after Alex's death in June 1929.

The Great Depression swept away all of Alex's benefactions to his
labor force that had marked the start of his presidency in 1902. Within
months of the stock market crash, the effects of the crisis were felt at Smith
Carpets. About 4,500 workers were laid off, and the 3,000 who remained
suffered first a 10-percent pay cut in the spring of 1930, followed less than
a year later by a second, equal cut. Work was only part time, alternating
three- and four-day weeks. Thomas Ewing III, who became president soon
after Alex's death, died unexpectedly in 1933, although his passing did no
further damage to the by then much-diminished company. Still, Smith
Carpets remained in operation, and even made improvements. When
the English poet laureate John Masefield, who had worked in the Smith
factory as a teenager, returned for a visit in the 1930s, he reported finding
new machinery and great enhancements, saying "the system was changed
beyond belief."[39]

Nevertheless, only the Second World War brought prosperity back
to Smith Carpets, as it did for many other businesses in America. Once

enlisted in the war effort, the huge Yonkers plant ran 24 hours a day with 7,000 workers pouring out vast quantities of army blankets and canvas tents.[40] The old motto, "Keep the machines at full speed!" could apply again. There were prosperous days on the home front, and the firm remained lucrative until 1948, when it began to suffer heavy losses, tried to modernize its outdated plant, then experienced labor strikes in 1952 and 1954. Discharging 5,000 hands, it moved to Greenville, Mississippi, and almost immediately vanished in a merger with Mohawk Carpets. Four years later, shedding the Smith name and taken into "Mohasco," what was left of the company relocated to Mexico. The vast old factory in Yonkers—19 buildings on 38 acres—is now a historic district. Part was converted to artists' studios and workshops; a major fire on January 30, 2017, was limited, fortunately, to a corner of the sprawling plant.[41]

III

In the years Alex directly headed Smith Carpets, he did not chain himself to his desk. From early on, he assumed the role of a New York socialite and sportsman, which he played full-time after he withdrew from the company's presidency. He joined 13 clubs, all but one in New York, and had a part in organizing the Brook Club in 1903. He was among the many millionaires who founded the luckless New Theater.[42] He acquired a twin-screw steam yacht, the *Alvina,* in 1906, aboard which he took classmates to the tenth reunion of Yale's class of 1896 and a small group to Europe. He traveled to the Ottoman Empire and Persia in 1907 with a professor friend and, on another occasion, to Belgium on a carpet fact-finding mission. The next year, in England, he was introduced to fox hunting, which he loved and decided to make an annual pursuit whenever possible. This was also when his collecting of Elizabethan drama began.[43] The next year, in New York, he came by the sailboat *Avenger* and had success in racing it.[44] The alternation between horses and yachts, for both of which Alex had early training, was dominant in his life and became affirmed while he was president of Smith Carpets. His siblings followed suit. Brother William, a self-styled socialist who relocated to Baltimore, also loved horses and yachting, while Gifford became a full-time, successful turfman, with two wins each by horses of his in the Kentucky Derby and the Preakness.[45]

Alex's foremost occupation outside Smith Carpets was philanthropy, in which the Elizabethan Club held a comparatively modest place. What he did for his employees has been told in connection with his presidency. His generosity to Yonkers can only be mentioned selectively. Alex's parents had set a model for this beneficence, and he followed their example. William Francis Cochran's fame was specially attached to the establishment of a workingmen's club, the Hollywood Inn, which included a library, gymnasium, and meeting rooms, all housed in a handsome, purpose-built clubhouse, with playing field adjacent. Alex would become president of this generously conceived "saloon substitute for working men." Quaint to our ears, William even financed a drinking fountain in a Yonkers public square, the city's first.[46] Alex's mother, Eva, continued to foster her husband's Hollywood Inn, and she rescued Yonkers' oldest historical monument, Philipse Manor Hall, from neglect and decay. (Later, Alex applied $50,000 to its restoration.) Many of Eva's gifts were to the Episcopalian Church, whose foreign missions she often financed. She alone built the church of St. Andrew's parish, which was entrusted to the family friend Rev. James Freeman; she also provided him with a wooden church at the Cochran-Ewing summer place in Maine. Her benevolence did not omit hospitals, and she took an interest in the city's African Americans. At her death, Eva Cochran was remembered glowingly and credited with no less than $2 million in benefactions to the city and Smith Carpets' factory hands.[47]

With this awe-inspiring background, Alex exceeded his parents' generosity, as his practice leads us to expect. At his death, the *Yonkers Herald* listed numerous recipients of his liberality.[48] Many gifts continued support for organizations his parents had fostered, such as the Hollywood Inn, Episcopalian churches and chapels, a school for nurses, several hospitals, and a cemetery's upkeep. An orphans' home received a lump sum from him and an annual subscription. He gave $250,000 to found the Sprain Ridge Hospital for tubercular patients and also provided the city with land for another such facility. His funding was used to enlarge two other local hospitals, to one of which he left $500,000 in his will. He was president of Hollywood Inn, to which he is recorded as giving $120,000. He also encouraged newer organizations. The YMCA received $25,000, and the YWCA was given $56,000 for its building fund; $5,000 went to the Masonic Temple and $10,000 to the Knights of Columbus building fund. The head of the Jewish Community Center, "of which Mr. Cochran was an ardent supporter," praised him for giving the center $10,000. Upon Alex's death, the Chamber of Commerce said: "The city of Yonkers has sustained an irreparable loss. Throughout his life Alexander Smith Cochran was ever a benefactor of our city. No sculptured monument or tablet of bronze will be necessary to keep alive his memory." Much of his generosity was anonymous, as his mother's had been.[49] As the mayor of Yonkers declared, "He has left his mark on every public institution in the city. His charitable gifts were … without regard to creed or race. No worthy cause but had his support."[50] The employees of Smith Carpets and the citizens of Yonkers applauded Cochran's open-handedness and mourned his passing.

Outside Yonkers, Alex's costliest gift came near the end of his life, when his health was failing. Rev. James Freeman, the Cochran family friend, now the Episcopalian bishop of Washington, D.C., spoke to Alex about the College of Preachers, an institution for adult education that Freeman had established alongside the National Cathedral. Alex undertook to finance a building for the college in honor of his mother and to provide a suitable endowment. The price tag was $1.45 million.[51]

Although no other institutional benefaction of Alex's came close to this sum, his outlays for the First World War may have amounted to more. Early in the war Alex, an Anglophile and ardent ally supporter, distributed £130,000 among the English, French, and Belgian Red Crosses and added large sums for a fully equipped, 15-car hospital train and for two military hospitals in London. Not all his "princely gifts" were noncombatant.[52] He furnished the British Navy with six scout boats whose design anticipated the PT boats of World War II. They were built by the Lawley firm of Neponset, Massachusetts, which had launched several of Alex's yachts. Half a dozen 60-foot-long fighting motorboats could not have come cheap. King George V sent Alex a letter of thanks, which he treasured.[53] Not forgetting the Belgians, Alex spent $1 million for food to avert the famine threatening them owing to ruthless German requisitions.[54]

Fig. 1.6. This print by Theodore Diedricksen from 1920 shows the Elizabethan Club of Yale University. The Lizzie was founded in 1911, one year after Alex's sailing victories aboard *Westward.* Cochran bought the property and house to give to the Club's Corporation. He also paid for its thoroughgoing renovation by a New York architect. Yale University Library, Manuscripts and Archives

Alex's other sizable gifts, while more moderate, added up. In his will he left St. Paul's, his prep school, $250,000. To found the Elizabethan Club, Alex provided an endowment of $100,000, and was believed to have given another $75,000 for a clubhouse and its refurbishment. Further gifts from Alex to the Lizzie were its bank-sized vault and the structural alterations needed to install it at a cost of $25,000.[55] No precise estimate exists for the value of the superb collection of books Alex presented to anchor his Club, "the fruits of his brief excursion into the world of rare books."[56] The most precious component of this library—its Shakespeare quartos and folios from the Henry Huth library—cost £36,000 (about $180,000 at the time). The balance of the library, about 100 volumes in all, centering on works by Elizabethan-age playwrights, may have been bought for less. The monetary cost of the endowment, clubhouse, furnishings, vault, and books combined bring Alex's gift of the Elizabethan Club to Yale (fig. 1.6) to somewhat more than a half-million dollars. As a donor to his alma mater, he broke no records, but it is unarguable that his establishment became a transformative addition to Yale College, markedly affecting its "tone and atmosphere." His contributions to the college were not wholly confined to the Lizzie. Monetary gifts from the class of 1896, as noted above, were considered particularly generous, and Alex, although unnamed, was credited with having a large part in this result.

Almost from the first, the Elizabethan Club's endowment proved inadequate for its expenses, and Alex made up the small sums needed to balance its accounts. He never carried out an expressed wish to increase the endowment, and neither the Lizzie nor Yale was included in his will. In the time after his foundation, his interests moved elsewhere; in 1921, his friend and early Club member Maitland Griggs reported to the Club officers that Alex had lost interest in the Lizzie, believing that his gift was unappreciated.[57] To some extent Alex soon shed this gloomy thought and sent friendly letters, but without subsidy. Even without further support from the founder, the leadership at the Lizzie made ends meet, and the Club has endured and prospered, unlike the much costlier College of Preachers at Washington Cathedral, which folded in 2009.[58]

Alex's generosity did not end there. In 1913, to commemorate a voyage he had made to the Ottoman Empire and Persia in 1907, he gave the Metropolitan Museum of Art in New York a collection of fine Persian manuscripts that had been catalogued by his friend A. V. Williams Jackson, a professor at Columbia University with whom Alex had traveled.[59] The museum's website includes pictures of all of Alex's varied gifts.[60] Still another benefaction with cultural content comprised 60 portraits, half of U.S. presidents and the balance of other great Americans, lent to Philipse Manor Hall, the Cochran-patronized historic mansion in Yonkers. Philipse Hall is now a New York State Historic Site, and Alex's portrait collection continues to be noted as a major tourist attraction in that city.[61] The loan became a bequest valued at nearly half a million dollars.

Concerning the founding of the Elizabethan Club, the secretary of the Yale class of 1896 wrote: "This is the sort of thing Cochran gets real pleasure out of. He doesn't enjoy just giving money to carry out other people's ideas. What he likes is working on one of his own."[62] Two other benefactions that he may have conceived were the portrait collection for Philipse Hall and the six motorboats for the Royal Navy. He constantly received appeals for contributions, and he made myriad gifts large and small, most of them anonymous and unrecorded. Year after year the Metropolitan Museum of Art listed him among its benefactors. During his life, St. Paul's School thanked him for donations to its annual fund. He was said to have contributed much to American polo, but typically the only such gift definitely attributable to Alex is a playing field named after him at the Meadowbrook Club. A scattering of recorded examples of his small-scale bounty remain. For example, the founder of the English Speaking Union (E.S.U.) frequently received checks for £1,000. Alex could claim to be the organization's cofounder, and he enthusiastically approved of its program. Columbia University received $2,500 and another $1,000 on another occasion. $5,000 went to a Red Cross disaster fund and £5,000 toward the restoration of Nelson's flagship *Victory*.[63] It is likely that many hundred more gifts of this kind were made throughout his life. Bishop Freeman, who had been pastor of St. Andrew's parish in Yonkers for 10 years, wrote: "As the privileged dispenser from time to time of many of his benefactions I was under obligation to reveal to no one the source of the gift."[64]

IV

Philanthropy aside, how did Alex dispose of his riches? From time to time, reporters speculated that his fortune must have grown very much from what had come to him in 1903. Amounts of $80 or $100 million or even more were conjectured. The reality was different. Alex left his main heir little more than one-quarter of what he himself had inherited. A few months after his death, the stock market crash of 1929 quickly led to further shrinkage by 1933, when Thomas Ewing III, his nephew and principal heir, died tragically young.[65] This decrease can be explained only in part by Alex's philanthropy. Still less may it be attributed to reckless spending for pleasures, let alone to gambling.

Despite leading an irreproachable life, Alex ran through a lot of money. He spent as though his resources were limitless, accumulating and shedding houses, horses, and yachts. He shouldered heavy and not clearly necessary expenses, such as the underwriting of an America's Cup trial boat without the help of a syndicate, acquiring five additional ranches to expand his already huge Colorado estate, and maintaining 13 club memberships. When he gave up playing polo, the sale of his ponies was "probably the largest of its kind." He planned to build the tallest apartment building in New York at its time.[66] He accumulated houses, most of which he did not occupy. There were two apartments in London, a town house in Paris, and a hotel apartment in Monte Carlo. He had a cottage at Sorrento, Maine (Bar Harbor), another at Newport, Rhode Island, as well as a fox hunting property with a small house in Aiken, South Carolina, and another in North Carolina. Fox hunting in the English Midlands occasioned the immediate purchase of a lodge. Uninterested in the Scottish-style castle that went with his 8,000 acres in Colorado Springs, he built an imposing "cottage" that he virtually never saw. He died in Saranac Lake, New York, the tuberculosis refuge in the Adirondacks, where he had "one of the largest and finest private homes." For what was to be his last winter, he bought a house with a noteworthy garden in Redlands, California.[67] In 1916, at the height of his enthusiasm for polo, he acquired the superb Long Island estate called Brookholt, which adjoined the Meadowbrook Polo Club. Hunters, polo ponies, thoroughbreds, and western mounts passed through his stables. He had a pack of hounds, and purebred cattle stocked his Westchester farm. In his few months of participation in thoroughbred racing, he acquired a pricey stallion that soon went, with the rest of his racing mounts and paraphernalia, to Gifford, his able-turfman brother.[68] Alex briefly owned a Wright biplane, and kept more than a dozen motor cars. He was one of the earliest American buyers of Rolls Royce automobiles (he bought 11), and his choice of Rolls models, tourers rather than limousines, shows him to have been an active motorist.[69]

Houses aside, yachting made the largest calls on his fortune. Over time he owned at least 11 power and sailing vessels, all of which had to be maintained and manned. An accident to one of his yachts cost $100,000 in repairs. The steamers tended to be second-hand, but almost all the sailboats were built to his order. This was the case with the wonderful *Westward* (fig. 1.7), the largest schooner ever launched by the famous Herreshoff shipyard; it marked the zenith of Cochran's racing career and had a long life after he sold it.[70] Also bespoke were *Vanitie,* his bronze-hulled America's Cup contender, "one of the most costly racing yachts ever built";[71] *Dolly Bowen,* a 40-foot racer; *Restless,* a bespoke steamer; and *Vira,* a stunning, record-size wooden sailboat. His most expensive order, also of record size, was the ocean-going auxiliary schooner *Sea Call,* with the largest gasoline engine yet built and, as an experiment, its entire steel hull sheathed in Monel, a new, very costly nickel-copper alloy. "[N]o expense [was] too great for the *Sea Call* and thus when completed she will be the very finest of the American yachting fleet."[72] Soon after its launching, *Sea Call*'s metal hull was infected by electrolytic corrosion, so that it had to be scrapped within six weeks of being commissioned by the builder, taking with it "a small fortune." Undaunted, Alex immediately ordered the *Dolly Bowen* and soon bought the huge ex-Vanderbilt oceangoing steam yacht *Warrior.* Alex acquired in 1924 the 40-foot racing yacht *Iris,* which he apparently never used, perhaps because of his deteriorating health. His coffers must have been replenished often with dividends from Smith Carpets, but spending on this lavish scale was a way to shrink one's fortune.[73]

As the amount of his outlays suggests, Alex's active participation in sports was so central a part of his life that it deserves special attention. The

Fig. 1.7. Alex ordered *Westward* from the famed Herreshoff
shipyard. This painting, Westward *in Full Sail,* is by Montague
Dawson RMSA, FRSA (1890–1973), a renowned marine artist.
It belongs to John Cochran. Courtesy of John Cochran

enthusiasm for fox hunting that he gained in England in 1908 was nursed annually, when possible, in South Carolina, France, or England. His Baltimore nephew (and namesake) suggests that Alex spent "most of his adult life hunting in England and the Carolinas"—certainly an exaggeration. The sport's drastic curtailment in England at the outbreak of the First World War interrupted this agreeable activity.[74] Polo attracted him intermittently, occasioning large purchases of ponies and equipment, and he was praised for his playing.[75] He spent two expensive years racing thoroughbreds, but apparently had scant success.

Sailing occupied Alex most. Having competed with success in his first sailboat, *Avenger* (1909), he longed for something bigger and ordered the racing schooner that would be the largest then afloat, the *Westward* (1910). Alex sailed it to England, then to the Kiel Regatta to compete against the German yachting fleet, graced by the participation of Kaiser Wilhelm II (who had Alex to dinner). Alex never captained his own yachts, so to command *Westward* in its European campaign, he engaged Charles Barr, his friend from *Avenger* days, who already was famed as the most skilled of racing skippers and winner of three America's Cup defenses[76] (fig. 1.8). With Barr at the helm, *Westward* won all but one of its 11 races in Germany and England, an extraordinary record. Alex never again had the good fortune he did in the 1910 season. Barr died of a heart attack in January 1911 at the age of 56. When *Westward* raced that year in American waters it disappointed, and Alex, who believed that "things would never be the same again aboard [*Westward*] now that Charlie had gone," sold the craft to a German consortium. (In 1924, it was acquired by a self-made millionaire from the island of Jersey, who raced it with great success for many years.)[77]

The bronze-hulled sloop *Vanitie,* very costly for its time, was Alex's next major order. It was destined for the defense of the America's Cup in 1914, racing *Resolute* for the right to meet the English challenger. Alex's undertaking payment for the whole defense himself marked the first time this had been done since 1887. *Vanitie* out-sailed *Resolute* in the trials, but, when handicaps were taken into account, the victory went to *Resolute.* The outbreak of war in Europe cut short the competition.[78] The next year, Alex had to endure the calamity of *Sea Call,* the biggest schooner yacht in the

Fig. 1.8. Cochran (left) at the helm of *Westward* with Charles Barr, his racing skipper. The zenith of Alex's competitive yachting was the racing season of 1910, when Barr captained *Westward* at a regatta off Kiel, Germany. Alex was unable to repeat this success in U.S. waters after Barr's untimely death, and he sold *Westward* to a German consortium. Courtesy Gifford W. Cochran

world, for which he had spared no expense and had planned a global cruise. In 1919, after the war's end, when the America's Cup series began again, *Vanitie* and *Resolute* came out of storage and resumed their rivalry. Alex's boat did not win, but it enjoyed a succès d'estime in some yachting circles.[79] (In other hands, *Vanitie* later had a happy life racing in New York waters.) Alex was deeply disappointed by *Vanitie*'s loss to *Resolute,* about which he soon after unburdened himself to the beautiful Polish singer whom he was courting aboard the liner taking them to Europe. In 1916 and 1924 he acquired 40-foot vessels and won a race with the first of them, *Dolly Bowen.* The boat was named after his niece who had christened *Vanitie* when she was six years old. But a taste for yachting in this class never wholly seized him.[80] The last sailing vessel ordered by Alex was *Vira,* the breathtaking, long-lived three-masted schooner, the world's largest wooden sailing craft, whose unhappy time in his possession will presently be told.

V

Alex's First World War blew hot and cold, then hot again when he was made an officer of the British Navy, until his health forced him back reluctantly to civilian life. At the war's outbreak in August 1914, Alex was much involved in racing *Vanitie.* Then the war suspended the America's Cup challenge. Since at the outset only a short conflict was foreseen, Alex could anticipate a second try against *Resolute.*[81] For an Anglophile of his stamp, England's participation had a pronounced effect. He poured a very large sum of money, perhaps as much as $650,000, into the Red Cross in England, France, and Belgium and, in addition, gave the large gifts detailed above to hospitals. Alex also set in motion a military present for Britain—six powerful motorboats for the Royal Navy. The letter of thanks from King George V was posted in the chart room of Alex's steam yacht *Warrior.* The total cost for all these gifts might easily have exceeded $1 million, and there was another million in food charity for Belgium. It would not be surprising if Alex's various war contributions added up to the largest philanthropic expenditure of his life outside the city of Yonkers.

Offerings of this kind and size from a private foreigner were extraordinary, but Alex did not stop there. In November 1914, he shipped out with his most powerful car and a chauffeur aboard the Cunard liner *Orduna* to take part personally in the action. This departure of an ostensibly neutral American multimillionaire for the war zone caused a sensation. Before leaving, he spoke to the press about what he hoped to do. The November 19 issue of the *New York Times* reported that he meant "to aid war sufferers personally"; the *New York Tribune* added that Alex, who had studied the carpet industry in Brussels, was on his way to do relief work among the "homeless thousands in Belgium." The account of Alex's departure in the *Baltimore Sun* the next day sounds less neutral. It reports that Alex hoped to be a dispatch bearer for the British Army; he was taking his best car, which he considered to be the most effective way to carry dispatches; he had influential friends in the British Army and hoped for a position that would take him to the front.[82]

Alex's hopes for either course of action did not long survive his landing in England. Belgium, then in German hands, was off limits, and British dispatch bearing was too serious and dangerous a responsibility to entrust to a foreign civilian volunteer.[83] But a realizable possibility opened up soon after Alex's arrival. The U.S. embassy in London was having trouble communicating with its counterpart in Berlin. Alex offered to carry the diplomatic pouch himself by traveling by rail through neutral Holland. In spite of his two passports (one as a diplomatic courier) (figs. 1.9–1.10), the Germans arrested him at the frontier town of Bentheim.[84] He spent the night as a prisoner on the cold floor of the frontier guardroom. The next morning he succeeded in having his credentials recognized, and the American embassy in Berlin remonstrated with the German Foreign Office. Alex was released, but his role as a courier ended almost before it began; the arrest made him persona non grata with the Germans.[85] Early in 1915, he donated an ambulance to the American volunteer ambulance force.[86] Other than in the philanthropic sense, Alex's first venture into the war did not work out. It is unclear how he spent the balance of his time in England. Fox hunting, his favorite occupation, was drastically limited by the war.[87] Although the date and the name of the ship on which he returned home are not recorded, he definitely was back in New York by late March 1915.[88]

The centerpiece of that year for Alex was the tragedy of *Sea Call*, which was then under construction at Lawley's shipyard as the world's

Fig. 1.9. Cochran's passport portrait, 1914 (age 40). Courtesy of the National Archives and Records Administration / FamilySearch.org

Fig. 1.10. The U.S. was neutral in 1914 when Cochran went to England to join in the European war. Unable to find employment with the allies, Alex was enlisted by the U.S. embassy in London to carry dispatches and was given a diplomatic courier passport. The document was not honored by the German border guards, who arrested him and aborted his courier run to the U.S. embassy in Berlin. This original document is safeguarded in the Ewing Family Archives. Courtesy of Caroline Ewing.

record–sized pleasure schooner (fig. 1.11). The yacht was launched at the end of April, then underwent completion and running in. In early May, the *New York Tribune* reported that "Cochran rejoices over his new yacht."[89] Planning a world cruise for 1916, Alex commissioned *Sea Call* on July 15. One week later the yacht showed signs of metal corrosion; on August 1, it was thought that the plates might be replaced; ten days later *Sea Call* was scrapped, a victim of its Monel metal sheathing.[90] According to press reports, Alex took the loss of his prized yacht philosophically, "as an unfortunate but not necessarily discouraging result of an experiment." He declined to sue the builder.[91] This stoical, perhaps nonchalant public

THE PERSON TO WHOM THIS
PASSPORT IS ISSUED HAS DE-
CLARED UNDER OATH, THAT he
DESIRES IT FOR USE IN VISITING THE
COUNTRIES HEREINAFTER NAMED
FOR THE FOLLOWING OBJECTS

Going to Germany Austria Hungary France Turkey Servia Belgium Holland bearing despatches. England and United States. Bearer of United States despatches.

THIS DOCUMENT EXPIRES *February 6th 1915*
UNLESS RENEWED.   THE HOLDER HAS
APPLIED TO THE DEPARTMENT OF STATE AT
WASHINGTON FOR A REGULAR PASSPORT.

Embassy
of the
United States of America,
at
London, England.

To all to whom these presents shall come, Greeting:

I, the undersigned, Ambassador Extraordinary and Plenipotentiary of the United States of America,

hereby request all whom it may concern to permit

_____ a Citizen of the United States _____

safely and freely to pass, and in case of need to give him all lawful Aid and Protection.

Description

Age *40* Years

Stature *5* Feet *11* Inches Eng.

Forehead *medium*

Eyes *blue*

Nose *regular*

Mouth *medium*

Chin *round*

Hair *brown*

Complexion *fair*

Face *oval*

Signature of the Bearer

Alex Smith Cochran

Given under my hand and the Seal of the Embassy of the United States at London, the ___ day of _____ in the year 191_ and of the Independence of the United States the one hundred and ___

Walter Hines Page

No *4314*

Fig. 1.11. This newspaper illustration conveys some of the three-masted *Sea Call*'s magnificence. The record-size cruising vessel cost Alex a small fortune, but it had to be scrapped a few months after its launching because of unexpected and irreversible corrosion brought about by the use of the new alloy Monel. What *Sea Call* might have looked like in full sail is suggested by the exhilarating picture of *Vira/Creole* (see fig. 1.13). Courtesy of Caroline Ewing

face probably masked profound feelings of regret and loss. His log, which Alex suspended keeping on July 20, when all still seemed well, suggests how deeply he was affected. A year passed before he took up his pen again, in July 1916, to write a last, regretful entry: "The history here interrupted was sad. On inspection the plating was proven a failure. *Sea Call* was sailed to Boston and dismantled."[92]

The plan for a world cruise suggests that Alex was turning his back on the war, but not entirely. Eager for the U.S. to participate, he left his doomed yacht in early August and, in spite of tenuous health, joined many other socialites at the first of the Plattsburg Movement's training camps in northern New York State, where volunteers acquired military fitness and training with a view to providing cadres for a future army. Alex's tuberculosis must have been securely in remission at that time for him to be able to endure the rigors of the month-long encampment.[93] Soon after the camp dispersed, he sailed to England and, in December, was at Melton Mowbray, his fox hunting base, where the sport was severely pared down: "[M]asters and hunt servants were away in uniform. Hunts were kept going by women, old men, committees and unexpected candidates. Prodigies of menial work in kennel and stable were done by the families of masters."[94] Alex is unlikely to have shared in these austerities.

As war raged on the continent in 1916, Alex's participation continued to be wholly civilian. In March he returned to the U.S. aboard the neutral Dutch liner *Rotterdam,* but first he stopped by Quaritch's in London to buy books for the Elizabethan Club, the last addition he would make to his founding gift. Late that month, his six motor boats for the British Navy were delivered.[95] In June his 40-foot racer *Dolly Bowen,* which he had ordered from the Heereshoff shipyard after the loss of *Sea Call,* won a race. His main sporting activity that year was polo, in which his performance in the back position was praised. He bought Brookholt, a showpiece Long Island estate near the Meadowbrook Polo Club, in August, but too late in 1916 to serve as his polo hotel. No record confirms his having ever resided there.[96]

Alex had not abandoned his plan for a world cruise. He had bought from the estate of the *Lusitania* victim Alfred Gwynne Vanderbilt the very large, graceful steam yacht *Wayfarer,* to which he restored its original name, *Warrior.* When Alex took guests on a summer cruise in waters near Newport, his captain ran the ship onto a boulder at Fishers Island.[97] (With earlier owners, *Warrior* had been beached off Colombia in 1914, but, a charmed ship, it lived to be a naval auxiliary vessel in three wars before finally being sunk by German bombs in the Second World War.) The damage was repaired and, with a long cruise in the offing, *Warrior* underwent further work in September. Alex set sail in October 1916, unaccompanied by other passengers, with a captain and a crew of 39. He left New York in the first days of the month and reached Honolulu in November, swam off Waikiki, then turned back. The yacht pulled into San Francisco on November 20 and retraced its course through the Panama Canal.[98] In January 1917, *Warrior* reached Kingston, Jamaica. Here, finally, Alex joined the war from which the U.S. was still absent.

> 9th February, 1917
>
> Dear Mr Hughes,
> I have great pleasure in telling you that our gallant friend Cochran has put his Yacht and himself at the disposal of the Admiralty. We have gratefully accepted his generous offer and he is to be put in command with the rank of Commander R.N.R. He especially telegraphed to me to write and tell you about it. I am sure that he will not only be of the greatest service to us, and will also have some exciting times himself, which I feel certain he will much enjoy.
>
> W.J.R. Hall
> Director of Intelligence, Admiralty [99]

As Hall points out in this note, *Warrior* had been lent, gratis, for British service, to be returned to Alex after the war ended. Its civilian crew was sent back to New York on a passing freighter, and the yacht was converted into a cruiser with two guns. Alex's commission as Commander, Royal Naval Reserve, was posted in the *London Gazette* on February 20.[100] Hall's letter puts beyond doubt not only Alex's rank, but more particularly his appointment as captain of *Warrior.*

This new position raises interesting questions. Although Alex was an experienced sailor, he never captained his yachts. He always had a "sailing master" who would take over when Alex wished to leave the wheel or needed to for reasons of health.[101] He had no training for command of naval ratings or for firing cannon. A letter from the admiralty to Alex two months later, on April 20, 1917, may shed light on this problem: "I hear you have just commissioned as a fully commissioned Man of War."[102] The period from February to April was taken up with the conversion of *Warrior* into a warship. The major naval dockyard of this command was in Bermuda, to which Alex had taken his yacht from Jamaica. The same weeks may have witnessed Alex's own conversion from civilian to commissioned officer. He would have been trained, probably by junior but experienced naval personnel, in the running of his ship as a vessel of war. By April, H.M. Armed Yacht *Warrior* was ready to join the North America and West Indies Station and was charged with escorting and patrolling duties in the Caribbean.[103] The ship's log traces these journeys—some to Halifax, Nova Scotia; others to Belize; Havana; Charleston, South Carolina; and New York—but mostly cruising from island to island in the Caribbean. A lot of formal conviviality is recorded. The place of this British Navy service in Alex's recollections (such as the Yale account of his war or his portrait in uniform [see Appendix 1.10D]) suggests that these days of naval command were among the best of his life.

They ended too soon, perhaps because his health failed him. In a message of October 18, 1917, the admiral commanding the North America and West Indies Station tells Commander Alexander Smith Cochran:

> Admiralty acquaint me that your application to resign your commission in the Royal Naval Reserve has been accepted, and Their Lordships desire me to thank you for your generosity in placing your Yacht gratuitously [i.e., without cost] at their disposal. ... Your commission should be returned to me for cancellation.[104]

Another paragraph provides for interim command of *Warrior* by a Lieutenant until a replacement officer came from England. This took place when *Warrior* had berthed in New York harbor. The *Warrior* log records the last days of Alex's captaincy (October 21–29, 1917).[105]

Having relinquished his charge and rank, Alex was not content with a mere eight months of naval service. He went to ground; traces of him disappear. He may have spent at least part of the next six months in a sanitorium or a place with a climate suited for his health. A letter to Maitland Griggs dated December 7, 1917, reports, "I hear that Alex is in town [New York]." There is no clear sign of his whereabouts. When traces of him appear, in 1918, he seems still to be serving as a British officer. On April 15, 1918, the Cochran estate office in New York replied to a query with: "Mr. Cochran is on active service," and probably unreachable.[106] Among the subscriptions to a U.S. war loan on May 5, Alex is listed as "commander of British naval forces." Toward June 1918, he was in London, where he dined with an English friend without intimation that he was in the navy, but the August 3 announcement of bonuses for the workers of Smith Carpets specifies that Alex was "now an officer in the British navy."[107] By then he had returned to the U.S. and was in the mountain air of Colorado Springs, a guest at the Broadmoor. At the end of the month, he bought Glen Eyrie, a huge property in Colorado Springs. The *New York Herald* of August 31, 1918, reports that the purchaser was an "American now serving in the English navy…. [he] is in command of the *Warrior*."[108] In September a fuller account of his status came from East View, New York, near the Cochran farm:

> Alexander Smith Cochran Recovering: Commander in the British Navy Has Been Ill in Colorado
>
> East View, NY, Sept 27 [1918]. Alexander Smith Cochran [is] recovering from illness in Colorado, and is arranging to return to his duties as Commander in the British Navy. The announcement is the first intimation of Mr. Cochran's illness which necessitated a furlough. Mr. Cochran gave his yacht *Warrior* to the British Navy before the US declared war on Germany and was made a Lieutenant. Later he was promoted to Commander.[109]

The fiction, first found here, that Alex was first made a Lieutenant and later promoted to Commander adds a new twist to his career, lengthening and complexifying the start of his service. At the end of the war, in November 1918, Alex was in the U.S., which made it easy for him to resume civilian life.

The Royal Navy returned *Warrior* to him at the very end of the year, and it was refurbished in Brooklyn in 1919. Alex sold it in 1920 to Sir Thomas Lipton, who used it for his tender in the forthcoming America's Cup races.[110]

Alex was proud of his war record and service in the British Navy, and he retouched its course. Starting with the *Quarter-Century Record of the Class of 1896 Yale College,* the account of his war experiences in Yale alumni publications, which he must have supplied, blends fact and fib. (The details he provided were redacted for publication.)

> [*Index*] War Record of the Class of 1896. [A.S. Cochran] *Commander, Royal Naval Reserves, British Navy.* Relief work in Belgium; U.S. Embassies' Courier between London and Berlin in 1914. Capt. H.M.Y. "Warrior" attached to North Atlantic [*sic*] and West Indian Squad[ron].

> [*Description*] He was next heard of as a special dispatch bearer to Germany under the direction of the British Foreign Office; a volunteer courier between the American Embassies in London and in Berlin. [Quotes Gerard, p. 424, "he was arrested.... This ended his aspirations to be a courier."]

> In January, 1917, he turned over to the British Navy his steam yacht "Warrior" and was commissioned a Lieutenant and afterwards a Commander in the British Royal Naval Reserve and placed in command of the "Warrior," which was converted into an armed cruiser. Later he was engaged in other activities connected with the British Navy until the end of the war, when he received the decoration of Commander of the Order of the British Empire.[111]

This summary is notable for recalling and realizing the ambitions Alex revealed to the press in 1914 when embarking on the *Orduna*—to engage in Belgian relief and carry dispatches in British service. Another addition is "other activities connected with the British Navy," which presumably filled in between the *Warrior* command and the end of the war. The British decoration is first heard of here. Alex's Yale obituary adds nothing, but confuses dates by setting his earliest service in 1917 rather than 1914; he also is said to have been promoted to Commander in February 1916 (one year too soon), and to have been captain of *Warrior* until 1918. As usual, his squadron is renamed "North *Atlantic*" in lieu of "North *America.*" An oddity first found in the East View dispatch of September 1918 is the claim that he was first made a Lieutenant, then a Commander. This story of a nonexistent promotion may redefine the period of training for command of *Warrior* that Alex is likely to have undergone in the winter and spring of 1917, while his yacht was being armed. In his memoir of Alex, Bishop Freeman offers an expanded version of this promotion, even involving training on the *Aquitania.* The decoration is also arresting. U.S. publications, other than daily newspapers, that took notice of Alex's death, such as American biographical dictionaries, Yale class books, and the Elizabethan Club website, assert that he was named Commander of the Order of the British Empire, but no such mention occurs in the official *London Gazette* or his English obituary notices in the *London Times* and *The Spectator.*[112] Embellishments like these were unlikely to be noticed among the confusions of a world conflict. To sum up Alex in the war, after three on and off years, he ultimately gained a gratifying, but too brief, naval command. Disappointed by its premature ending, he set about discreetly adjusting the record of his service, even awarding himself the Order of the British Empire.

VI

While crossing to England aboard the *Aquitania* in July 1920, Alex (fig. 1.12) was introduced to Ganna Walska, a Polish beauty and aspiring opera singer, who was the widow of a New York doctor. Apparently smitten, he courted her for two months, and they quietly married in Paris in September 1920. They lived together for six months, during which they briefly resided in New York and made a trip to Yonkers. It was a memorable occasion at the Smith Carpet Mills: "Alexander, breaking all precedents, brought his bride on a visit. The Mill workers had turned out as for the advent of royalty, cheering and demonstrating."[113] (Alex did not also bring Walska to New Haven to be cheered by the members of the Elizabethan Club.) The

workers.

ccounts. He
ə cost of a
: of wool in
of machin-
and produc-
ıe while he
ıimself with

s free to do
ıeld himself
ınd insisted
:d like any
ınd not as
vner of the
d the secret
l the knowl-
ıandle men
gh learning

Fig. 1.12. Alex rarely was photographed unbidden—all other
pictures of him in this book are portraits. This unposed, candid
view from around 1920 shows how he looked about the time he
met Walska. Newspapers typically printed this image, and it also
accompanied numerous versions of his obituary. Courtesy of
Caroline Ewing

couple returned to Europe in December and, by April 1921, Alex had had enough of marriage. He never took to its constraints, and he found that it stood in the way of his normal routine and occupations. Despite being in the weak position of having no grounds for divorce, he proceeded to sue. Not undeservedly, Walska demanded a rich settlement from her multi-millionaire. She was offered $10,000 per year, which later was doubled to $20,000, but neither sum was anywhere near what Walska believed and expected his liberty to be worth. Alex's lawyer, Samuel Untermyer, was one of the most skilled in America. He dredged up information in Poland and elsewhere making it possible to threaten Walska with annulment on grounds of bigamy. Monetary terms were agreed upon on May 1, 1922, and the divorce became final in June. The settlement, later claimed to have cost Alex $3 million, was severely limited to a trust fund guaranteeing Walska $20,000 annually for life. She could also keep the opulent gifts with which he had showered her.[114]

Ganna Walska was a colorful, enterprising, and self-confident woman, two out of whose six husbands were very rich. Her crucial husband was Alex's successor, Harold Fowler McCormick, of the reaper millions, whose unstinting generosity fostered her musical career and fame. In Walska's memoirs, *Always Room at the Top* (1943), she devotes much negative attention to her marriage to Alex. She lived well into her nineties (d. 1984), and in the years after her last marriage—almost half her life—she developed extraordinary gardens in the Montecito district of Santa Barbara, California, that she named Lotusland. They are now open to the public. Although brief, Alex's part in her social ascent was important. She was his only known romantic entanglement.

The marriage was a watershed in Alex's life. When he returned to New York from the Paris divorce in 1922, the *New York Times* quoted him remarking that he had nothing to say for publication on any subject.[115] In the seven remaining years of his life, while suffering deteriorating health, he provided only rare traces of his existence. Neither fox hunting nor polo is recorded. His Long Island estate surfaced in the news fleetingly when sold. He bought the 40-foot yacht *Iris* in 1924, but he is not known to have ever raced it. He had *Restless,* a large steamer yacht, built for himself in 1922 and may have cruised in it around the world in 1923, as he had once planned to do. *Restless* definitely reached Hong Kong.[116] He was in Colorado Springs in 1924–25, long enough to build himself a large "cottage" and venture into a real estate development that quickly failed.[117] In 1927, he appears to have made a second attempt to acquire a champion pleasure vessel when he commissioned his ultimate boat, the three-masted wooden schooner *Vira* (fig. 1.13), named for Vira Whitehouse, the close woman friend who had launched *Sea Call*. The ill-fated *Sea Call* had been the "ultimate" boat in 1915, and it was evidently on Alex's mind in 1927. *Sea Call* was recalled by being named after the friend who had launched it, by having three masts, and by being built of wood to avert another metal disaster. Ominously, it took three tries for the champagne to shatter at its launching. After *Vira* was delivered, "intimidated by the very size and power of the yacht," Alex, in failing health, made alterations to the masts and ballast that spoiled its sailing qualities. It was sold within a year.[118] His pattern of enthusiasm followed by loss of interest, which has been observed several times and will concern us presently, surfaces particularly in the fate of *Vira*.

Bishop Freeman tells that "long before the final [health] crisis came, [Alex] disclosed increasing physical weakness and experienced periodic severely painful ailments incident to the disease he had long combated." He passed long, exacting periods in hospital and sanitorium where he underwent repeated and exhausting operations.[119] His tuberculosis, slowed for a long time by fresh-air activity and travel, finally became medicalized. In the autumn of 1928, in New York, he was stricken with a severe case of pneumonia and came close to dying. He survived, but now was in need of a prolonged recovery. With his divorced sister, Elizabeth, and 12 servants and medical staff, he wintered in Redlands, California, near Los Angeles, in a house with notable gardens that he bought.[120] In April 1929, accompanied by many canisters of oxygen, his sister, and the entourage, he was rushed in a special four-car train from California to New York. He spent some weeks in his Savoy-Plaza Hotel apartment, then moved to Yonkers. To escape great heat in June, with his life ebbing, he was taken north to his house at Saranac Lake in the Adirondacks, but found no relief. Within days of his arrival, he died in the arms of his long-serving valet, Fisher.[121]

Fig. 1.13. *Vira,* Alex's final yacht, may have been intended as an improved *Sea Call.* He ordered it from an English builder in 1927, when his health was failing. Overawed by its power, Alex damaged its sailing qualities, and sold it in 1928. A later owner restored the yacht to its original specifications and renamed it *Creole.* Since then, it has been wholly refitted twice and now, nearing 100, is still in commission. ©Beken of Cowes

In Yonkers Alex's death occasioned an outpouring of grief. "With every flag in the city at half mast, the bells of almost every church tolling and all Yonkers out to pay final tribute … [the funeral] not only was the most impressive but the largest the town has had." The mayor suspended all city business. Alex was widely remembered as a generous employer and an exemplary philanthropist, supporting every institution in the city, carrying on the Cochran tradition of openhandedness. As thousands of well-rewarded Mill workers stood among the mourners, Cochran and Ewing relatives came from far and wide. The open casket, lying in state for two hours, was viewed by an estimated 5,000 persons. Distinguished honorary pallbearers were appointed. Large crowds stood outside the overfull St. John's Episcopalian Church, where Bishop Freeman conducted the funeral service and delivered the eulogy. With an escort of thousands, the casket was taken to Oakland Cemetery, the family burial ground, and interred.[122]

VII

How is one to form an opinion of this Yale benefactor? In roughly chronological order, here is a summary of his many activities. After schooling at St. Paul's, Alex at Yale was a member of two fraternities and the Wolf's Head secret society; he earned a just-passable degree.[123] He had a five-year-long apprenticeship at Smith Carpets; was made its president; had his first bout of tuberculosis; inherited a very large fortune; began a lifelong practice of philanthropy; joined a near-record number of New York clubs; took Yale friends cruising aboard his first steam yacht; traveled to the carpetmaking Near East with a professor friend; rode to hounds in the English Midlands; collected an extraordinary assemblage of Tudor and Stuart first editions; built and successfully raced a record-size schooner; dined with his racing rival, the German kaiser; gave his rare books to the Yale club that he founded and endowed for students with literary tastes;[124] bought a biplane and took flying lessons;[125] joined Theodore Roosevelt's breakaway Progressive Party and was its largest single contributor; named as a delegate to the party's national convention, but instead of attending, needed to nurse his health in southern France;[126] acquired one Rolls Royce after the other;[127] raced thoroughbreds at Saratoga and Belmont Park; built and independently financed an America's Cup contender, but lost the qualifying races; after the outbreak of the First World War, gave liberally to Allied causes; went to war-torn Europe intending to bring relief to the Belgians and carry British dispatches; had one wartime run as a U.S. diplomatic courier to Berlin; built and lost a grand auxiliary schooner; participated in the military training camp at Plattsburg; played polo; cruised to Hawaii on *Warrior,* then lent it to the British Navy and was its captain; bought a castle in Colorado Springs; married and divorced a beautiful Polish would-be diva; commissioned a steamer yacht and took a lengthy cruise; dabbled in a real estate development in Colorado Springs; commissioned "the largest wood sailing yacht in the world"; contributed $10,000 to Al Smith's presidential campaign;[128] financed a major addition to the Washington Cathedral complex; and left generous legacies to his siblings, their children, and many others.[129] Most of all, from age 28 to the end of his life, he ruled the Alexander Smith & Sons Carpet Company, and was known to do so.[130]

Except for his lifelong leadership of the family enterprise, few of his many pursuits engaged Alex for long. The high point of his lifetime activities outside business came early; it coincided with his retirement from the presidency of Smith Carpets and the flaring up of his illness in 1910 and 1911. These were the years of *Westward*'s triumphs and of the foundation of the Elizabethan Club. Nothing of equal moment later came his way. Bishop Freeman said, "Repeatedly, through a long and intimate friendship, I was astonished by the extent and variety of his interests." Two perceptive observers drew attention to his pattern of embarking on something, then almost at once turning away.[131] His abruptly ended marriage was perhaps the most noteworthy example of Alex's inconstancy. Chance cut short endeavors that might have lasted longer: Charlie Barr died; *Sea Call* had a fatal flaw; his British naval command was abridged. Smith Carpets aside, philanthropy was his one steady occupation. His medical gifts to Yonkers endure; so do many others, notably those to churches. The quarter-million dollars that he bequeathed to St. Paul's School became the endowment of an instructorship in ancient Greek that remains in place today.[132] Judging from the scale of his posthumous generosity, he prized St. Paul's more highly than either the Elizabethan Club or Yale University itself. His main fortune, or the diminished amount left after the Crash of 1929, descended to his niece-in-law Lucia Chase Ewing, through whom it played a large part in supporting the American Ballet Theater. Ganna Walska heard of this and rejoiced that Alex's riches had finally been applied to the arts.[133]

He was described in 1920 as having modest and retiring ways—a quiet, earnest, reserved man of many experiences and serious purposes.[134] Bishop Freeman noted that Alex "consistently avoided all forms of publicity."[135] John Sloan, a business associate, was equally admiring: "His brilliant mind and winning and considerate personality always left a lasting impression." Richard Selzer aptly said of Alex's lifelong philanthropy, "[he] was the embodiment of generosity without thought of recompense."[136]

The longest and most attentive appreciation of Alex is by Clarence Day, Jr., in the *'96 Half-way Book* (1915). Day, a noted author, was a contemporary of Alex's at both St. Paul's and Yale:

> In character he is much what he always was, a reserved unassuming sort of chap…. He has a good brain, a good organizing ability…. Could probably command a high salary if he ever needed it. In so far as he possesses distinction or personal flavor, it expresses itself in his acts rather than in other channels, except that his appearance too is distinguished…. He is generous but not to be imposed upon; very pleasant; conscientious; decisive; only moderately social; only moderately happy.
>
> He keeps hoping he has found something very absorbing; but no, for its flavor won't last, and he searches again. Like a man without much appetite, who hopes a good dinner will give him one.[137]

To his nephew and designated heir Thomas Ewing III, Alex had been "his role model, his mentor, the anchor and inspiration of all he aspired to and believed about life, business, and family."[138]

Some held less positive opinions of this complex man. He could be notably brusque *en famille* (his reproof of brother Gifford on one occasion caused a stir). Ganna Walska complained that, when they were in Paris, Alex would order a midday dinner at home for friends, then at the appointed hour telephone to say he was eating out.[139] Walska, whose shabby divorce gave her reasons for scorn, thought Alex had no idea of what happiness might be, even in theory. He was, she said, the most miserable (i.e., inwardly unhappy) man she had ever known. He was always bored and "lived only to kill a day." She taxed him with "insane selfishness" and "limitless egoism."[140] He was not designed for a lasting union.

Long before he married, Alex's own words suggest a perceptible lack of joie de vivre. He had had a varied and stimulating life in the ten years after graduating from Yale (1896–1906). Heading the great family business, he was considered "one of the wealthiest active manufacturers in the world."[141] He participated in New York social life and belonged to many clubs throughout his life. His mother was still alive, and he had many siblings, for whom he felt responsible as head of the family. He had even traveled to exotic Tunisia to repatriate the body of his uncle. Yet, when invited to write for the Yale *Decennial Record of the Class of 1896,* he presented himself to his classmates as being mainly occupied by "loafing" by himself in the country north of Yonkers, "leading a pastoral, bucolic existence." Absent from the class report was the fact that his tuberculosis had been detected in 1902. For recovery, which Alex did experience for a time, he retired to Grasslands, the family farm. Like his mother, he was uninterested in farming, hence the advertised "loafing." To Alex, at least in this context, the many experiences he had had in the years since his college graduation were overshadowed by the disease he left unmentioned. The result was a spare and sad self-portrait.[142]

Walska was not alone in finding Alex difficult and wretched. His Baltimore nephew called him a "poor, lonely, lonely person," and an English well-wisher found him to be "a curious disgruntled person." Dudley Field Malone, Walska's divorce lawyer, observed that, "as soon as he gets anything, immediately he is weary of it." This, Malone said, was how Alex had treated his bride.[143] Clarence Day attributed Alex's behavior to ennui and restlessness: "He keeps hoping he has found something very absorbing; but no, for its flavor won't last, and he searches again." The moves listed above form a pattern of repetitive behavior; he would do something, at times wonderful, such as building the *Westward* or founding the Elizabethan Club, then turn his back on it and head toward something else. His recurrent tuberculosis, which has been considered to induce restlessness, cannot have moderated his lifelong inclinations.[144]

Two documented traits of Alex's catch the eye. His *New York Times* obituary notes that he was admired for his democratic ways, easily engaging with persons from all walks of life. Several quotations relating to his time at Yale and to his employees, cited above, associate his name with the word *democratic*. His years on the floor at the Smith Carpets factory after graduating from Yale, as well as his recruitment and training of hired racing crews, may have developed this gift.[145] Then, too, in correspondence with the leadership of the Elizabethan Club he continually insisted that the Lizzie must have no initiation fees and membership dues, presumably to permit access to poorer students.

The Elizabethan Club is not Alex's only lasting monument. Two great sailing ships built to his order — *Westward* and *Vira* (renamed *Creole*) — survive to this day. *Vira/Creole,* after association with the scandalous deaths of Eugenia Niarchos and Maurizio Gucci and needing two complete refits after ill use, now belongs to Maurizio's daughters.[146] Called by the photographer Gilles Martin-Raget, "a boat outside all the norms of size, aesthetics and history," it remains in commission and is available for charter. *Westward* was scuttled by its owner in 1947, but it lives on in an exact replica (called *Eleonora*) built in 2000, and in a *Westward* Cup instituted as a competition among very large sailboats.[147] These are substantial relics of Alex's passion for yachting.

Still, as a goal for a Cochran pilgrimage, the Elizabethan Club in New Haven is more accessible than yacht anchorages. Here it sits at the heart of the Yale campus. "As a realized idea," Gilbert Troxell said, "it is the unique, perfect expression of one individual's intelligence and generosity."[148] Club members show guests its rooms, large garden, and the queen's portrait in its elaborately carved frame. They offer tea and food and, on Friday afternoons between 4:30 and 5:30, invite inspection of "some of the most precious of English books" in the massive vault. Overseeing the vault room is a portrait of Alexander Smith Cochran, in whose honor the Club holds an annual birthday banquet. Alex himself moved discontentedly from one activity to the next, but at least one seed that he planted took root and assured that he would be remembered and thanked.

Notes

1 Lewis, pp. 112–13. The Yale colleges date from 1933 onward.

2 Strachey, p. 117.

3 Used by his family (see Ewing, *Bravura*). His normal signature was "Alex." Ganna Walska consistently calls him "Alec"—a form he hated—in her memoirs (ART). The *Yale Class Book '96* (p. 29), uses the alternative surname "Cockerane."

4 Cochran to William Lyon Phelps, July 26, 1921. MSSA, RU36, box 3, folder 156.

5 Tuberculosis, a bacterial disease, became curable with the advent of antibiotics. Drug-resistant strains have recently appeared and "worldwide, the disease kills more than 4,000 people a day" (*New York Times* [September 25, 2018]: D3). "Socially shaming" disease: *Times Literary Supplement* 5986–7 (December 22 and 29, 2017): 17. Some believed, even in his home town, that Alex died of pneumonia: Cochran "expires from the effects of illness contracted last fall" (*Yonkers Herald* [June 1929]: n.p.); with thanks to Marianne Winstanley, Yonkers Historical Society Archive Committee. The *Dictionary of American Biography,* vol. 2 (1961), p. 250, gives the correct cause of death, as do other sources. For background information, see the books listed under "Tuberculosis" in the Part 1 bibliography.

6 Alex with his mother in California, where she came down with her final illness: EFA, Ewing 2, p. 127. Diagnosis in 1902: *Quarter-Century Record of the Class of 1896 Yale College* (hereafter *Quarter-Century Record*), p. 85. For the sanitorium, see Appendix 1.1, "Alex Cochran, 'Billy' Phelps, the Books, and the Club."

7 Smoking: Hamilton-Adams, p. 12. He tried quitting when crossing to Europe aboard *Westward,* but failed. A year's abstinence: EFA, Ewing 2, p. 376; on the verso is Anna Ewing's handwritten note about Alex's rest at Grasslands. Alex's difficulty walking the length of *Vira*: Hampton, n.p. Disease not known to Ganna Walska: ART, p. 191. Many of his obituaries offer slightly different ages at his death (EFA, Scrapbook, ff. 22–32).

8 "Alexander Smith Carpet Mills Historic District." https://en.wikipedia.org/wiki/Alexander_Smith_Carpet_Mills_Historic_District

9 Joe Kelly, "When the Mill Pulled the Rug out from under Yonkers," *New York Times* (July 29, 1979): WC15 (an excellent source on the mill through the 1970s). www.nytimes.com/1979/07/29/archives/westchester-weekly-when-the-mill-pulled-the-rub-out-from-under.html (retrieved March 2, 2019).

10 Jordan, p. 32.

11 EFA, Ewing 2, p. 125. An otherwise totally unknown family member is recorded in the *New York Sun* in 1917: "Death at 76 of Mrs Mary L.T. Smith, second wife of Alexander Smith, founder of Smith Carpets, who died 15 years ago [that would have been in 1902, but Smith died in 1878]. She died at 355 Palisade Ave [later Alex's Yonkers address]. Step-grandmother of Alex, William, and Gifford" (*New York Sun* [March 20, 1917]: 6). Alexander Smith's date of death is the only error in this strange report. He had, in fact, died 39 years earlier, when this second wife would have been 37. Might Mary have been the second wife of the founder, scorned and excluded by the main families? While this interpretation is not unbelievable, the alternative but unlikely explanation is that the notice was a malicious hoax.

12 About William Francis Cochran and Eva Smith Cochran, see EFA, Ewing 2, pp. 100–117. On the children, see Appendix 1.8.

13 Yonkers is about 40 minutes commuting distance from Manhattan. Eva did not like Duncraggan, the Yonkers house William built for her, so she settled the family at 5 East 45th Street in New York City for winters. Where all the children were schooled is not recorded. As noted, the sons went to St. Paul's, a socially celebrated prep school. Anna Cochran married Thomas Ewing II, who was active in municipal affairs. (His father—here considered as "I" [i.e., the "first"], even though he had ancestors of that name—had been a Civil War general, Ohio politician, and a lawyer in New York; he settled the family in Yonkers.) Anna and Thomas II had "the most elaborate church wedding . . . that had ever taken place in Yonkers" [EFA, Ewing 2, p. 137, from the *Yonkers Statesman*]. Thomas II, a patent lawyer, became U.S. Commissioner of Patents under President Wilson.

14 EFA, Scrapbook, f. 19, column 1: from an unidentified newspaper, ca. June 21, 1929. For the "table runners," poor classmates whom one was expected to tip, see Judith Ann Schiff, "Uncommon Leadership," *Yale Alumni Magazine,* 32/4 (March–April 2019): 23.

15 Yale University, *Decennial Record of the Class of 1896* (hereafter *Decennial Record*), p. 276.

16 For quotations, EFA, Ewing 2, pp. 134, 135, and 161.

17 EFA, Ewing 1, p. 108.

18 Jordan, p. 33.

19 Quotations, EFA, Ewing 2, p. 161.

20 EFA, Ewing 2, p. 161. Perhaps William Cochran moved to Baltimore to keep a distance from his older brother (Weeks, p. 4). William had an enviable, somewhat eccentric life clear of Alex, but did not cease to be on good terms with him. (See Appendix 1.8.)

21 EFA, Ewing 1, pp. 110, 141.

22 On Alex's inheritance, the exact size of which is disputed, see Selzer, p. 48. (Others offer different amounts, but I think Selzer is right.) Like many other commentators, Selzer adds, in error, that the "amount rapidly grew to uncountability until the Crash." On the contrary, it seems as though Alex notably diminished his inheritance. Despite what is claimed in EFA, Ewing 1, p. 144 (and repeated in EFA, Ewing 2, p. 201), Eva did not leave the "residue" of her fortune to Alex. Each of her six children received the same amount, $1.3 million (*New York Times* [October 9, 1909]: 8; Anna Ewing added a pencil correction to this effect to EFA, Ewing 2, p. 201).

23 EFA, Ewing 2, pp. 432–33; https://en.wikipedia.org/wiki/W._%26_J._Sloane

24 *New York Journal of Commerce* (June 21, 1929), in EFA, Scrapbook, f. 24.

25 Jordan, p. 32.

26 Hamilton-Adams, p. 29.

27 The principal source for the details of Alex's benevolence is Jordan, p. 34.

28 EFA, Ewing 1, p. 110. Alex's labor policy is noted in biographical dictionaries, such as the *Cyclopedia of American Biography,* vol. 32 (1945), p. 479; and *Dictionary of American Biography* vol. 2 (1961), p. 250. (In Part 1 bibliography, see entries under "Alexander Smith Cochran" and "French, Robert D.," respectively.)

29 Yale College Class of 1896. '96 *Half-way Book* (hereafter *Half-Way Book*), p. 84.

30 Jordan, p. 32.

31 Formalities: *Quarter-Century Record,* p. 236; periodic descents: EFA, Ewing 2, p. 187. "Cochran Estate Inventory," p. 5, indicates his divestiture on July 14, 1920.

32 EFA, Ewing 2, p. 187.

33 About Robert P. Perkins, see Bigelow-Sanford Carpet Company, pp. 49, 54–58; in the First World War, Perkins headed the U.S. Red Cross Commission in Italy. Ganna Walska: ART, p. 75. Aboard Alex's sailboats *Westward, Sea Call,* and *Vanitie*: logs from *Westward* and *Sea Call.* Italian mission: *New York Times* (February 11, 1918): 2, and (May 24, 1918): 3. Cooperation in business: see Halcyon Skinner obituary: *New York Times* (November 29, 1900): 1.

34 EFA, Ewing 2, pp. 354, 385. Alex saw no need for change.

35 Ewing, *Bravura,* p. 16.

36 EFA, Ewing 2, p. 451.

37 EFA, Ewing 2, pp. 386–87.

38 EFA, Ewing 2, p. 430.

39 Pay cuts and part time: EFA, Scrapbook, undated loose clipping from the *Yonkers Herald* (1931); death of Thomas Ewing III, Ewing, *Bravura,* pp. 20–21, and EFA, Ewing 2, pp. 520–24; Masefield quotation: Smith, p. 132; also see Appendix 1.9, "John Masefield at Smith Carpets and the Elizabethan Club."

40 Ewing, *Bravura,* p. 16; Kelly, "When the Mill Pulled the Rug out from under Yonkers." The merger of Smith Carpets with Mohawk Carpets took place in 1956 and involved more than a renaming and move to Mexico: the Smith name vanished.

41 In 1979, Kelly's "When the Mill Pulled the Rug out from under Yonkers" contemplated reuse of much of the plant, a rosier situation than now exists. 2017 fire: Matt Spillane and Ernie Garcia, "Yonkers' Art District's Future in Question after Fire," *The Journal News.* www.lohud.com/story/news/local/westchester/yonkers/2017/01/30/fire-yonkers-artist-community/97233972/ (retrieved November 4, 2018).

42 With a short commute between the cities, being active in New York did not cut Alex away from Yonkers. In Manhattan, he lived at the family's house at 5 East 45th Street, then at 10 East 41st Street. Later, Alex never built himself a New York mansion, but rented luxury apartments. For a time he was at the Ritz-Carlton Hotel (*Quarter-Century Record,* p. 84). The 13 clubs to which Alex belonged—second in number only to the 16 memberships of Cornelius Vanderbilt, Sr.—were: the Ardsley, Brook, Knollwood, Lambs, Larchmont Yacht, New York Yacht, Racquet, Riding, Turf and Field, Union League, University, Yale, and in Washington, D.C., the Metropolitan Club. Alex joined all of these within a decade after his Yale graduation, and he still maintained memberships in all of them on the eve of his death. About the New (later Century) Theater, see Mary Jane Matz, *The Many Lives of Otto Kahn* (New York: Pendragon, 1963), pp. 68–78.

43 Yale men to the reunion, *Decennial Report,* p. 277; to Europe, *Quarter-Century Record,* p. 84. The fact-finding journey to the Ottoman Empire, et al., is commemorated in Williams Jackson's travel book of 1911 (dedicated to Alexander Smith Cochran). The trip to Belgium recalled: *New York Tribune* (November 19, 1914): 1. Fox hunting: *New York Times* (December 13, 1908): SM4. Alex promptly bought a hunting lodge in Melton Mowbray with stabling for nine horses. Also Phelps Laudation. Book collecting: see Appendix 1.1.

44 *Avenger*: "The transfer [of *Avenger*] was made late in the season, and after a few weeks of racing," Alex ordered a much larger craft. Yves Gary, "Cochran, Alexander Smith (1874–1929)," at America's Cup 1851–1937: http://america-scoop.com/index.php/en/actors/owners/1414-cochran-alexander-smith-usa (retrieved June 16, 2017)

45 On Alex's siblings, see Appendix 1.8. Neither riding nor sailing was a Yale sport, but boating took place on the Hudson in Yonkers and at the Cochran summer home in Maine. Alex had a small sloop, and he learned sailing early; see

Gary, "Cochran, Alexander Smith (1874–1929)."
Practice in horsemanship went without saying.
There were stables at Duncraggan, Grasslands,
and the New York properties as well as at
the summer retreat in Maine. Riding was the
favorite sport of Alex's father: EFA, Ewing 2,
pp. 110, 114, 117.

46 Photograph of Hollywood Inn:
In Memoriam William Francis Cochran (n.p.,
1902), opposite p. 71.

47 EFA, Ewing 1, pp. 141–42; EFA, Ewing 2,
pp. 199–200; African Americans, p. 124. James
E. Freeman, *In Memoriam Eva Smith Cochran,
1845–1909* ([n.p.], 1911).

48 *Yonkers Herald* (June 20, 1929), in EFA,
Scrapbook, f. 12.

49 EFA, Scrapbook ff. 12 and 13; "Ewing
Memorandum."

50 EFA, Scrapbook f. 10, col. 4; "Ewing
Memorandum."

51 Freeman, pp. 25–38; failing health, EFA,
Ewing 2, p. 442. The endowment was for
$1 million and the remainder of the gift was for
the building. The contribution was completed
after Alex's death (see "Cochran Estate
Inventory").

52 *New York Times* (March 2, 1930): 50
(reprinted from the *London Times*). The
quotation is from the obituary notice for Alex
in the *Spectator* 142 (June 29, 1929): 997.

53 *The Rudder* 32 (1916): 189.

54 Alex's obituary, *New York Journal of
Commerce* (June 21, 1929): [n.p.], in EFA,
Scrapbook f. 24, col. 1. Alex's relationship to
relief work in Belgium is detailed below.

55 Legacy to St. Paul's School, see "Cochran
Estate Inventory." For the Elizabethan Club,
see Appendixes 1.1 and 1.2. The amounts of
his gifts for the clubhouse and vault are not
certain (see Appendix 1.3, "The Mysterious
Purchase Price of the Clubhouse").

56 Bell, p. 21. For Alex's books, see Appendix 1.1.

57 MSSA, RU36, box 3, folder 157.

58 About the Club's finances, see Appendix 1.4,
"Downs and Ups of the Club's Finances." The
College of Preachers (later called Cathedral
College) suspended operations April 1, 2009,
owing to the severe economic hardships
experienced by the cathedral. Nicholas Fandos,
"National Cathedral's Repair Work: Finials,
Finance and Faith," in *New York Times* (July 4,
2015): A10, reports that "the Cathedral College
was among the first budget items cut."

59 Metropolitan Museum of Art, *A Catalogue
of the Collection of Persian Manuscripts.*

60 For photographs of these works, www.
metmuseum.org/art/collection/search-
results#!/search?q=alexander%20smith%20
cochran. Includes the Persian manuscripts,
a superb sixteenth-century Afghan carpet,
and some miscellaneous items. For a careful
discussion of the carpet, see *American Carpet
and Upholstery Journal,* vol. 26 (1908): 235.

61 *New York Times* (February 22, 1912): 7:
"The collection is an important one, brought
together after many years' effort.... Most
of the portraits were painted from life, by
American artists." See Appendix 1.5, "ASC's
Other Collections." It may be in connection
with these portraits that Alex was elected to
the exclusive Walpole Society, composed of
collectors of Americana, in 1915. He is listed in
the members' list (http://findingaid.winterthur.
org/html/HTML_Finding_Aids/COL0386.htm;
retrieved March 14, 2019). There is no Cochran
material in the society's archives.

62 *Half-way Book,* p. 85.

63 On the founding of the E.S.U., see *The
Landmark* 1:1 (1919): 59; page 231 also discusses
a gift by Alex that enabled the organization
to get started. The second gift to Columbia
University's department of Indo-Iranian
languages connected to his friend Professor

Williams Jackson (*New York Sun* [February 6, 1918]: 7). *Victory*, EFA, Scrapbook, f. 21, col. 2.

64 Freeman, p. 12. Again, "repeatedly in large gifts that I was privileged to administer for him, he insisted that no one was to know who the donor was" (unattributed clipping of June 1929, EFA, Scrapbook, f. 11, column 2). Eva Cochran also wanted her gifts to be anonymous (EFA, Ewing 2, p. 121).

65 Inflated estimates: Selzer, p. 48; many other estimates, none authoritative. His wife's divorce lawyer said Alex's fortune was $17 million, but that must be an error (*New York Tribune* [October 16, 1921]: 6; *San Francisco Chronicle* [October 17, 1921]: 1). Shrinkage: the $35 million Alex inherited in 1903 was the rough equivalent of $70 million in 1929, but his net estate, valued in 1932, was about $39 million ("Cochran Estate Inventory"). He bequeathed $19.6 million net—about 28 percent of the inflation-adjusted sum that originally came to him—to his principal heir. Death of Thomas Ewing III: Ewing, *Bravura,* pp. 21–24. The estate Ewing left was less than one-fifth of what he inherited from Alex (*New York Times* [February 9, 1933]: 17, and [February 19, 1933]: 11).

66 No syndicate for *Vanitie*: *Boston Globe* (October 25, 1913): 6; polo-pony sale: *New York Times* (June 13, 1920): 24A; apartment house, *New York Times* (July 23, 1916): XX8. He later changed his mind and had various plans for the lot.

67 Much of the foregoing is from the *Washington Post* (October 20, 1920): 64. For the Saranac Lake house, see "Historic Saranac Lake: Alexander S. Cochran," localwiki.org/hsl/Alexander_S._Cochran (retrieved June 16, 2017); hunting lodge: *New York Times* (December 13, 1908): SM4. Redlands, a suburb of Los Angeles, was noted for its dry climate. For details, see Appendix 1.10B, "ASC's Residences."

68 He acquired thoroughbreds and engaged in racing them in 1913 and 1914. Gifford's "principal stallion will be His Majesty ... for which [Alex] paid $20,000 three seasons back and sold to him," in *Vanity Fair* 5:5–6:4 (January–June 1916): 87.

69 For the plane, see Appendix 1.7, "ASC as a Sportsman." Memorandum (based on several sources) about Alex's Rolls Royces kindly supplied to me by Thomas Murray, Yale University Organist, Elizabethan Club member, and authority on these cars. With gratitude. Much motoring (in England) is noted in Cochran, *Westward* log.

70 Details in Hamilton-Adams.

71 *New York Times* (July 17, 1924): 13.

72 *Boston Sunday Globe* (April 4 1915): 63. Alex even bought *Minerva,* an 80-foot cruiser, to serve as tender to *Sea Call* (*The Rudder* 31 [1915]: 32), but he cannot have owned it for very long.

73 See Appendix 1.7. The *Sea Call* log mentions that Alex bought an auxiliary schooner, *Intrepid*. It is referred to nowhere else and, presumably, was disposed of in a short time.

74 Roger Longrigg, *The History of Foxhunting* (New York: Crown Publishers, 1975), p. 199: "[H]unting suffered from lack of people, feed, horses and money." Because of a shortage of feed and popular pressure, "a great many hounds were put down and very few bred." (In fox hunting hounds are more important than horses.) Praise for his riding and polo playing: *New York Tribune* (July 30, 1916): A3.

75 *New York Times* (December 13, 1908): SM4.

76 In keeping with Alex's practice of disregarding the crews of his yachts, Barr is never mentioned in the *Westward* log, and neither is the captain of *Warrior* for Alex's Pacific cruise in the log for that craft. They are in pasted-in photographs, however. (See Appendix 1.6, "ASC's Yacht Logs").

77 "Things would never be the same…":
Hamilton-Adams, p. 36; the German purchase,
ibid., p. 44; the last owner, Thomas Benjamin
Davis, and his races, ibid., pp. 54 ff.

78 Shouldering all expenses: *New York Tribune*
(May 15, 1914): 13; also "Ewing Memorandum."
For details about *Vanitie* and its races, see:
Plain Talk … [for Port Washington, N.Y.], ed.
Henry Kuizer Landis (Port Washington, N.Y.:
North Shore, n.d. [1914?]), p. 172. On 1920 races:
The Rudder 36 (1920): 159; also see America's
Cup website: http://america-scoop.com/
index.php/en/20-2/vanitie (retrieved June
16, 2017). This internet account has two parts
(not marked)—one written in 1914; the other
based on Alex's standard c.v. and written after
his death. The first part includes valuable
biographical information. *Vanitie*'s later life:
Boston Globe (October 14, 1934): A27.

79 Succès d'estime: *New York Times*
(December 19, 1924): 28.

80 ART, p. 66.

81 According to the International
Encyclopedia of the First World War, "many
people in the government, military and civilian
population imagined that the conflict would
be short" (https://encyclopedia.1914-1918-
online.net/article/willingly_to_war_public_
response_to_the_outbreak_of_war). But by
1915, in a letter to Andrew Keogh, Alex said:
"I imagine there will be plenty of time before
this war and the next will be over" (MSSA, RU36,
box 3, folder 157). "The next" is intriguing.

82 *New York Times* (November 19, 1914): 4;
New York Tribune (November 19, 1914): 1;
Baltimore Sun (November 20, 1914): 4. The
need for relief work in Belgium (especially
food to avert starvation and shelter to replace
destroyed homes) was widely publicized by
American news organizations in these months.
See Nash, *Hoover*, vol. 2, pp. 17–66.

83 Alex evidently did not join in the London-
based efforts of Herbert Hoover's newly
founded, American-centered Commission for
Relief in Belgium to feed the starving Belgians
(see "Commission for Relief in Belgium," https://
en.wikipedia.org/wiki/Commission_for_Relief_
in_Belgium; in general, see Nash, *Hoover,* vol. 2,
pp. 66–67, and chapters 3 and 4 *passim*). The
name *Cochran* does not occur in the index to
Nash's biography of Hoover.

84 His diplomatic courier's passport survives
in the EFA. See fig. 1.10.

85 Credentials recognized: *New York Herald*
(June 21, 1929) in EFA, Scrapbook, f. 22, col. 2.;
the embassy's intervention: *New York Tribune*
(March 17, 1917): 5. James W. Gerard, *My Four
Years in Germany* (New York: Doran, 1917),
p. 424: "In the piping times of peace he had
been the guest of the Emperor at Kiel." No one
tells us whether Alex's batch of diplomatic mail
reached the Berlin embassy.

86 *The Nation* 101 (July–December 1915):
709–10: he was noted as a particularly
generous contributor to the American
Volunteer Motor Ambulance Corps.

87 Siegfried Sassoon, *Memoirs of a
Fox-Hunting Man* (London: Faber, 1928),
pp. 298–99: "[O]n a starved grey November
morning … [t]he opening meet would have
been last week if there hadn't been this war."

88 Alex in New York, March 21, 1915: Wrench,
p. 132.

89 *New York Tribune* (May 2, 1915): A6. His
purchase of the 80-foot steam vessel *Minerva*
to be *Sea Call*'s tender is noted above. The
engine was not delivered in time for the launch
(letter of February 1, 1966, in *Sea Call* log).

90 Commission, *Sea Call* log; *New York Times*
(July 23, 1915): 23; *Boston Globe* (August 1, 1915):
53; *New York Tribune* (August 11, 1915): 1; *New
York Sun* (July 28, 1915): 4, has a featured article
about a conference of those concerned with

the yacht (i.e., Alex and its builder, engineer, etc.) to determine the fate of *Sea Call*, which still seemed salvageable; it includes details about construction and costs. See also George S. Hudson, "The Passing of *Sea Call*," in *Motor Boating* (February 1916): 10–11.

91 Quotation: *New York Tribune* (August 11, 1915): 4; not suing: Hamilton-Adams, p. 58.

92 The log of *Sea Call* shows that, after his loss, Alex acquired *Intrepid,* another auxiliary schooner, but he seems to have disposed of it shortly afterward. It disappears from the log almost at once and is mentioned nowhere else. His next major yacht was *Warrior.*

93 On the Plattsburg camp, see Donald M. Kington, "The Plattsburg Movement and Its Legacy," in *Relevance: The Quarterly Journal of the Great War Society,* www.worldwar1.com/tgws/relo11.htm (retrieved June 18, 2017); and "WW I—Plattsburg Training Camp," Historic Saranac Lake Wiki, https://localwiki.org/hsl/WW_I_-_Plattsburg_Training_Camp (retrieved June 18, 2017). Alex was at Plattsburg from August 10 to September 6 (*Hartford Courant* [August 15, 1915]: X7).

94 Alex in London, October 1915, and at Melton Mowbray, December 1915: Wrench, p. 145 and chapter 10. For fox hunting during the war, see Longrigg, *History of Foxhunting,* p. 199.

95 Return on *Rotterdam*: *New York Times* (March 6. 1916): 3. Quaritch book purchase: MSSA, RU36, box 3, folder 157, February 26, 1916; Quaritch notifies Keogh, the Club librarian, that he had sent Alex's purchases and attached a list (now lost). Boats for British Navy: Alex Cochran, "one of the most popular yachtsmen in this country, has recently made a gift to England of six patrol cruisers which he had designed" (*San Francisco Chronicle* [June 4, 1916]: 19). Alex's "designing" them may have been the newspaper's invention, but perhaps not; see also Wrench, p. 145.

96 Praise for polo performance: *New York Tribune* (July 30, 1916): A3. Brookholt purchased: *Chicago Tribune* (August 27, 1916): F5; also see "Brookholt" https://en.wikipedia.org/wiki/Brookholt. *Dolly Bowen* wins a race: *New York Tribune* (June 4, 1916): A4.

97 Purchase of *Warrior*: *The Rudder* 32 (1916): 244. *Warrior* at Fishers Island: *New York Times* (July 20, 1916): 11. For Alex's account of the grounding and its aftermath, see Cochran, *Warrior* log; "HMS *Warrior* (1917)," https://en.wikipedia.org/wiki/HMS_Warrior_(1917), (retrieved September 24, 2018.)]

98 Extensive work being done on *Warrior*: *New York Tribune* (September 2, 1916): 13. *Warrior* arrives from Honolulu: *San Francisco Chronicle* (November 20, 1916): 1. The cruise is skeletally chronicled by Alex, in Cochran, *Warrior* log. Alex kept busy while in the Bay Area. He was preparing to join the polo season beginning January 1: *Ogden Standard* (December 11, 1916): 8. Something must have changed his mind and decided him to resume cruising.

99 Letter from Cochran, *Warrior* log. The addressee is probably the F.R. Hughes who is mentioned several times in the *Westward* log (e.g., May 28, 1910, in England; joined *Westward* for the North Sea racing; July 3, "left for London"); evidently he was a good friend of Alex's. "R.N.R." are the initials of the Royal Naval Reserve.

100 Crew returns to New York: *Baltimore Sun* (February 23, 1917): 2. *Warrior* is often said to have been "presented" (or a similar verb, even "sold"), but correctly it was a free loan. Naval appointment: "Royal Naval Reserve, Alexander S. Cochran to be tempy Cdr, 15 Feb 1917," *London Gazette* 29954 (February 20, 1917): 1772 (p. 10 of 82): See also *The Rudder* 33 (1917): 327, by which U.S. yachtsmen were informed.

101 EFA, Ewing 2, p. 223.

102 Letter preserved in Cochran, *Warrior* log.

103 Nick Metcalfe's "HMS Warrior," at Sacrifice website, https://ww1sacrifice. com/2015/02/17/hmswarrior/ (retrieved, June 19, 2017) is an important article on *Warrior* in the First World War (although it lacks any reference to Cochran's *Warrior* log). The yacht was attached to the North America and West Indies Station, although information proceeding from Alex substitutes *Atlantic* for *America*. See also "Royal Naval Dockyard, Bermuda," https://en.wikipedia.org/wiki/ Royal_Naval_Dockyard%2C_Bermuda

104 Cochran, *Warrior* log.

105 Ibid. Alex's replacement by a Lieutenant illustrates that a craft of *Warrior*'s size normally would not have been captained by a Commander.

106 MSSA, RU36, box 3, folder 156: letter to Maitland Griggs, December 7, 1917, and letter from estate office (527 Fifth Avenue, New York) of April 15, 1918. The yacht, no longer captained by Alex, served as Admiral Sir W. L. Grant's flagship during a visit to Washington, D.C., where it participated in a ceremony on Memorial Day 1918 ("HMS *Warrior* [1917]"). Metcalfe, "HMS Warrior," focuses on this official visit. The *Warrior* log was suspended when Alex resigned, with an added line about the yacht later being the admiral's temporary flagship. The log was resumed between the time *Warrior* returned to Alex and its sale.

107 War loan subscription: *New York Times* (May 5, 1918): 1; lunch in London: Wrench, p. 325; Smith Carpets bonuses: *New York Tribune* (August 3, 1918): 13.

108 The Broadmoor, still a luxury hotel, calls itself "an iconic Colorado Springs resort" (MSSA, RU 36, box 3, folder 158, *New York Herald* [August 31, 1918]: 8): Glen Eyrie purchase: *The Spur* (September 15, 1918): 36. Alex reputedly paid $1 million for Glen Eyrie. The Elizabethan

Club archives contain a real estate company's illustrated, glassine-wrapped brochure from 1932 showing Alex's "cottage." It lists the lands (8,000 acres) and the productive possibilities of the attached ranches, all for sale at $500,000. (I believe there were no takers.) The "Cochran Estate Inventory" shows the property assessed at $400,100.

109 Unattributed clipping (MSSA, RU 36, box 10, folder 248).

110 *Warrior* sold to Lipton: *New York Times* (February 8, 1920): 2; Alex in London autumn 1919: Wrench, p. 445.

111 *Quarter-Century Record*, p. 122.

112 Freeman, p. 21. Another particularly fanciful version reports that Alex "put himself through a stiff course in navigation" and served on *Warrior* as second in command: EFA, Ewing 2, p. 277. *Thirty-Five Year Record of the Class of 1896 Yale College* (1932), pp. 182–83. The faulty dates may partly result from errors made by the obituary writer. For the decoration: e.g., "Obituary Record of Graduates of Yale University, 1928–1929," *Bulletin of Yale University* (November 1, 1929): 142-43. None of the June 1929 U.S. obituaries refers to the British decoration (EFA, Scrapbook, f. 22–32). British obituaries: *London Times* (June 21, 1929); *New York Times* (March 2, 1930): 50, copying a later notice in the *London Times*; *The Spectator* 142 (June 29, 1929): 997, honors his "princely gifts" and naval service. To put Cochran's enhancements of his war record into perspective, see the many autobiographical improvements in Hoover's memoirs; one set is pointed out in Nash, *Hoover,* vol. 2, p. 13.

113 EFA, Ewing 2, p. 377.

114 Ganna Walska and the Cochran marriage are detailed in Part 2. Walska is often said to have divorced Alex, but it was the other way around. During the many months of the separation, Alex traveled in Britain. On the divorce, see especially Appendix 2.2, "Arcadie Eingorn and the Cochran Divorce." *New York World* (June 21, 1921): n.p. (EFA, Scrapbook, f. 22) is unusually well informed about the financial side of the divorce. Untermyer, a prominent Zionist, was a Yonkers neighbor of Alex's and possibly a personal friend; about him: *Who Was Who in America, 1897–1942* (Chicago: Marquis, 1942), p. 1254. An article in the *Washington Post* (July 12, 1916: 5) reports his having bought from Alex Duncraggan, the main Cochran house in Yonkers, which adjoined Untermyer's land.

115 *New York Times* (November 18, 1922): 24.

116 Brookholt sold: *New York Times* (November 18, 1923): X11; purchase of *Iris*: *New York Times* (July 17, 1924): 13; *Restless* ordered: *Boston Globe* (January 7, 1923): 40; *Restless* in Yokohama: MSSA, RU36, box 3, folder 256; card from Hong Kong: Freeman, p. 26.

117 *New York Times* (March 21, 1925): 7. There also is the real estate circular of 1932 mentioned above in note 108.

118 Mrs. Norman D. R. Whitehouse (1859–1930). "Ultimate" yachts: "Gucci's Creole," The Islander, theislander.net/gucci-s-creole. Ominous launching: Hampton, [n.p.]; "intimidated by very size": Hamilton-Adams, p. 38. *Vira* was sold in 1928 (*Chicago Daily Tribune* [January 13, 1929]: H11). More will be said of it.

119 Quotation, Freeman, pp. 25, 27.

120 The course of his final illness is related in many of his obituaries: EFA, Scrapbook, ff. 22–32. *Los Angeles Times* (December 15, 1928): 8, he bought "a large home [that] has one of the most beautiful gardens in Redlands." The following press reports raise a perplexing problem to which I have no answer. The October 14, 1928, *Washington Evening Star* (p. 4) states: "Alexander Smith Cochran will return in Washington this week to open his attractive suite in the Hay-Adams House. He expects to remain during the winter season." A complementary article appeared in the same newspaper two months later (December 23, 1928, part 3, p. 7); paraphrasing, it says that Alexander Smith Cochran would lease a house at Massachusetts Avenue and 23d Street—the address of one of the most imposing mansions in the city, which includes noteworthy gardens. It had been untenanted for three years, and Mr. Cochran was having it renovated. Meanwhile, he was at the Hay-Adams. The gross discrepancy raised by this information is perplexing. While neither Washington article can possibly refer to our Alexander Smith Cochran, his namesake behaves very like the Yonkers Cochran. The only other known Alexander Smith Cochran was brother William's son, the future architect, who was 14 at the time.

121 Savoy-Plaza Hotel: Alex must have been among its first residents, since this hotel opened only in October 1927. The move to Yonkers is noted in EFA, Scrapbook, f. 22, col. 1. Saranac Lake was the site of Dr. Edward Livingston Trudeau's famed Adirondack Cottage Sanitorium for treating tuberculosis patients. Although Alex owned the house in which he died, which was among the largest in the area, no source known to me records earlier visits by him to Saranac Lake. Perhaps some occurred in his poorly documented last years. EFA, Scrapbook, ff. 22–32, contain obituaries from far and wide; folio 26 has an odd, semi-humorous, and very faulty obituary from the *New York Evening World* (ca. June 20, 1929). Valet at death: EFA, Ewing 2, p. 452.

122 "With every flag": *New York World* (June 24, 1929): [n.p.]. The statement on behalf of Smith Carpets was issued by its treasurer, Richard Edie; it is a good capsule summary of Alex's business life (EFA, Scrapbook, f. 10). In his eulogy, Bishop Freeman said that Alex was "self-effacing almost to a fault, diffident, reticent, amazingly so" (EFA, Scrapbook, f. 17). Funeral: EFA, Scrapbook, ff. 9–19 and 33; also Ewing, *Bravura*, p. 1.

123 Yale's Chief Research Librarian, Judith Schiff, informs me that Alex's standing was "the lowest honor grade." My thanks to her for this information. Yale social clubs: *Quarter-century Record*, p. 235.

124 Although the books and their increase were given formally to Yale University, it was with the understanding that they would be lodged at the Club and subject to its rules (see Appendix 1.1).

125 Flying: *Baltimore Sun* (June 7, 1911): 2; *Town and Country* 66 (May 1911): 55; *Washington Post* (May 24, 1911): 7. Belmont Park was the center of this activity.

126 Weeks, p. 6; Alex's very brief involvement in politics is the most obscure part of his biography. Largest contributor to the Progressive party: *Chicago Daily Tribune* (November 1, 1912); *Half-way Book*, p. 85. See also *New York Times* (July 27, 1912); *New York World*, June 21, 1929, EFA Scrapbook, f. 22, col. 3. Congressional candidacy: Hall writes that Alex "has entered the race for Congress from Westchester County, New York" (p. 889). Southern France: *New York Times* (May 15, 1912): 1, and (July 27, 1912): 3. This political activity is very faintly recorded in the Yale class books or anywhere else.

127 Memo from Thomas Murray.

128 *New York Times* (October 17, 1928): 2: Alex suspended his usual support of the Republicans. Al Smith's promise to end Prohibition decided him; Alex was a "wet" and regarded Prohibition as hypocritical.

129 For the details, see "Cochran Estate Inventory."

130 The obituary in the *New York Journal of Commerce* (June 21, 1929), in EFA, Scrapbook,

f. 24, emphasizes the continuity of Alex's headship of Smith Carpets even after he divested himself of ownership.

131 Freeman quotation: Freeman, p. 18; the observers were Dudley Field Malone and Clarence Day, cited below.

132 Instructorship at St. Paul's, "The Rector's Letter" 10:1 (Spring 1930): Articles 6; message to me from Beth Flynn, director of stewardship at St. Paul's School, June 1, 2017 (for which, my thanks). Also Freeman, p. 30. Other contributions from Alex to the school included its annual fund and endowment.

133 Main fortune applied to ballet, detailed in Ewing, *Bravura*; ART, p. 195.

134 *Detroit Free Press* (October 10, 1920): E7 (a syndicated feature article, often cited herein, that coincided with Alex's return to the U.S. with his bride; also in the *Washington Post*, same day).

135 EFA, Scrapbook, f. 11, col. 3.

136 EFA, Scrapbook, f. 24, col. 2. (Sloan headed the New York firm through which Smith carpets were marketed.) Selzer, p. 55.

137 '96 *Half-way Book*, p. 86.

138 Ewing, *Bravura*, p. 18.

139 EFA, Ewing 2, p. 388; ART, pp. 68–69, 90.

140 ART, pp. 67, 189–90. "Selfishness" and "egoism" may refer to Alex's inability to change his bachelor way of life.

141 *Decennial Record*, p. 276.

142 Alex in Tunisia: EFA, Ewing 2, p. 167. *Decennial Record*, p. 276: "My principal occupation at present is loafing up here [at Grasslands in East View, New York]," he wrote that spring. "When you get tired of Class Records let me know and run up and spend a night   Will be delighted to post you on these matters first hand and show you the

delights of a pastoral and bucolic existence."
The report's editor, Clarence Day, interpreted
this remark to mean "temporary resting,"
which was, in part, true. On Grasslands, see
EFA, Ewing 2, p. 142. After about a year at the
farm, Alex returned to the Smith Carpets
presidency and took part in strenuous sports,
but said nothing of them or other activities in
the report. He portrayed himself in solitude,
ostensibly wanting company. (The *Decennial
Record* also details other activities, notably his
business life.) Uncommunicative class notes
were his habit, as witness his contribution
to the *Sexennial Record, Class of 1896* (p. 79):
"I really have nothing interesting to write of
my career. Since 1896 I have been right here in
Yonkers in the manufacturing business, with an
occasional trip off, and am at present President
of the Alex. Smith and Sons Carpet Co." For
the *Triennial Record of the Class of 1896* (p. 28),
Alex's contribution amounted to three words,
whereas his friend Maitland Griggs wrote five
lines (p. 36). Alex provided a *curriculum vitae*
but offered no comments in later class books.

143 Baltimore nephew: Weeks, p. 5; also
"somewhat aloof." English well-wisher: Wrench,
p. 466. Malone: *New York Times* (May 2, 1922):
1. Earlier, the *New York Times* (October 2,
1921): 9, reported Malone saying: "Alexander
Smith Cochran has been joy riding all over this
world, buying houses and yachts by whim and
caprice.... If Mr. Cochran thinks he can dispose
of his wife the way he disposes of toys and
playthings when tired of them, then he is much
mistaken."

144 Day meant his comment in a frank but
friendly spirit (*Half-way Book,* p. 86). Alex
must have known what Day wrote about
him; as noted above, he named his last steam
yacht *Restless* (1922). He moved among his
many residences, never settling anywhere
(see Appendix 1.10B). According to Selzer,
"restlessness is said to be part of the hectic,
febrile course of tuberculosis" (p. 51).

145 Obituary, *New York Times* (June 21,
1929): 25.

146 These are famous names, Niarchos
associated with ship owning, Gucci with luxury
fashion.

147 On *Creole,* see Keith Dovkants, "The Curse
of Classic 63m Sailing Yacht *Creole,*" www.
boatinternational.com/yachts/editorial-
features/the-curse-of-classic-63m-sailing-
yacht-creole--28755 (retrieved March 1, 2019);
includes the Martin-Raget quotation; also
Abigail Haworth, "The Gucci Wife and the
Hitman," *The Guardian,* www.theguardian.
com/fashion/2016/jul/24/the-gucci-wife-and-
the-hitman-fashions-darkest-tale (retrieved
March 8, 2019). On the end of *Westward,* see
Hamilton-Adams, p. 103. A second *Westward*
was built by Alex's nephew Drayton Cochran.
It also was a schooner, but neither a replica
of its namesake nor a racer; rather it was a
cruising vessel often taken around the world,
and it still remains in use. (Thanks to John
Cochran for this information.)

148 Troxell II, p. 28.

Fig. 1.14. William Lyon ("Billy") Phelps, assistant professor
in Yale's English department. Considering that he was a Yale
celebrity, the university's Manuscripts and Archives collections
hold few photographs, and most of those show him in middle age.
This portrait was made during his early professorial years, about a
decade before he had a leading part in founding the Elizabethan
Club. Yale University Library, Manuscripts and Archives

Appendix 1.1

ALEX COCHRAN, "BILLY" PHELPS, THE BOOKS, AND THE CLUB

William Lyon "Billy" Phelps (1865–1943) was a prominent figure in American letters and a towering presence at the Yale of his time (fig. 1.14). By 1910, when he enters our story, he was the Lampson Professor of English Literature, noteworthy for having widened the Yale English curriculum. Phelps was Alexander Smith Cochran's (ASC's) crucial Yale contact, who worked out the club details with him, mobilized other members of Yale to support the enterprise, overcame presidential resistance at the university, and brought the Elizabethan Club into existence in less than a year. Phelps wrote the original and most influential account of the Club's foundation immediately after ASC's death in 1929, both to honor his memory and to commemorate his gift of the Club to Yale. The first, very abbreviated version of Phelps's narrative appeared in the *New York Times* on June 24, 1929 (p. 15), four days after ASC's death. A fuller version, referred to here as the "Phelps Laudation," incorporates the brief original. It was published on August 4, 1929, in both the *Hartford Courant* (p. E5) and the *Washington Post* (p. SM16); it is likely it also was included in newspapers elsewhere. The essay is in the *Yale Alumni Weekly* and, accompanied by a brief addition by Phelps, was reprinted in part in *The Elizabethan Club of Yale University 1911–2011: A Centenary Album,* edited by Stephen Parks (13–14; hereafter referred to as Parks I). Slightly abbreviated, it was incorporated into James E. Freeman's *A Revealing Intimacy: A Friend's Tribute to Alexander Smith Cochran* (13–18). The Phelps Laudation was quoted at length in other publications as well (e.g., Troxell I and II; Selzer 1998). It served as the basis for the retouched account of the same subject that Phelps included in his *Autobiography, with Letters* (292–93). The Phelps Laudation was much admired and praised for its completeness and precision (e.g., Griggs to Phelps, MSSA, RU36, box 3, folder 159).

Phelps wrote his Laudation 18 years after the founding of the Elizabethan Club, not from notes or documents (as far as is known) but from memory, with the intention to praise the just-deceased ASC rather than to provide a careful chronicle of his life. Phelps did not minimize his own role in this first recollection of the Lizzie's beginnings. The remarks of the board of governors of the Club on the occasion of Phelps's death in 1943 faithfully echo his authoritative narrative: "In a unique sense [Phelps] directly inspired the conception and later development of the Club. It was his magnetic teaching and contagious love of books that led a member of his earliest class in Elizabethan Drama ... to found and to endow the Elizabethan Club" (Parks I, p. 52). An early member adds that the Club was founded "on the encouragement of [Phelps]. The latter believed that Yale undergraduates interested in writing and the arts should have a place to congregate" (Lewis, p. 112). It seems that Phelps "directly inspired the conception" of ASC's club and "deserves equal prominence ... in the story of the founding" (Parks I, p. 13). Is this so?

Phelps's account overstates his own part, and Alexander Smith Cochran needs to be restored to his foremost place in starting the Club. When suitably trimmed, the Phelps Laudation of 1929 allows ASC's role its due stature.

> [ASC wrote to Phelps in 1910 that he was living in England, where he] mainly engaged in riding after hounds ... [he] amused himself by collecting ... plays, poems, &c published during the reign of Queen Elizabeth.... he said he was about to return to America, that he had a plan of his own for the books.... He appeared at my house in New Haven [for lunch, on November 3, 1910], and began to talk on a project that he had been developing in his mind for a year.... [T]he one thing he had missed most as an undergraduate was good conversation.... He was sure that many men wanted to talk about the things that really interested them ... [and felt so strongly about this] ... that in his Senior year he had organized a small eating club with a few congenial spirits.... There men talked freely and intimately about literature, art, and religion.

Now he had come to the conclusion that the one thing needed at
Yale … was an opportunity for the free and unaffected exchange
of talk. In order to have this, there must be the right atmosphere.
Accordingly he proposed to give his Elizabethan collection, not to
the university library, but to the students. He thought it would be
a good idea to have an Elizabethan Club, with this collection of
books as a center and nucleus. There were to be no entrance fees
and no dues; but only those students should be elected who were
seriously interested in the finer things of life, and unafraid to talk
about them.

One of [ASC's] most important and enduring monuments is the
Elizabethan Club at Yale. The idea of it originated with him, the
plans of its constitution and membership and program were
designed by him…. It is the offspring of his mind.

These lines seem unqualified in reporting ASC's role as the sole founder.
The preeminence Phelps allotted to himself in the Laudation was in the
story of the Elizabethan Club book collection. In a brief comment to the
Club in 1933, Phelps showed awareness of how he sounded: "I dislike to
magnify the ego … for after all, the 'only begetter' of this Club is Alexander
Smith Cochran" (Parks I, p. 33). As Phelps realized, his ego stands out at the
start of the laudation, which begins with himself:

I began teaching English literature at Yale in the autumn of 1892;…
[after] two years, it occurred to me … to offer … a course in
Elizabethan drama…. Among the juniors taking my course was a
boy named Alexander Smith Cochran…. Twelve or thirteen years
later, I received a letter…from [him]…. [He said that] owing to the
interest aroused in him by studying the Elizabethan drama … he
had amused himself by collecting…plays, poems, &c., published
during the reign of Queen Elizabeth.

Phelps's surmise that ASC's exposure to a course on Elizabethan drama
inspired his book collecting and what came of it was exaggerated. ASC's
association with rare books had a more complex genesis. In an article

published in 1952 that is crucial for details of the Club's foundation (see
Appendix 1.2), Gilbert McCoy Troxell, the Club's second librarian, reported
inquiries by a Yale professor of English that shed light on ASC's earliest
book buying:

> As the great interest of the Club is concentrated in the superb
> collection of books given by Mr. Cochran, it is fortunate that
> Professor Karl Young should, several years ago, have looked into
> the history of Mr. Cochran's early bookbuying. According to
> Mr. E. H. Dring, the president of Quaritch's in London at the
> time of Mr. Young's visit in February, 1928 [the year before ASC's
> death], Mr. Cochran first planned to collect English poets. Bernard
> Quaritch [son of the founder of this great London bookseller],
> thinking of Thomas J. Wise's immense purchases in that field
> (this was in 1907–8), suggested it was overcrowded, and urged Mr.
> Cochran to substitute English drama instead. Mr. Cochran thought
> this over for some time, and finally on December 11, 1908, yielded,
> and immediately bought for about £2,000 seven of the interludes
> [early form of English play] Quaritch had acquired at Sotheby's in
> 1906 at the so-called "Irish Find" sale. With this foundation, Mr.
> Cochran went on, and during the next three years acquired the
> greater part of his collection (Troxell II, 23–24).

Expert advice in London, rather than Yale reminiscences, guided ASC's
book collecting.

Dislodging Phelps from a role as inspirer of ASC's book collection and
as cofounder of the Club should not diminish recognition of his golden
part in the Club's life during its first decades. After ASC himself, he was the
principal contributor to the development of this project, overcoming resistance from the university's president, and seeing that the Club came into
existence in as little as seven months. A few willing helpers assisted him.
Phelps's leadership in animating the first years of the Lizzie may have been
even more admirable than his role in its foundation. His place in the Club
is best recalled in Frederick Pottle's address to the Founder's Dinner in 1961:

My most vivid recollections of the place are confined to the period of fifteen years following [1920 or 1921]. In 1920 [Phelps] was fifty-five, at the peak of his charm and not much declined in vigor.... [He] was bringing all the most famous writers of the English-speaking world to address the public in Sprague Hall and to meet the Elizabethan Club before or after.... [A]s the scenes rise in my memory, I see Phelps sitting under the portrait of Queen Elizabeth radiating zest for life, friendliness, and unaffected goodness, basking in our admiration, showing off shamelessly, happy and making everybody in the room happy.

Pottle added, "Phelps had been the Club's first President, and was President of that mysterious inner entity, the Elizabethan Club Corporation, but I always remember him simply as a member" (Parks I, pp. 70–71).

To return to the story of the Elizabethan Club's book collection, Troxell, as quoted above, relates that the purchase of seven "interludes" marked the start of ASC's accumulation. On the same day in December 1908, Quaritch also sold ASC a Shakespeare First Folio. This book, given by ASC to the Lizzie, became a duplicate after the acquisition of the superb Huth First Folio. The now-duplicate First Folio was sold back to Quaritch in February 1912 for what ASC had paid for it in 1908. Quaritch then sold it to the great Shakespeare collector Henry Folger, whose fiftieth First Folio it became (West, vol. 2, p. 179, no. 108; and Curatorial File for Folger STC 22273 f. 1, no. 50).

Bernard Quaritch Ltd was central to Cochran's book buying, but ASC also bought from other sellers. The purchases of those three years focused on Elizabethan drama and formed the larger, though not the salient, part of the final collection. The acquisition that made ASC's library world famous took place after the Club's founding on June 4, 1911 (see Appendix 1.2). As Troxell says, Mr. Quaritch *fils* turned him away from poets, ASC's first idea, and toward drama. The turn toward drama came from material considerations: poets were "overcrowded," and there was greater scope in drama for advantageous purchases.

ASC's acquisitions in England between 1908 and 1910 were itemized in letters to Phelps, and this set in motion the sequence of events that led to the Club's founding. The quality and value of the books mentioned in these letters startled Phelps. In 1929 and, especially, in 1939, Phelps's recollection of this list was faulty; he anachronistically spotlighted purchases from the Huth sale, which were not made until November 1911. What the early list sent to Phelps did include is an elusive question. In theory, it would consist of the "original books," the gifts from ASC minus the Hoe and Huth additions. But the only systematic indication of provenance known to me is the attractive (generally red) stickers imprinted "Ex museo Huthii" in the Huth books. A bold bibliographer might take on the problem of approximating the list of 1910 centered on the Elizabethan drama other than Shakespeare that made Phelps almost drop from his chair.

A massive complement to the "first collection" was acquired in 1911, the year the Club was founded. In April, the large Robert Hoe sale took place in New York. Andrew Keogh, reference librarian at the Yale University Library and the Elizabethan Club's first librarian, attended on ASC's behalf, guided by less than clear instructions. He acquired 11 choice items that together cost ASC a little more than $2,000.

The Huth acquisition was more complicated, and Phelps's Laudation muddles its circumstances. Phelps wrote: "When it was announced some years ago that a famous library would be sold at auction in England, Mr. Cochran went over, and bought in advance for the club the four folios of Shakespeare." It sounds as though ASC's transatlantic crossing took place well after the foundation of the Club ("some years ago," i.e., before 1929), for the sole purpose of book buying, and that he acquired only one prize (the first folio) and three lesser complements (folios 2, 3, and 4). Again, Phelps is an imperfect guide.

The Huth purchase is most fully set out in Alan Bell's introduction to *The Elizabethan Club of Yale University and Its Library,* the Club's catalogue (Bell, 14–17; also Troxell II, pp. 24–25). It occurred a few months after the first meeting of the Club on June 17, 1911, and less than a month before the clubhouse opened its doors on December 6. ASC went to Europe late in the summer of 1911 primarily for his health. In September he was a patient at the recently opened Kurhaus Semmering, a tuberculosis sanitorium 50 miles from Vienna. ASC was aware of the coming sale of Henry Huth's library and was attracted to its Shakespeariana. He wrote to Keogh, inviting him to visit London at ASC's expense so as to meet him between October 10 and 20: "My idea for the Elizabethan Club collection now is to confine ourselves principally to really well-known and rare books. That is, not to get a lot more of the less important writers but fewer of really well-known ones" (Troxell II, p. 25). ASC very much wanted to confer with Keogh about the coming sale, but a health "set back" early in October, kept him at Semmering. Keogh's trip was cancelled, and ASC's own appetite for Huth purchases abated. He wrote again to Keogh on November 4, when the sale was less than two weeks away: "The only books I was really tempted with at the Huth sale were the five or six first edition Shakespeares. But Quaritch [central to the transaction] seemed to think the five I selected would bring about £12,000 or more, so I decided to drop the question" (Troxell II, p. 25). Quaritch took the matter in hand and turned the transaction around:

> Quaritch had discovered that the Huth heirs were willing to sell as a whole the forty-two Shakespeare items listed for November 11, the eighth day of the sale, if they could get from a private collector what they considered a good price, and when they were offered £36,000 on behalf of Mr. Cochran on November 9, they gasped and accepted, delighted with the amount. (Troxell II, p. 25)

The ensuing triumphal cable came to Keogh from Semmering on November 19: "Confidential Have secured entire collection Huth sale Shakespeares." ASC's acquisition of the complete lot of Huth Shakespeares by private sale disappointed the great American collectors Henry Huntington and Henry Folger, even though each of them had often resorted to the same maneuver (Grant, pp. 131–32; a more dramatic account of the purchase is in Mays, pp. 176–77).

The clubhouse opened on December 6, 1911. Phelps was on sabbatical in Munich and could not attend. ASC also stayed away, although he had returned from Europe in late November (*New York Times* [November 23, 1911]: 11). Almost concurrent with the opening, the Elizabethan Club gained possession of 42 quartos and folios of Shakespeare's works. Henry Huth had required "that his books should be bibliographically perfect and in good condition" (Bell, p. 25). He also had them sumptuously bound. For a time they were America's leading collection of early Shakespeare editions. Later surpassed by those of the Folger and Huntington libraries, and other collectors, the Lizzie and Yale University Library can still pride themselves on having one of the foremost collections in America (*New York Times* [December 19, 1929]; EFA Scrapbook, f. 53). The Huth purchases are the jewels in the crown in an otherwise not contemptible gathering of other Tudor and Stuart authors, often in first editions. Thanks to ASC's munificence, the Elizabethan Club houses "some of the most precious of English books" (Strachey, p. 117).

Authorities disagree on the cost of the 42 Huth additions: Bell says it was 30,000 guineas (£31,500; see Bell, p. 16), while Troxell cites the amount of £36,000 (Troxell II, p. 25). If the higher price included a commission of £4,500, the additional charge was money well spent. The dollar equivalent in 1911 of the larger sum was about $180,000, which would have equaled roughly $4.25 million in 2016. To gauge how much of a bargain this purchase of 42 books was, *just one* of the items included in the Huth purchase fetched more than $5 million at a Sotheby's sale in 2006. Many other items in the collection (e.g., *Hamlet* quartos, the sonnets) are much rarer than the First Folio. And the Huth purchase accounted for a fraction of ASC's acquisitions, the first state of which had stunned Phelps. The ASC-donated core of the Elizabethan Club library, identified in Parks's catalogue, consists of 142 volumes (*Yale Daily News* [October 5, 2007]). Additions have been made by gift and purchase.

In *Pleasures and Palaces* (Lazarovich-Hrebelianovich, p. 188), the Princess Lazarovich-Hrebelianovich offers an unexpected sidelight on the Huth books: "I had, too, the pleasure of acquaintance with the early rare editions of Shakespeare in the famous Huth library at Bolney House.... The most magnificent fancy-dress ball of the time was given by the Huths, and that night we danced, surrounded by those treasures." (*Pleasures* refers to the vast Huth library in its entirety, not just the volumes of Shakespeare.)

It seems to have been thought around the Club (e.g., by Keogh,) that
ASC intended to continue enriching the library, as he did, magnificently,
with acquisitions from the Hoe and Huth libraries. But this was not to
be. Prodded by Keogh, ASC made further small purchases for the Club in
1915 (including the Florio translation of Montaigne's *Essays*) and in 1916 at
Quaritch's in London. On February 26, 1916, Quaritch notified Keogh that
he had sent ASC's listed purchases (MSSA, RU36, box 3, folder 157; the list is
lost). ASC's three-year "excursion into the world of rare books" ended with
no plan to continue purchases except, perhaps, "to confine ourselves principally to really well-known and rare books" (Bell, p. 21). It seems as though
he perceived the Elizabethan Club library as having a strictly limited need
for enrichment. As Carl Cannon suggested in his 1941 account of American
book collectors, "Alexander Smith Cochran should perhaps be classed as a
philanthropist rather than a collector" (Cannon, p. 333).

One of the founder's wishes was that the undergraduate members of
the Club, for whom this invaluable collection was destined, should be
free to handle and avail themselves of the book treasures. Troxell reports
that "Mr. Cochran wanted his books to be used by undergraduates, and
believed at one time that, if the books wore out, they would be replaced"
(Troxell II, p. 26). But this lighthearted idea was never taken seriously by
Club librarians. Normally, the vault is shut. Exceptions are made for special
occasions; for research, when Club books are taken to a secure location; or
on the initiative of members of the Club's library committee. Being a Club
member gives no privileged access. In general, the Lizzie book collection
is approachable, under supervision, only for one hour per week—from
4:30 to 5:30 PM on Fridays—during the university term, at which time the
vault is opened and a member of the library committee offers appropriate
commentary. For Club members, this is when the vault comes into its own
as the place to take one's guests, especially expert ones, to wonder at and
envy the Club's treasure.

By virtue of a prudent condition imposed by the university in an
agreement of June 19, 1911, the Elizabethan Club books, the gift of its
founder, belong to Yale. They are deposited at the Club in its massive

vault (see Appendix 1.3), "subject to such regulations as the corporation will determine." The vault combination is known only to members of the library committee, who, in rotation, display the books as described above (Parks I, p. 61). If books in the Elizabethan Club are needed for research by a reader at Yale, they are transferred to the nearby, secure Beinecke Rare Book and Manuscript Library for reading there. That is also the only way Lizzie members may consult the Club's treasures.

ASC, often alone, was an avid reader. In 1914 he gave the Lizzie his collected modern books (Board of Governors minutes, April 24, 1914, MSSA, RU36, box 1, folder 49), some of which may occupy shelves of the Club's Governors' Room. The books in ASC's possession at his death were valued at just under $9,000 ("Cochran Estate Inventory").

The precious books given by ASC distinguish the Lizzie from other societies at Yale and elsewhere, making it the one of the many Yale clubs that invites the attention of the world at large. The importance of the Club's remarkable library was recognized by the university from the moment the clubhouse opened: "The unique collections also presented to the Club by Mr. Cochran have served to bring to the University visitors from far distant institutions" (*Report of the Treasurer of Yale University*, 1910–16, p. 17). The library is a guarantee of the Lizzie's future well being. "And thanks to [ASC] for the talismanic spellbinding propinquity of the books in the vault. They are more than books; they are presences. They are the genius of the place" (Selzer, p. 55).

Appendix 1.2

THE TROXELL NARRATIVES ON THE FOUNDING OF THE YALE UNIVERSITY ELIZABETHAN CLUB

Gilbert Troxell's appealing accounts of the Elizabethan Club's creation can be regarded as definitive. The applicable parts drawn from his articles are reprinted below. To facilitate understanding of these passages, the excerpts are preceded by a chronicle of selected events during the founding period as a point of departure that supplies relevant dates and summarizes the sequence of events.

June 12, 1897. ASC buys at a Christie's auction the portrait of Elizabeth I now hanging in the Club.

December 11, 1908. ASC begins collecting early editions of Elizabethan drama.

Early autumn 1910. ASC writes to William Lyon Phelps and tells him of his book collecting in England. In an undated follow-up letter (ASC to Phelps, MSSA, RU36, box 3, folder 156), ASC promises to send Phelps a provisional list of books and explains the sort of club he has in mind.

Autumn 1910. Phelps, impressed, consults Andrew Keogh, the Yale reference librarian. They ask ASC for bibliographical information and, upon seeing it, are enthusiastic.

———— ASC writes to Phelps that he is about to return to the U.S., and he will come to visit and discuss his plan.

November 3, 1910. ASC meets with Phelps for lunch at the professor's house at 110 Whitney Avenue, New Haven (still standing). Also present is Frederick Wells Williams, assistant professor of Oriental languages at Yale, a friend of ASC's who will be much involved in the founding and early life of the Club. ASC discloses the plan he has been developing. He wants his books, which he is giving to the undergraduates, to be the nucleus of a club composed of men "seriously interested in the finer things of life, and unafraid to talk about them" (Phelps Laudation). It was to have neither an entrance fee nor dues. Phelps and Williams applaud this plan and presumably help define its details.

Winter 1910–1911. Phelps and Keogh approach J. C. Schwab, University Librarian, with ASC's offer of books. Schwab's response is negative. Advised by Schwab, President Hadley rejects the books and club.

Winter 1911. Phelps and Keogh, joined by George Parmly Day, treasurer of the university, Anson Phelps Stokes, its secretary, and others, strongly protest the president's refusal of ASC's books. They are helped by a friend of ASC's, Abraham Valentine Williams Jackson, professor of Persian at Columbia University, who indicates that Columbia will welcome what Yale declines. Hadley's resistance crumbles.

March 24, 1911. Hadley writes to ASC telling him of his support for the creation of the proposed club. He urges patience lest the undergraduates be alarmed (Parks I, p. 14): ASC replies from Grasslands, the Cochran farm, "pleased to see the apparently genuine interest being taken in the Elizabethan Club" (ASC to Hadley, MSSA, RU36, box 3, folder 157).

April 1911. A first step is taken toward buying the property whose building will become the clubhouse. (For the acquisition of the club property, see Appendix 1.3.)

June 4, 1911. Articles of Association are drawn up for the Yale University Elizabethan Club Corporation [titular owner of the Club]. The original Incorporators—ASC, Keogh, Phelps, and Williams along with George Parmly Day and Chauncey Tinker—sign the document. (ASC, absent at the signing, added his signature two days later in New York.) Article 6 provides that, if the Corporation is dissolved, all its property will vest in Yale University and be conveyed to it. This is the Club's foundation charter.

June 17, 1911. The organizers of the Club, including ASC, meet at Phelps's house. The Club's rules are laid out in detail, and an initial slate of officers is chosen.

———— ASC instructs Williams, his trustee for the property he bought at 123 (now 459) College Street, to sell this property for no consideration to the Club Corporation.

June 19, 1911. Finalization of the agreement by which the Elizabethan Club and ASC stipulate that ASC has given Yale University "a number of books and pamphlets." Yale becomes the owner of the Elizabethan Club Collection "and all additions thereto," and it accepts ASC's requirement that the Collection and all future additions will be deposited on the premises of the Club subject to such regulations as the corporation will determine.

July 11, 1911. Deed of gift by ASC to Yale University. To establish the endowment, ASC gives Yale $100,000 "together with such additions as may hereafter be made thereto," and Yale University accepts the gift for the uses of the Club, promising to make quarterly payments to the Yale University Elizabethan Club Corporation as prescribed in detail. Also stipulated is that, should the Elizabethan Club Corporation ever be dissolved, the $100,000 "with any and all increases thereon shall immediately vest" in Yale University. Signed by ASC, Day, and Yale's President Hadley.

October 11, 1911. Frederick Williams, trustee for ASC, sells 123 College Street for $1.00 and further consideration to the Elizabethan Club Corporation.

October–November 1911 (dates uncertain). The clubhouse is remodeled according to plans by the New York architect George Chappell; ASC supplies furnishings.

December 6, 1911. The clubhouse opens for the first time. Members examine its exhibited treasures.

As said at the beginning of this appendix, the most authoritative accounts of the Club's founding are articles published in 1933 and 1952 by its second librarian, Gilbert McCoy Troxell. Although they overlap in some respects, they also complement each other, and the parts relevant to the founding of the Club warrant reprinting here. The earlier of the two articles, entitled "The Elizabethan Club of Yale University" (cited as Troxell I) appeared in 1933 in issue 27 of the *Papers of the Bibliographical Society of America*.

At the time of its foundation the Elizabethan Club of Yale University symbolized, to its academic world, the advent of radicalism. For years the dangers of originality had been avoided with such care that they were believed to be imaginary. The various college institutions were well established and almost venerable, and as undergraduates regarded them with the reverence and awe tinged with hysteria that serve usually to protect traditions, everything seemed to be satisfactory. Suddenly a club, centered about a collection of sixteenth- and early seventeenth-century books, reported to have cost thousands of dollars, had come into being, established quite frankly for the purpose of encouraging undergraduates, chosen for their special abilities, to talk to each other about art or literature or whatever intellectual interests absorbed them at the moment. No one had ever heard of such an institution before, and very few thought that it was destined for anything more than complete and rather dismal failure. The late president of the university, Dr. Arthur Twining Hadley, admitted once that he had been opposed to it at first. He had tried to imagine how his own class—that of 1876—would have felt under the circumstances, and the result had not been stimulating. But, as he explained, there seemed to have grown up in college since his time a generation that, because of its contact with certain members of the faculty, wanted to read, and wanted to talk about itself and about books—he did not pretend to understand it, but at least its individuality had to be acknowledged even in the midst of a conservative society. (Troxell I, pp. 83–84)

Troxell continues with a summary of and a quotation from the Phelps Laudation. He goes on:

> On the sixth of December, 1911, the building Mr. Cochran had had remodeled, according to plans made by Mr. George H. Chappell, was opened for the first time to the Club members. The *Yale Alumni Weekly* in its account remarked, "There were no formal ceremonies, but a large majority of those persons already elected who live within reach of New Haven were present to inspect the club house, and to see the first exhibition of books, prints, and paintings contained in the club's library." From that time, the Elizabethan Club, in spite of occasional jeers, has become a recognized part of undergraduate life—it has, with certain limitations, managed to fulfil Mr. Cochran's intentions in a manner that must have been a satisfaction to him during his life, and it has provided an asylum for many individuals. The organization is the usual one of president (who serves for a term of two years), vice-president (who is elected annually), secretary (always an undergraduate member of the club), librarian, board of governors, and committee on admissions. Candidates for admission are proposed and seconded as they are elsewhere: the qualifications for membership are rather indefinite, but at least it is assumed that members should be interested in books and reading, in collecting of some kind, or should have the ability to write or to talk well. There are five kinds of membership: faculty, graduate, associate, undergraduate, and honorary.[1] The number of undergraduate members from any single class can never be more than twenty-five. There are no initiation fees, and no dues. Tea is served each afternoon during the college year, and the safe in which Mr. Cochran's books are kept, together with a few others belonging to the same general period that have been acquired by gift since 1911, is opened regularly once a week, and at other times at the request of members. Occasionally, artists, writers, critics, actors, and singers give informal talks: these "club nights" were suggested

1 In 1932, two additional classes of members were added: university and foreign.

by Mr. Cochran, as he believed undergraduates would like to be brought into closer relationship with prominent men and women who ordinarily come to New Haven under more formal conditions. It should be emphasized that the Elizabethan Club was never given to the university: it was actually given to five individuals, the incorporators [six in the list of original incorporators (January 3, 1911)], who, as members of the university, hold the Club in trust for the undergraduates. These men interfere with nothing, and even their existence was not known officially until recently. (Troxell I, pp. 85–86)

In 1952, Troxell published "The Elizabethan Club: Its Origins and Its Books" (cited as Troxell II) in the *Yale University Library Gazette*.

In the New Haven world of 1911, the advent of the Elizabethan Club suggested only the appearance of radicalism: undergraduates had long-established activities, athletics, singing, Dwight Hall; if they ever read, there was Rudyard Kipling in the shiny, brown "Outward Bound" edition, or there were novels by contemporary exponents of the romantic school, George Barr McCutcheon, Meredith Nicholson, and John Fox, Jr.; there were also Victor talking machines, and a few automobiles. And into this academic serenity a "club" created for the purpose of encouraging undergraduates to talk about literature, or art, or themselves, whatever might absorb them at the moment, had been projected, endowed both with money and with a library of sixteenth- and seventeenth-century plays, several titles of which could not be mentioned in a mixed company. It was new; it was different; it was not what anyone had ever, by experience, been led to expect. (Troxell II, p. 19)

Here, too, Troxell includes a summary of the Phelps Laudation and quotes from it.

"This [Elizabethan Club] seemed to me a magnificent plan, and I naturally entered into it with enthusiasm. 'If you will find a house,' said he [ASC], 'I will buy it.' I found one, and he immediately bought it for about $75,000. Then he gave $100,000 for endowment."

But much more had gone on before the happy conclusion of the $100,000 endowment. Mr. Cochran's original list of books had been simply a catalogue of titles without dates or identifications of any kind: Mr. Phelps showed it immediately to Mr. Andrew Keogh, at that time Reference Librarian in the University Library, and they decided to ask for more information. When that arrived, and when there followed the suggestion of a club built around the collection of books, Mr. Phelps and Mr. Keogh went to Mr. Schwab, the University Librarian, to ask his help in inducing President Hadley to accept the gift. Mr. John Christopher Schwab was a kindly man, very good to his staff; but first editions of early English dramatists meant little to him, and he advised Mr. Hadley to decline—the whole idea was too experimental. Mr. Hadley, who, possibly, remembered that Mr. Cochran had shown no interest in supplying the Divinity School with new dormitories, followed the advice and refused. In the storm that followed this action, there suddenly appeared the figure of the Professor of Persian at Columbia University, Abraham Valentine Williams Jackson, an old friend of Mr. Cochran's, who offered everything Columbia had for the Cochran collection. This was too much, and what Mr. Henry W. Farnam called "the bibliophilic dainties" were accepted by Yale, along with the club for which the Administration anticipated only a dismal future. Mr. Hadley, later on, in an alumni address confessed his original opposition to the entire club idea: he had tried, he said, to imagine how he and his classmates would have felt about such an organization, and the result had not been encouraging; but, apparently, since his time a generation had grown up that liked to read and liked to talk, and even though he did not pretend to understand it, it existed.

With the official acceptance accomplished, the work of organization could commence. Mr. Cochran had as his collaborators three invaluable people, Mr. Phelps, Professor Frederick Wells Williams, and Mr. Keogh who not only knew a great deal about books, but could be depended upon to do the hard work of supervising, cataloguing, and making detailed reports. In March, 1911, the portrait of Elihu Yale was bought; in April came the sale of Elizabethan books in Mr. Robert Hoe's library; on June 17, the first meeting of the Club was held at the Phelps house to adopt the first constitution, and to elect members and officers. Mr. Phelps was the first president, Mr. Williams vice-president, Mr. Keogh librarian, Julian Cornell Biddle secretary (an undergraduate position), H.E. Joyce treasurer, Professor C.B. Tinker chairman of the admissions committee, and Dr. William Pitt McCune chairman of the house committee. The honorary members who, in the language of the constitution, "shall be ineligible for office, shall have no vote in meetings of the Club, and shall not serve upon any of the standing committees," were headed by President Hadley, Mr. Stokes, and Mr. Schwab, and included Simeon E. Baldwin, Professor Lounsbury, George Pierce Baker, Beverly Chew, Dr. H.H. Furness, Professor A.V.W. Jackson, Barrett Wendell, and George E. Woodberry. It was not until the sixth of December, 1911, however, that the clubhouse at 123 College Street, remodeled according to Mr. George H. Chappell's plans, was opened for the use of the members. The *Alumni Weekly*, nervous as usual about its readers, was inspired to ask Mr. Keogh to write about this event, and about the Club itself:

> There were no formal ceremonies, but a large majority of those already elected who live within reach of New Haven were present to inspect the club house, and to see the first exhibition of the rare volumes, prints, and paintings contained in the club's library.... The Elizabethan Club, which was formed "to promote in the community a wider appreciation of literature and of social intercourse founded

upon such appreciation" is, in no sense, a part of the traditional Yale undergraduate secret society system. It is, rather, an open club for the use of its chosen undergraduate and graduate members, who may or may not belong to existing societies, together with a certain number of faculty members ... and a limited number of honorary members, among whom will be included scholars occupying places in the faculties of other institutions, as well as private collectors ... of note in this country and abroad. While the membership of this unique Yale literary club will naturally be limited, as in the case of any such social organization, it is of interest to note that the members are at liberty to bring in guests. The qualifications set for membership cannot be very easily defined, but in a general way are those which obtain in any club formed for the use of men of discriminating tastes and appreciations. It has been suggested by some observers that the Elizabethan Club will be a miniature combination of the Century, the Grolier, and the Players' clubs of New York. Perhaps this will best indicate the desired character of its membership. Under the Elizabethan Club's standards the mere fact that a student has written for any of the undergraduate publications, or has become an editor of one of them, will not entitle him to membership unless, with literary ability, he possesses the rather indefinable qualities of originality and individuality which combine to make a medium of social intercourse of distinction....

At the second annual meeting of the Club, there were two sets of nominations for all the offices, one presented by a nominating committee which had had the idea of introducing entirely new names, the other by the Club's members who thought the original officers should be continued; as a result of this conflict, the constitution was gone over and amended.

The Club had become established, and it had succeeded....
[T]he entertainment committees were extremely active. Colonel
Theodore Roosevelt wrote Professor Lounsbury that he grudged
the Elizabethan Club to Yale; and Mr. Cochran wrote: "It is indeed
good to hear of the success of the club. I hear outside, every once in
the while, of how much it is thought of. Gilbert Murray was the last,
telling a friend what had interested him most in America, and it got
back to me. Well, it was done right." (Troxell II, pp. 20–23)

President Hadley's only other letter that is connected with ASC, dated
December 26, 1911, supports his nomination to membership in the Century
Association, a New York club that centers on literature, to which Hadley
belonged (MSSA, Hadley, box 118, p. 511). Nothing came of this initiative,
and the Century was not among ASC's many clubs.

Appendix 1.3

THE MYSTERIOUS PURCHASE PRICE OF THE CLUBHOUSE AND THE ACQUISITION OF THE VAULT

The Clubhouse

The cost of the clubhouse is mysterious. It poses problems that may never be solved, at least not with the evidence currently available. Names distinguished in the history of Yale and the Club are involved, and they make the problems even more puzzling than the documents alone. The sources, including five hand- or typewritten documents and several lines of narrative, ought to suffice to clarify the purchase. Instead, they are so perplexing as to create insurmountable problems.[1]

The Documents

The documents on which this appendix is based are described below and listed in chronological order. Unless otherwise indicated, copies of all documents that once were in the Club office's files have been moved to MSSA RU36.

A. A handwritten docket, typed at its end, includes separate listings of transactions involving the Property between February 1911 and November 1974. It starts with a notice of the death of its owner, Wilbur F. Gilbert, on February 6, 1911. As of February 21, 1911, it was owned by Gilbert's estate and Helen G. Gilbert, who, although not his wife, probably was a close relative. Five other notices follow (mentioned below as they become relevant). Near the end of the docket, an assessment figure of 1973 for the property is given, which affected the Yale University Elizabethan Club Corporation.

---

1 The documents repeatedly detail the bounds of the property they concern, specifying its neighbors on all sides. Its address then was 123 College Street, but now is 459 College Street. I have simplified my discussion by omitting repeated expositions of the detailed bounds and include them all within the term the *Property*.

B. An unchronological entry in docket A dated March 24, 1911, records that the estate of Jane E. Gilbert, deceased, deeds the "undiv ½ int" (undivided half-interest) in the Property to Helen G. Gilbert. This is anomalous: Why would Helen Gilbert receive from Jane Gilbert's estate, in March, the share of the Property that she already seems to have owned as of February 1911?

C. An agreement dated April 28, 1911, by which Geo. Parmly Day (see Appendix 1.2) undertook to purchase the Property from Ella Gilbert and Helen Gilbert. Helen had "one undivided half portion," while Ella, Wilbur's wife and heir by will, had the other. Day purchases the Property from them for $35,800, which they split evenly, in a transaction set to be completed by June 1, 1911.

D. Executor's deed, dated May 8, 1911. Probate court authorized the executors of Wilbur Gilbert's estate to sell "the real estate hereinafter described" to Frederick W. Williams [see Appendix 1.2, November 3, 1910] for the consideration of $18,000 — "an undivided half-interest" in the Property. (This deed is summarized in docket A, above; it is recorded in New Haven City records vol. 666/98.)

E. A lost document summarized in docket A that specified "Ella H. Gilbert / Helen G. Gilbert / to Frederick W. Williams" and indicates "Con[sideration] $1 etc." What the document concerns is not stated, but the context (see document C, above) suggests it is the Property.

F. A lost document, the existence of which is suggested by documents D and E, above: purchase of the Property by ASC from Frederick W. Williams.

G. Conveyance of the Property by ASC, dated May 8, 1911, to Frederick W. Williams, who undertook to hold the Property purchased by ASC in trust and to convey it "to such person, firm or corporation" as would be named by ASC.

H. Letter dated June 17, 1911 (date of the first meeting of the Club), handwritten on William Lyon Phelps's note paper and signed by ASC, instructing Frederick W. Williams to convey "without consideration" to the Yale University Elizabethan Club Corporation "the Property recently conveyed to him by Helen G. Gilbert and Ella H. Gilbert and the Executors of the will of W. F. Gilbert" (MSSA RU36, box 1, folder 40).

I. October 11, 1911. Frederick Williams sells the Property to the Yale University Elizabethan Club Corporation for no consideration (New Haven City records vol. 676/69.)

This trail of deeds is neither clear nor straightforward, but its main puzzle is the relationship of the $35,800 (document C) to the $18,000 (document D). As best I can make out, the smaller amount relates to Ella Gilbert's share of the Property; for the indicated sum, which is included in the $35,800, Wilbur's half-share in the Property was detached from his estate and included as Ella's half of the Property in document C. The costs indicated by these documents are coherent: much of the documentation concerns the "undivided half-interest" in the Property, and $18,000 is just a little more than one-half of $35,800. It also is clear that the two half-interests were brought together by the buyers, so the figure given in the George Parmly Day document (document C) is coherent as far as the documentation goes.

The adventures of the Property are relatively uncomplicated by comparison with those of its price. Phelps's two basic accounts of the cost provide a starting point. In the Phelps Laudation, he reported, " 'If you will find a house,' [Cochran] said, 'I will buy it.' I found one, and he immediately bought it for about $75,000." Roughly ten years later, in his *Autobiography,* Phelps recalls that ASC "asked me to find a suitable building. I found one and told him the owner wanted seventy-five thousand dollars. 'I'll buy it,' said Cochran, and he did" (p. 293). An undated qualification is in a footnote in Troxell II (p. 20): "Mr. George Parmly Day, one of the original incorporators of the Club, has pointed out that this figure includes not only the price paid for the house and land, but also the amount spent on the complete reconstruction of the building." While perhaps true, this definitely is not the sense we get from Phelps's descriptions. The only available alternative to Phelps's statement of cost of $75,000 is in Day's agreement (document C), where he specifies $35,800.

Other figures must also be taken into account when considering the prices stated in the documents. The value of the dollar in 1911 was different from what it was in 2017. Going by inflation calculations derived from the Consumer Price Index (CPI), which was first reported in 1913, $1.00 in 1913 would equal $24.73 in 2017. Therefore, when calculated at the CPI for 1913, Phelps's 1911 figure of $75,000 rounds to a 2017 value of about $1.86 million. The City of New Haven's present assessment of the house and land at 459 College Street is an estimated market value of about $980,000, which places the 2017 adjustment of Phelps's price at about twice what the market value of the Property is considered to be today. (Today New Haven takes the market value of property, which changes every year, as its assessment value.) A similar calculation based on Day's $35,800 demonstrates that, if taken as one-half of Phelps's figure, it yields a much more reasonable 2017 market price of $534,100, which is considerably less than the notional $980,000 arrived at on the basis of the assessment, but too low for a lot as large as the Club's.

One final figure warrants consideration because it suggests that even Day's $35,800 was excessive. In 1973, roughly 60 years after ASC acquired the Property for the Lizzie, the City assessed it at $46,200. Applying the City's then standard formula for calculating market value (assessment + 30% assessment), the Property appears to have been worth $60,060 in 1973. This, of course, is much less than the Phelps's alleged price in 1911 of $75,000. But odd results are also attained with the price of $35,800 in Day's agreement. By using the inflation calculator, one finds that this amount in 1911 (1913) would have grown to about $165,000 in 1973, more than twice the Property's estimated market value for that year ($60,060). This oddity implies that the purchase price in 1911 would have been considerably less than $35,800—which those persons interested in real estate with whom I've talked about this problem believe was too high a price for New Haven property at that time.

It is possible that Phelps was insensitive to numbers and unacquainted with the real estate market; perhaps he simply did not worry about the $75,000 figure in his Laudation. Treasurer of Yale George Day, however, had a head for figures and would have had to be familiar with New Haven real estate prices. The $35,800 amount set down in his promise of purchase is also out of line with what, conjecturally, such a house is likely to have cost in 1911, but at least it is conceivable, whereas Phelps's $75,000 is not.

ASC was a businessman involved in real estate. Hillbright Corporation, his holding company for real estate properties, employed Harry Zuckert as its full-time lawyer, and it owned two large buildings in New York and others elsewhere. ASC bought and sold many houses and apartments for himself (see "Cochran Estate Inventory"). It is hard to think that he would have cheerfully replied "I'll buy it" to Phelps's announcement that the owner was asking $75,000, an amount equaling close to $2 million in 2017 and an enormous, highly improbable price for the Property. In the comment reported by Troxell, George Day affirms that he was content with Phelps's figure provided it was understood that it included a "complete reconstruction" of the house. Unless the reconstruction (often called a remodeling), which was carried out in a few months, cost more than the purchase price of the house and land, that figure is unlikely as well. Day further muddies the subject in a letter of 1949: "It was in the following year (1911) that [ASC] authorized me to purchase the house at 123 College Street, which he thereafter gave to the Yale University Elizabethan Club Corporation" (Parks I, p. 56). Cost is not mentioned, and reference is made to neither Frederick W. Williams—so central to the deeds summarized above—nor Phelps himself, whose autobiographical remarks, however exaggerated, cannot be wished away.

What is one to make of these various discordant numbers and statements? The one certainty is that Phelps's $75,000 is impossible. Otherwise, I have laid out the evidence I have found, and hope that a future researcher will find a way out of this morass.

The Vault

When the Lizzie opened, the clubhouse had a fireproof safe. The December 29, 1911, issue of *Yale Alumni Weekly* (21:12, p. 372) printed a response to a letter dated December 18, 1911, in which its writer had inquired about the safety from fire of the Elizabethan Club book collection. The editor replied: "The rare books at present housed in the Elizabethan Club... are kept in a fire-proof vault set into the wall of the exhibition room." Phelps also intimates the existence of this vault: a house was acquired, and "a vault was built for the books" (*Autobiography,* p. 293). To judge by language alone, the description published in December 1911 could describe something very like the present vault, but this probably is not the case. The minutes of the Club's Board of Governors' meeting of January 27, 1912, plainly indicates the perceived need for improvement: "In view of the addition of the Huth Shakespeares to the Club Library and the imperfect protection from fire and burglary afforded by the safe, it was agreed to secure plans and draw-ings for a better and larger safe to replace the present one.... It was voted that the Tudor and Stuart rarities be placed temporarily in one of the New Haven banks" (Parks I, p. 21). By March 12, the project had moved forward: "Plans and specifications for a new vault have been received from three safe works.... In the meantime, a fireproof safe has been rented and Tudor and Stuart rarities transferred from the safety deposit box" (Parks I, p. 21). In sum, the Club's existing vault was considered inadequate; a safety deposit box in a bank was rented, and the rare books were moved to it; next, a fireproof safe was rented to which they were moved from the bank. There the records end.

We know that the Club duly gained the bank-worthy vault that it has today (see Parks I, p. 50), and clearly it was an expensive purchase that required major work to be done to shore up a corner of the clubhouse: "The walls consist of masonry about sixteen inches thick," adequate for fireproofing (Parks I, p. 88). No clear-cut information states when this was done, what it cost, or how the costs were paid.

Fred Robinson's talk at the Founder's Day Dinner of February 2003 does include some information, however. In "Vaulting Ambition," a version of the speech published by the Club as an undated, unpaged pamphlet, Robinson gives no details of date, cost, or source, but he writes: "The founder pledged a sum of money for the new safe along with plans and specifications from three manufacturers that included York Safes and Vaults in New York City, which was selected for the job." The details of the choice of manufacturer show that although Robinson had a definite source, he was more interested in other aspects of the subject.

In the published version of a Founder's Day address of February 28, 1998, Richard Selzer, after speaking of the clubhouse, says: "He [ASC] also gave an additional $25,000 to renovate the house to accommodate a large vault for his collection" (Selzer, p. 49). There is no doubt that the clubhouse needed major construction at its southeast corner in order to receive the new safe. Selzer seems to be saying that, over and above the cost of the clubhouse and its remodeling, some months after the Club's opening ASC supplied an additional $25,000 for the vault and the construction needed to install it. Selzer died in 2016, making it impossible to determine where he got this detail. He was well placed to be informed, and perhaps it was the same source Robinson knew.

The Club documents suggest that a first, inadequate vault was replaced by the one the Club now has. In addition to the initial cost of the club-house and its renovation, ASC appears to have made a further gift to the Lizzie for replacement of the earlier safe, but again, if conversion to our dollars is done, the $25,000 price seems high.

Appendix 1.4

DOWNS AND UPS OF THE ELIZABETHAN CLUB'S FINANCES

The Club's endowment—initially ASC's gift of $100,000 (see Appendix 1.2)—was entrusted to Yale for the stated purpose of defraying the costs of the Club. It is pooled with the university's endowment. ASC emphatically expressed the wish that the Lizzie members should pay no dues or initiation fees, and he repeated this prohibition many times in his correspondence with the Club. After only a few years, the income from the endowment no longer sufficed to wholly cover the Club's expenses. ASC was asked for help with the shortage and gave it. In 1961 Frederick Pottle recalled "those carefree days when the Founder could be appealed to annually to bail us out" (Parks I, p. 71). In the earliest days of the Club, even a small improvement—the creation of a bowling green—was noticed and approved by ASC, who reimbursed its cost (Parks I, p. 21).

A more reliable financing by the founder eluded the efforts of Club leaders. In 1921, while experiencing a difficult marriage, ASC turned his back on the Lizzie, even harking back to the university's resistance ten years earlier. His classmate Maitland Griggs wrote a memorandum to Club leaders (February 22, 1921), in which he explained that Cochran had lost interest in the Elizabethan Club, and he was not likely to endow it further. Griggs did not think that it was of any use to ask him for money for books or other things at this time. He did not believe he would increase the endowment. The principal reason for this loss of interest was Mr. Cochran's belief that his gift was not appreciated. Apart from Mr. Phelps and [Griggs] and possibly one or two others, he did not think that anyone here cared about it, and he was certain that the administration did not look upon it with favor when it was first proposed. He was greatly disappointed at the reception he had from the administration in 1911 (MSSA, RU36, box 3, folder 156; also Selzer, p. 51). Griggs, ASC's lawyer and close friend, was an original member of the Lizzie and uniquely well situated to know about his sentiments. This estrangement from the Club was temporary, however. In its archives, Griggs's memorandum is flanked by letters from ASC that express pleasure at the success of the Club, affirm his continued interest in its well being and his concern for its upkeep, and show willingness to underwrite its refurbishment (letters from ASC of 1919, 1920, 1921, 1922, 1923, 1925, MSSA, RU36, box 3, folder 156). As George Parmly Day recalled in 1949: "[Cochran] had from time to time told us he meant [to add to the endowment] in order to make sure that its annual income would always be sufficient to meet its needs" (Parks I, p. 56). A letter from ASC dated July 10, 1927, aroused much hope: "I'll ... arrange to increase the endowment when I get back [from Paris] and can arrange details." That resolve was not carried out. A very discouraging letter came almost a year later, on May 19, 1928: "The matter of endowment can wait" (MSSA, RU36, box 3, folder 156). This proved to be ASC's last word on the subject. Even in his will (April 1929) he neither made any provision for the Elizabethan Club nor referred to it. (He passed over Yale University as well.) After ASC's death, the Club approached each of his six principal heirs, to whom he had made million-dollar bequests, suggesting that they might repair his oversight with gifts of $10,000 apiece, "as a memorial to their benefactor." No one replied (MSSA, RU36, box 3, folder 156).

The small deficits that the Lizzie already ran in the 1920s were offset by subsidies from ASC. This help stopped upon his death (June 20, 1929), just months before the onset of the Great Depression. The gravity of the situation was announced to the membership in December 1931 in a letter from the Club's president, Frederick Pottle, on behalf of the board of governors (Parks 1, pp. 138–39). To paraphrase it, ASC regrettably had not increased the endowment or bequeathed anything to the Club in his will. The founder's prohibition on dues was well known and heartily endorsed by the governors, but unless several hundred dollars were secured, the social pleasures of the Club would have to be limited severely, and necessary maintenance would be impossible. The governors therefore instituted a Founder's Fund to which active members would be invited to contribute annually. The suggested contribution was $10, but it was hoped that some would give more. The annual appeal could be ended if ten gifts of $5,000 each were added to the endowment. Pottle clearly set out the Lizzie's need. The new fund would be the more necessary because the Club's endowment took a hit in the 1930s, when the payout from the university endowment was lowered gradually from 5 to 3½ percent. In view of this, the founder's fervent wish that membership in the Club should be completely gratis had to be disregarded. Annual dues were instituted. They are recorded as $5.00 in 1934 and, by 1950, had reached $25.00 (MSSA, RU36, box 2, folder 136).

Although regrettable, this step helped balance the books, but it was not enough to prevent a deterioration of the plant: "Unfavorably impressed when visiting the Club by the inadequate electric fixtures, the dingy walls and outworn furniture, Mr. Griggs generously offered five hundred dollars to be expended for such renovations as seemed most urgent" ("President's Letter" of 1938, in Parks I, p. 141). Special appeals were made to pay for capital expenditures (e.g., roof repairs). A letter of November 30, 1949, from George Day to Charles P. Kellogg reveals that the Lizzie was still leading a hand-to-mouth existence (Parks I, pp. 55–56). An appeal to President Charles Seymour in 1950 for a university subsidy received a gentle refusal (Parks I, pp. 56–57).

By the start of the 1960s, the Club's finances remained very constrained. Only "sporadic gifts by graduates" allowed it to maintain a "precariously balanced budget" (letter from Frederick Pottle, April 1961; Club files). A fund drive was begun in the hope of doubling the Club's endowment, and an Incorporators' Fund was established. The endowment then stood at $151,000 and was soon augmented by the university's distribution of a capital gain of $15,100. Two years later, the endowment had grown to $199,000, and the long-absent tea sandwiches could be restored (Parks I, pp. 70, 72). The Founder's Fund continued to be a reliable and prized resource.

In the next three decades a major, though poorly documented, change in Club finances took place. The still-modest endowment of 1963 attained seven figures, $2.5 million, in 1993 (David Swensen, email to author, October 5, 1917), Swensen, Yale's chief Investment officer since 1985 and a former Lizzie Incorporator, has advised me that, in that period, Yale changed its endowment accounting from book value to market value. That alone would make a notable difference, but by itself it seems insufficient to explain the Club's rapid enrichment. During this 30-year period, the Club undertook a complete renovation and enlargement of the clubhouse. To assist with the costs, the endowment was drawn upon and, evidently, Club members also made additional generous contributions (see Parks I, pp. 105, 110–12; see also " 'The Elizabethan Club,' Kenneth Borson Architects," under Yale University, Elizabethan Club, in the Part 1 bibliography). At some point, which was not recorded, annual dues were eliminated, an action in keeping with the founder's fervent wish. By 1993, the Club's finances were in a different world from the short commons of its beginning and middle years. The subject deserves further study.

Appendix 1.5
ASC'S OTHER COLLECTIONS

The Elizabethan Club books are just one of several instances of ASC's acquiring a collection then rapidly disposing of it. The others involved Persian manuscripts given to the Metropolitan Museum of Art (MMA) in New York; a gallery of patriotic American portraits, mainly of U.S. presidents, lent then given (by bequest) to Philipse Manor, the main historical site in Yonkers; and the pictures that originally hung on the Lizzie's walls as well as other Club furnishings that are believed not to survive.

To commemorate his journey in 1907 to the Ottoman Empire and Persia—carpet lands—with his friend Professor A.V. Williams Jackson, ASC bought a precious assemblage of mainly illuminated Persian manuscripts through the London Quaritch firm, which obtained them on ASC's behalf from the noted Swedish scholar and collector Fredrik Robert Martin. The transaction took place during the same months of 1911 that Quaritch assisted with the Huth purchase (Bell, pp. 15–16). After Jackson catalogued the collection (MMA, *Catalogue of the Collection of Persian Manuscripts*, 1914), it was gifted to the museum in 1913. The total cost is unknown, but Alan Bell (p. 16) mentions that one particularly precious item cost £6,000. Jackson's catalogue indicates neither the dealer involved nor the source of this collection, let alone its price. (These details are not found on the MMA website, where photographs of all ASC's gifts are included: https://metmuseum.org/search-results#!/search?q=alexander%20smith%20cochran). The Yale University Library has many publications by Martin, including a book on Persian miniatures. ASC made smaller gifts to the MMA that include a magnificent sixteenth-century Afghan carpet, furniture, an Aubusson carpet, and a tapestry. He was made a Life Member of the MMA.

Philipse Manor is a Yonkers landmark with interesting relevance to the history of Loyalists at the time of the American Revolution (see William H.

Nelson, *The American Tory* [Oxford: Clarendon Press, 1961]). ASC's mother saved it from terminal neglect, and thanks to the Cochrans, the manor has been a New York State historical monument since 1908. ASC put 60 patriotic portraits on permanent loan to the site. Half of them depict U.S. presidents, and all were collected while Alex was president of Smith Carpets and shortly afterward. This noteworthy assemblage of Americana earned ASC a place in the Walpole Society in 1915. Shortly after the paintings were hung, the collection began to be mentioned in travel guides of the day. For example, the 1922 *Rand McNally Guide to New York and Its Environs* (New York: Rand McNally, 1922, p. 7) refers to it as "the extraordinary collection of portraits of Presidents of the United States and other great Americans"; and *Rider's New York City and Vicinity* (New York: Holt, 1916, p. 396) rates it a one-star sight and includes a full list of the portraits' subjects. The "Cochran Estate Inventory" refers to the group as "one of the most important private collections of oil portraits of Presidents of the United States in existence." Upon ASC's death, the loan became a bequest, which at the time was valued at close to a half-million dollars.

ASC supplied the Elizabethan Club with "many valuable paintings and pieces of furniture" (Phelps Laudation). The centerpiece of the paintings was a portrait of Queen Elizabeth I, then thought to be a contemporary likeness by Federico Zuccaro, also known as Zucchero. Today the portrait is the subject of much study by specialists, and it has been demoted as it comprises two parts, the second of which dates to the late nineteenth century. Remarkably, ASC acquired this painting of Elizabeth at a Christie's auction in 1897, a year after his graduation from Yale, and ostensibly years before he first contemplated the Elizabethan Club. Complementing the likeness of Elizabeth I was the third known portrait of Elihu Yale, bought in 1911. "Besides the paintings the club possesses thirty-one engravings, some of them executed at the earliest period of engraving on metal in England." A list of the original collection is included in the pamphlet, "Opening of the Elizabethan Club" (Yale University, Elizabethan Club, "Opening …"). The "Check List of Paintings and Prints" in the *Year Book of the Elizabethan Club* (pp. 89–102) provides information about the collection as it stood in 1933. A new inventory is needed.

An interesting sidelight of ASC's biography is that much of his collecting (after the Elizabeth portrait of 1897) took place simultaneously in virtually the same years. Except for the book purchases of 1915 and 1916 for the Lizzie, ASC spent the last 15 years of his life without assembling any new collections. According to the "Cochran Estate Inventory," however, he had "many paintings" (six are named) in his Savoy-Plaza apartment at the time of his death.

In a letter to his wife, Ganna Walska, ASC wrote, "I sent word to Duveen to send the four pictures, brought in under bond, back to America" (Adams, p. 92). Evidently, he dealt with this famous art dealer about paintings, and there seems to have been further association. S. N. Behrman relates that Duveen, in a patient multiyear campaign, conned ASC ("the Yonkers carpet man") into buying $5 million-worth of objets d'art (Behrman, pp. 168–69), including no paintings. Parts of this story—notably, that ASC socialized with Duveen, especially on shipboard—are believable. But the multimillion-dollar purchase is highly unlikely. Nowhere except here is ASC recorded as ever paying $5 million for anything—he was not so rich that he could casually part with such a sum—and the "Cochran Estate Inventory" of his possessions at death includes no category or value estimate for objets d'art.

ASC owned paintings, but apparently had no intention to form a new collection. Casual comments by Walska indicate that he occasionally visited antique shops (ART, p. 68) and bought paintings as gifts (such as one, reputedly by Gainsborough, given to his sister Elinor [ART, pp. 68–69]) as well as for his own walls.

Appendix 1.6

ASC'S YACHT LOGS

The closest one comes to ASC archives are the six logbooks he kept for seven of his yachts. These handwritten, skeletal aides-mémoires of ASC's prized activity were rescued by John Cochran, of Palm Beach, Florida, ASC's great-grandnephew (descendant of ASC's youngest brother, Gifford).

A ship's log seems to depend for its design on whether it is drawn up from the standpoint of the ship or of a person, notably its owner. Little obligatory content is required in the logs of small, simpler craft, such as yachts. The questionnaire is flexible, open to choice, determined by the log maker as a record of whatever he wishes to remember. ASC's logs are written from his standpoint: they include some nautical details but focus on the owner's whereabouts—the yacht drops away when the owner leaves it.

Two logs were brought to me in New Haven by the kindness of John Cochran for a brief examination, and he has supplemented them with photographs, some of which show pages from other logs. He also gave me an invaluable typescript of the *Westward*'s log, recording the cruise and races that proved to be the high point of ASC's yachting.

The log of the *Westward* starts with the launch of the yacht in the spring of 1910 and ends with its being taken out of commission on August 14, 1912. The early entries, which concern its transatlantic journey on the open sea, are rich in nautical detail: weather; the winds, the sea, and their changes; course; setting of the sails; the distance traveled; and latitude and longitude. These details are much curtailed when well-signposted waters are reached. As a sample, here is a particularly full entry about the yacht's departure for its run from England to northern Germany for the 1910 German regatta: "Tuesday, 14th [June]—Hughes joined 12:30 and we left dock under tow. Set sails 1 p.m. Cowes 3:30 bound for Cuxhaven. Passed Cowes Li[ght] Ship 8:30. Beautiful day. Evening light, fair wind. Trysail set instead mainsail."

(F. R. Hughes, a friend of ASC's, was often mentioned.) Although an appreciable number of nautical details is recorded, the design of this log is narrative rather than formulaic. The focus of the quoted passage could be the owner, but is not decidedly so, whereas in other entries he definitely is. An entry in England is particularly illustrative of ASC's centrality. Having gone to London by train on July 29, he writes: "Saturday, July 30, 1910—Joined 12:30 with Bob Perkins. Got under way at once and ran to Cowes. Fine day. Ashore at Royal Squadron for tea and dined aboard." When the *Westward* was in German waters, the scene for dining is most often the *Greta,* which arrived with a load of ASC's friends on June 19. The *Greta* is never explained; it must have been *Westward'*s tender, a powered craft, perhaps leased, that served the needs of the racer and afforded a better place for meals than the probably stripped down *Westward.* On racing days, the focus appears to shift from owner to yacht, but the personal note remains:

> Friday, July 1st—Left anchor at 7:30 for race to Travemunde. Squally, cold and blowing hard—got away first on run of 30 miles and rounded mark first. Blowing very hard. We lead on next reach of 14 miles and last close reach of 29 beating *Germania* 1:38 min. boat for boat. Most interesting race yet and a great performance. Ar. Travemunde about 3. Went ashore after dinner on *Greta* and received the prize Emperor's Cup.

Here and in the other entries detailing races, the log takes life. Nevertheless, it is the owner who gets the prize for this "great performance." There is no room for the exploits and supreme skills of the skipper, Charlie Barr, or for the disciplined maneuvers of the crew. ASC highly valued his great—but never mentioned—captain, and he took pains recruiting and exercising the crew. In his log, they are invisible employees, not companions in a joint adventure. The schooner itself is absent from a number of entries that are devoted wholly to ASC: "Saturday, [July] 25th—Fair mostly. Few showers. Ashore walking, etc. Dined on *Greta.* Townsend left us." This log, then, is ASC's sailing diary. The owner, his weather, his movements, his comfort, and his friends monopolize it; even the races seem to belong to him. ASC is laudably free of one trait of a diarist, namely, posturing for posterity. He may have muted a possible hero, his racing skipper, but he did not usurp the role himself.

In grasping these details, I was enormously helped by the transcript of the *Westward* log given to me by John Cochran. The *Warrior* log, seen only in its original handwriting, was harder to digest. ASC's handwriting is clear and regular, but the ink has faded somewhat. *Warrior* was a steamship with auxiliary sails, a very large, graceful vessel meant for luxurious cruising rather than racing. A characteristic concern here was fuel: the ship periodically had to be coaled, even to the point of piling coal on the decks to extend its range. Its main adventure when in ASC's possession occurred when he lent it to the Royal Navy in 1917 for the duration of the First World War. The value of the log to me came mainly from a group of letters pasted on blank pages that concern ASC's relations with the British Navy— when appointed captain of his loaned ship, when his ship was ready for service (having been converted into a warship), and when he resigned his commission. I owe my access to these letters to John Cochran, who kindly sent photographs of them to me. In the log proper, the features that caught my eye (not necessarily the most important) were the yacht's itinerary and, when island hopping, the frequency of entertainment ashore offered to Commander Cochran by the local officers in charge. The entries from when *Warrior* was cruising are, in general, very short and unconcerned with junior officers and crew.

The pages of the *Sea Call* log that John Cochran photographed for me also were very enlightening. They are the basis for much of what is said about this luckless ship in my biographical essay.

Appendix 1.7

ASC AS A SPORTSMAN

The following selected list of ASC's sporting activities includes records only for those events that I can positively confirm. It cannot claim to be exhaustive.

Sports other than yachting

Fox hunting, United Kingdom, 1908, 1909, 1921; Pau, France, 1920 (?); Aiken, South Carolina, 1920.

ASC is not recorded as joining the Suffolk Hunt Club, even though it was easily accessible from New York City (*Bit & Spur* 10 [1911]: 33). His Baltimore nephew and namesake exaggeratedly believed that ASC divided his time between fox hunting and yachting (Weeks, p. 5). ASC was very fond of this sport; he had stables at Aiken, South Carolina, and Melton Mowbray, U.K. He even left Ganna Walska's company, though newly wed, in order to ride to hounds.

Polo, 1915–20
The Spur (November 1, 1915): 23, reports that ASC has bought five mounts to form the nucleus of a polo stable; he has given an additional field at the Meadowbrook Club. ASC is among the polo players going to the Plattsburg military-preparedness camp. Is praised as a player (*New York Tribune* [July 19, 1916]: 6). Photographed mounted as a polo player (ART, opposite p. 72). Polo in Pasadena, California, hope he's in good health (carbon copy of unsigned letter to ASC, February 17, 1919, MSSA, RU36, box 3, folder 156). ASC sold his polo ponies in a record sale; he was leaving the sport (*New York Times* [June 13, 1920]: 24).

Thoroughbred racing, 1913–14
ASC plunged in with large means, buying a stallion for $20,000, but he withdrew after two seasons. His brother Gifford, a successful turfman, benefitted from ASC's departure from the sport.

Western mounts, 1918–25 (?)
ASC's 8,000-acre Colorado estate had many miles of riding trails. There must have been stocked stables on the property. Whether ASC availed himself of these mounts is not recorded.

Motoring
ASC owned eleven Rolls Royces, some of which he kept permanently in England. Five were bought prewar, six postwar; two were made in the United States. Information (with thanks) from Yale University Organist Thomas Murray, an Elizabethan Club member and authority on these cars. He advised me that ASC's Rolls Royce models show that he was an active motorist (i.e., they were not limousines). A chauffeur in ASC's company, if mentioned, would have been along as a relief driver and mechanic. Early cars often broke down. The casual note that ASC had twenty cars (*Washington Post* [October 10, 1920]: 64) suggests that he did not confine himself to Rollses. There are no indications of where his cars were kept.

Aviation, 1911
ASC is learning to fly and has bought a standard Wright biplane (*Baltimore Sun* [June 17, 1911]: 2). He is never seen making use of this plane.

Yachting
Surviving logs in the possession of John Cochran are marked with asterisks (*).

Sail (all bespoke except *Avenger, Intrepid,* and *Iris*)
Avenger (1909); *Westward** (1910); *Vanitie** (1914); both *Sea Call* and *Intrepid** (1915; *Intrepid* is ephemeral); *Dolly Bowen* (1916; *New York Tribune* [May 15]: 13); *Iris* (1924; *New York Times* [July 17]: 13); *Vira* (1927), sold in 1928 and renamed *Creole. Creole* is in commission today. (For further information, see note 147 in Part 1 biographical essay).

Steam
*Alvina** (acquired 1906); *Mohican* (acquired 1911; sold to Robert Perkins 1916); *Warrior** (acquired 1916; lent to the Royal Navy 1917–18; sold to Sir Thomas Lipton, 1920 [*New York Times* (February 8): 2]); *Restless** (built to order, UK, 1922).

Appendix 1.8

ASC'S SIBLINGS

Anna Phillips Cochran Ewing (1872–1943), the eldest of the Cochran children, married Thomas Ewing II, from a Yonkers family, and stayed in Yonkers. The Ewings lived originally at Duncraggan, the Cochran family seat, which ASC sold in 1916; they then moved to a house named Kinross. Thomas Ewing II was the son of a noted Ohio politician who had moved to Yonkers and practiced law in New York. (He, too, was named Thomas, here Thomas I.) Thomas II was very active in Yonkers affairs. A lawyer like his father, with whom he shared a practice, Thomas II was a patent specialist and was named U.S. Commissioner of Patents by Woodrow Wilson. The Ewings had seven children. Their eldest son, Thomas III, was ASC's main heir; he died of pneumonia in 1933 at age 36. A younger son of Anna's succeeded him as president of Smith Carpets.

William Francis Cochran (1876–1950). William was his father's namesake (see Hall, pp. 889–91). His earliest schooling was in Switzerland, but probably not for long. He went to a private school near Yonkers before attending St. Paul's School for six years, then Yale, where he chose its engineering branch, the Sheffield Scientific School, and graduated in 1898. Although he left Yonkers and moved to Baltimore in 1901 (allegedly to avoid his older brother [Weeks, p. 4]), he remained a director of Smith Carpets for much of his long life. The William Cochrans were "wildly generous"; their house was the social center of their neighborhood, with stables famous for thoroughbreds and hunters. William was the original developer (1915) of "Sherwood Forest" in Anne Arundel County, Maryland, an exclusive and extremely successful summer community that still exists. His wife, a Baltimorean, "embraced the polite traditions of her native [city]," whereas William, several times over a millionaire (by bequest) and a successful developer, was the "proponent of all manner of left-wing ideas" (Weeks, p. 4) and an avowed socialist, who eventually supported the New Deal. Much of his philanthropy, like his mother's, was associated with his church and its missions. In 1915 he invited "suggestions as to how to get rid of his wealth," thinking it wrong that nine-tenths of the nation's wealth belonged to one-tenth of its population (*New York Times* [March 7, 1915]: SM11]). Nothing came of this initiative. William was a leading Prohibitionist, whom H. L. Mencken called the "rich but imbecile leader of the uplift in Baltimore" (Mencken, p. 321). (The *uplift* was Mencken's word for "the professional saviors of the world.") A biographical article from 1912 affirms that William was "prominent in Baltimore society" (Hall, p. 891). Socialism did not detach him from the upper class and its diversions. With ASC's friend Maitland Griggs, William was an executor of his brother's will.

William's five children included Alexander Smith Cochran II, named after both his uncle and his Smith grandfather, who had established the family fortune. He became a significant modernist architect active especially in Baltimore. Much the longest lived of the Cochran children, William died in 1950. His obituary is in *New York Times* (July 4, 1950): 17.

Gifford A. Cochran (1880–1930) was William Francis and Eva Cochran's third son; his name also came from an earlier member of the Cochran family. An alumnus of the Yale Class of 1903 and an early member of the Elizabethan Club, Gifford married a Philadelphian in 1906, had two sons and a daughter, and divorced in 1927 after a long separation. He was often in ASC's company and briefly succeeded him as president of Smith Carpets. He too was tubercular, but less severely than his brother. Sustained by million-dollar bequests, Gifford was a successful turfman, with victories in major races. Unusually, he established his racing stable in New York state. He was a good-natured and hard-living man (called an alcoholic in his obituary), who died of a heart attack at 50 (*New York Times* [December 6, 1930]: 17), one year after ASC. He left an estate of about $3.5 million (*New York Times* [August 15, 1934]: 34). Walska mentions him with fondness ("dear Gifford"), even though she cannot have known him more than fleetingly (ART, p. 68).

Elinor DeWitt Cochran Stewart (1873–1933) married Wall Street lawyer Percy Hamilton Stewart (1867–1951; Yale 1890, Skull and Bones) in Jacksonville, Florida, in January 1899. They resided in Plainfield, New Jersey, Percy's hometown (known as a "Wall Street suburb"). The Stewarts also had an apartment in New York at 903 Park Avenue.

Elinor and Percy had two daughters. Elinor was an avid stamp collector and is the Cochran sister most often referred to in connection with ASC. She was his guest on *Westward* (log), hostess at a dinner with Walska at home (ART, p. 69); she also received ASC as a house guest in New York after his divorce (*New York Times* [November 30, 1922]: 19). Succumbing to heart disease in a Baltimore hospital, she appears in her *Baltimore Sun* obituary (January 31, 1933: 7) as, surprisingly, "one of the country's richest women," and was noted for large gifts to charity. (She had million-dollar bequests from father, mother, uncle, and ASC.)

Elizabeth Cochran Bowen (d. 1941), ASC's youngest sister, resided in Greenwich, Connecticut. Her marriage ended in divorce. Dolly, her daughter, launched *Vanitie* when she was six years old, and ASC later named a 40-foot sailboat after her. Elizabeth was with the convalescent ASC throughout his last winter (1928–29), but not at the time of his death.

Appendix 1.9

JOHN MASEFIELD AT SMITH CARPETS AND THE ELIZABETHAN CLUB

When he was a teenager, the future English Poet Laureate John Masefield (1878–1967) came to America as a sailor on a windjammer. Tired of life at sea, he jumped ship in New York and eventually found work at Smith Carpets in 1895 at age 17. Long after, he described his 22 months in Yonkers in an autobiographical book, *In the Mill.* He took to the life there and was an able worker, steadily promoted. He prized having regular free hours, during which he read voraciously. Yonkers is where he first encountered and became enchanted by Keats and Shelley; it was during his time at Smith Carpet that he found his vocation as a poet. *In the Mill* includes a description of the Smith Carpet factory:

> Soon, I saw ahead of me on the right of the road a great red brick building, three storeys high and of immense length and breadth. Other buildings stretched away behind it, with smoking chimneys. The road was black with crowds going in at the gates. The trolley cars were in their rush-hour service, bringing people to work: the morning flood was running … I had never been associated with any building so big. It loomed up above the road, like a gigantic ship taking in passengers at dockside. As I drew nearer, I heard the enormous murmur of its engines, and saw a general quickening in the steps of those entering. It was now almost seven o'clock. (Masefield, pp. 4-5)

These were the days when ASC, newly graduated from Yale, started to familiarize himself with the family firm, working up from the factory floor. Not surprisingly, he and Masefield did not meet; the name *Cochran* is absent from *In the Mill.*

A review concludes, "*In the Mill,* the story of the days when he was an intelligent young workingman, [is] one of the most engaging of his books"

(*Time* [August 11, 1941]: 73). Further details about Masefield's mill days are
in C. B. Smith (pp. 35–46).

Masefield's factory work had an unexpected complement. In January
1916 (during the First World War), Masefield came to America on a lecture
tour, which he thought "could be an excellent means of serving the Allied
cause" (C. B. Smith, p. 134).

> The engagement which he considered the most important, and
> which he greatly enjoyed, was at Yale. "The spirit of the young
> men is very much that of Oxford," he told [his wife], "and their
> freshness and affection is irresistible, so I did not lecture, but read
> from my poems and had a jolly afternoon…. I find the young men
> enthusiastic about poetry, and all the old arrogance seems changed
> to a kind of humble self questioning and doubt." (C. B. Smith,
> pp. 139–40)

One relic of Masefield's visit to Yale is his small, precise signature in the
Elizabethan Club's guest book (folio 4, verso). In those days, through an
endowed lectureship, "Billy" Phelps was able to bring the most noted
Anglophone writers to speak to the public in Sprague Hall, and he escorted
them across the street to meet the Lizzie members (Frederick Pottle
in Parks I, p. 70). This post- or pre-lecture visit must have been when
Masefield signed the guest book. What neither he nor his hosts realized is
that the Cochran fortune, on which the Club was built, was generated by
the factory in which Masefield had worked 20 years before.

Appendix 1.10

MISCELLANEA

A. ASC as a Yale Benefactor. William Lyon Phelps enthusiastically called ASC "one of Yale's greatest benefactors" (Phelps, p. 293). He may have meant this opinion in a moral sense, which is hard to dispute. In dollar terms, ACS's financing of the Yale Elizabethan Club is overshadowed by the enormous gifts others (such as John William Sterling, Edward Stephen Harkness, and Paul Mellon) have made to the university, not to speak of donors' recent offerings in the nine figures. ASC did not include Yale in his will. He was on a committee intended to encourage the fine arts at Yale, which had been instigated by Maitland Griggs, ASC's friend and a distinguished art collector (*New York Times* [November 21, 1925]: 12). ASC may have contributed to the arts at Yale when associated with this committee. Further anonymous gifts of his are also possible (such as with the class of 1896), but they could not have been large.

B. ASC's Residences. Ganna Walksa's divorce lawyer claimed ASC had houses in various places throughout the world. Although this is an exaggeration from an unreliable source, the allegation had a factual core. Not all the houses listed here would have been owned simultaneously, of course, but many were and are likely to have stood unoccupied for long stretches of time.

One house ASC did not have was a New York mansion. The family house on 45th Street appears to have been sold in the 1910s, at about the same time as Duncraggan, the Cochran homestead in Yonkers, was sold to Samuel Untermyer, the famous lawyer, to enlarge his already very large grounds, now a public garden (*Washington Post* [June 12, 1916]: 5]). ASC's New York address in 1920 was 820 Fifth Avenue (*New York Times* [December 25, 1920]: 10). For this apartment in a building noted for its luxury, ASC was reputed to pay $20,000 per year as rent—a record high sum for New York City (*Arizona Republican* [August 9, 1920]: 3). He and Ganna Walska did not occupy this apartment during their New York stopover from September to December 1920. When ASC moved into 820 Fifth Avenue and how long he rented it are not known. His letters to the Elizabethan Club in the 1920s come from several different New York addresses, one of which was the Ritz-Carlton Hotel (his base according to the *Half-way Book*). He could also stay temporarily at one of his clubs and, at one time, was received in the Park Avenue apartment of his sister Elinor. In 1929, when he died, his New York residence was an apartment in the Savoy-Plaza Hotel, on Central Park South. ASC probably had left his rented luxury apartment on Fifth Avenue long before, but at his death he owned a vacant apartment on Fifth Avenue.

Outside New York City, it is not surprising that he kept a base in Yonkers. Although I have no record of his occupying this house at 355 Palisade Avenue, an appreciable amount of his personal property was there ("Cochran Estate Inventory"). Yonkers was also the home of the Ewings, the Yonkers-based family of his eldest sister, Anna. On his intermittent visits to supervise Smith Carpets, ASC was sometimes a guest at the Ewing house, Kinross.

In 1915, he acquired a major suburban house, Brookholt on Long Island (*Chicago Tribune* [August 27, 1916]: F5), a showplace estate that may have been a bargain when he bought it (see *New York Times* [October 17, 1915]: 12). There is no definite sign that ASC ever lived there or put it to any use during the seven years he owned it. The purchase was too late in 1915 to have served as ASC's bivouac when he played polo. When it was sold to make way for a new golf club (*New York Times* [November 18, 1923]: RE1), it may have fetched a half-million dollars, but ultimately it never became a golf course. The mansion was later used for the distilling of bootleg alcohol, and it burned to the ground in March 1934 (*New York Times* [March 3, 1934]: 15.) In 1929, ASC had a suburban house in fashionable Locust Valley, Long Island ("Cochran Estate Inventory").

Another grandiose house—better termed a castle—stood within the 8,000-acre Colorado Springs estate Glen Eyrie, enlarged by five ranches, that ASC bought in August 1918. Although dubbed "million-dollar," Glen Eyrie is unlikely to have cost that much. ASC found the castle, with its 11 bathrooms, too large for him, and instead built the Pink House, a "cottage," on the property. The Pink House was very substantial, meant to accommodate tuberculosis sufferers when ASC did not occupy it. ASC sojourned in Colorado Springs for some months in 1924–25. Whether he ever returned is not recorded. The property was transferred to ASC's holding company (*New York Times* [June 12, 1922]: 11), which put it up for sale in the 1920s but had no takers, leaving it still ASC's property at his death.

ASC had a modest house in Aiken, South Carolina, a winter retreat and center for fox hunting (see *New York Times* [December 22, 1920]: 16). In Ewing, *Bravura,* a picture's caption records Thomas Ewing III's purchase from ASC of a small cottage on the Aiken property. There are at least two references to a hunting estate in North Carolina, not impossible but perhaps a case of confusion with South Carolina. For some time ASC also had villas in Bar Harbor, Maine (a family summer home in the satellite community Sorrento), and Newport, Rhode Island (*Detroit Free Press* [October 10, 1920]: E7), from which he yachted (*Baltimore Sun* [April 9, 1916]: SO6). He owned, rather than rented, the house in Redlands, California, in which he spent his last winter. It had probably been disposed of well before 1932, when ASC's estate was settled. Also disposed of before 1932 is likely to have been the large house in Saranac Lake, New York, in which he died.

ASC's foreign properties were impressive. A house at a good address in Paris; in London an apartment at the Albany (a famous apartment house in Piccadilly) and another at 6 Balfour Mews; and an apartment at the Park Plaza Hotel in Monte Carlo. All these were in his possession at his death. His main heir, Thomas Ewing III, and his wife, took a European tour to inspect them; they were delighted with the Paris house and resolved to keep it (EFA, Ewing 2). ASC's hunting lodge at Melton Mowbray was probably disposed of after the World War. The "Cochran Estate Inventory" lists a large tax payment to the Canadian province of Québec, but it omits stating what it was for.

C. ASC's Preference for Buying and for Large Sizes

(A list in approximate chronological order)

Lifelong club memberships, 12 in New York City, 1 in Washington, D.C. At the time, second only in number after Cornelius Vanderbilt, Sr., who was a member of 16.

Westward—largest sailing schooner launched by its celebrated makers, the Herreshoff Co. of Bristol, Rhode Island. Considered the largest in the world.

Standard Wright Biplane, bought, for learning to fly.

Stallion—"His Majesty," $20,000.

Largest single donor to Theodore Roosevelt's "Bull Moose" Party.

Largest American buyer of Rolls-Royce automobiles (possibly).

Sea Call—auxiliary schooner (i.e., combining sails and engine), with the largest gasoline (eight-cylinder) engine of its day (never fitted, arrived too late for launching), first with Monel-sheathed hull, "the finest sailing yacht in the world" (Hamilton-Adams, p. 37). "The Largest Schooner Yacht that Ever Sailed the Seas" (EFA Scrapbook, f. 4).

Vanitie—most expensive America's Cup contender.

Own expense, no syndicate, for America's Cup races (1914); first time since 1887.

Tallest apartment house in NYC planned (*New York Times*, July 23, 1916: XX8). Never built.

Apartment in ultra-luxury apartment house, 820 Fifth Avenue, record rent, $20,000 per year.

Philanthropy in war: money for medical purposes (including two London hospitals, a hospital train); six U.S.-built motor scout craft. "Princely gifts" (*The Spectator*, 1929)

"Brookholt," architect designed, ex-Belmont house and garden showplace, Long Island.

Warrior, one of the largest seagoing yachts then afloat.

Glen Eyrie, Colorado Springs: 5,000 acres with castle residence, bought with five adjacent ranches adding 3,000 acres more.

Auction of polo ponies, 1920, the largest of its kind.

Ganna Walska's wedding gifts: Paris town house in best district, million-franc sable coat, Rolls Royce limousine, her choice of jewel at Cartier, $100,000 per year pin money.

Saranac Lake, New York: one of the largest houses in the town.

Vira, three-mast wooden auxiliary schooner, the world's largest wooden sailing craft.

Mansion with a noteworthy garden in Redlands, California.

D. ASC's Postwar Yachting Costume. Two photographs of ASC, standing (fig. 1.15) and sitting, were evidently taken at the same portrait session. ASC wears a suit of naval cut that, at first sight, might be the uniform of a Commander in the Royal Navy, which ASC had been in 1917. Some captions, although not written by ASC, indicate precisely this.

That idea needs correction. The cap ASC wears is regulation, but the rest of the ensemble bears little resemblance to Royal Navy uniform specifications (https://en.wikipedia.org/wiki/Uniforms_of_the_Royal_Navy#Officers, retrieved April 14, 2019). Shoulder boards with three stripes are shown, and the cuffs lack gold-braid circlings. Except for the formal-dress uniform of admirals, a regulation uniform had no shoulder boards, and rank was distinguished by gold circles on the cuff (ASC's would have called for three circles). In the case of a Royal Naval Reserve member, which ASC was, the gold cuff bands would have had a wavy pattern ("wavy navy"; see illustration at https://en.wikipedia.org/wiki/History_of_the_Royal_Naval_Reserve, retrieved April 14, 2019), not the plain circle of the

Fig. 1.15. Contrary to general belief, Alex's costume in this photograph from about 1922 is not the uniform of a Commander in the British Royal Navy. Its specifications, such as the shoulder boards, are irregular. Note also the strange object on a chain in the breast pocket. I take this ensemble to be simply a reminiscence of Alex's months of naval service. Courtesy Gifford W. Cochran

Royal Navy. The stick ASC carries is either a cane or a swagger stick, which, although common for officers in the British Army, has no naval equivalent.

I suggest that what ASC is wearing is not his uniform as an RNR Commander but a specially designed, postwar yachting costume with reminiscences of his wartime service.

E. Was the Elizabethan Club Unique in American Academia? Some notices about the Lizzie maintain that it was unique of its kind. For example, "no one had ever heard of such an institution before" (Troxell I, p. 83). The anonymous report of the Club's foundation in *Yale Alumni Weekly* (21:12 [1911]: 294), says it "differs … from any club … heretofore known at Yale, or indeed at any American university." In connection with a reference to the *Yale Book of American Verse,* published by Yale University Press under the auspices of the Elizabethan Club, Theodore Roosevelt describes the Club as "the kind of club the possession of which every real university in the country must envy Yale" ("Productive Scholarship," in *History as Literature and Other Essays* [New York: Scribner, 1913], p. 209).

But there had long been another club of this kind in American academia: Harvard's Signet Society, founded in 1871, was oriented to literature and the arts in ways similar to the Lizzie, but it has neither a book collection nor, to its chagrin, an endowment. ASC's foundation clearly was not inspired by the Signet. The Yale of ASC's day seems to have been wholly oblivious to the existence of the club at Harvard, and even Harvardian Teddy Roosevelt was unaware of what his alma mater possessed. The similarity of the Elizabethan Club to the Signet Society, unnoticed in 1911, eventually came to light. The two clubs, neither of them socially exclusive, now have long had amicable relations, highlighted by intermittent croquet matches. A scattering of members (including this writer) take pride in belonging to both.

F. What Lizzie Members Talk about. As noted above, ASC's wish to let Lizzie undergraduates handle the Club's book treasures casually was not allowed by its officers. Another of his wishes did not come true: "If the founders of the Club had hoped that its members would be stimulated to discuss the profundities of life or acquire a taste for Elizabethan literature they were disappointed" (Lewis, p. 113, referring to 1915, the year he joined). Lewis adds impressions of the nature of the student membership, past and present (Parks I, p. 39). It hardly needs saying that today's Yale is very different from ASC's. For example, it no longer can be accused of being philistine. The Club now reflects the diversity of the university. Women were admitted to Yale College in 1969 and elected to membership in the Lizzie in that year as well. Since 1933 the residential colleges, rather than clubs, have had a large part in Yale's social life. Another change may come about in the years to come as a consequence of the establishment of a student center, almost directly across College Street from the Lizzie. None of these changes has inclined the membership to fulfill ASC's hopes of promoting edifying and elevating conversation: "The pleasures of the Club were social, not bibliophilic" (Lewis, p. 111). They still are.

G. The Elizabethan Club's Lock of Byron's Hair. One of the objects in the Club vault is a watch fob said to contain a lock of George Gordon, Lord Byron's hair (see Parks I, p. 28). Its descent from a close relative of the poet argues in favor of the authenticity of this relic. In a letter to William Lyon Phelps, Andrew Keogh wrote of a lock of Byron's hair "carefully preserved in a fob that Mrs. Sanderson's father used to wear. The hair was given to her father [Mr. Gaines, sometime U.S. consul general in Tripoli, Libya] by the poet's niece, Emily Leigh" (MSSA, Phelps, Phelps Correspondence H–Lz. Letter of Andrew Keogh to William Lyon Phelps, May 17, 1927).

Bibliography

Abbreviations: For those works for which abbreviations are used throughout, the applicable short version follows [in brackets] the title.

Primary sources are marked with asterisks (*).

Adams, Brian. *Ganna: Diva of Lotusland*. [N.p.]: CreateSpace Independent, 2015. See Part 2 bibliography.

"Alexander Smith Cochran," in *National Cyclopedia of American Biography: Being the History of the United States*, vol. 32 (New York: James T. White and Company, 1945), pp. 479–80.

Behrman, S.N. *Duveen* (New York: Random House, 1952).

Bell, Alan, "Introduction to the Catalogue of the Elizabethan Club Library" [Bell], in Parks II, pp. 13–45.

*Bigelow-Sanford Carpet Company. *A Century of Carpet and Rug Making in America* (New York: Bigelow-Hartford Carpet Co., 1925).

Cannon, Carl L. *American Book Collectors and Collecting from Colonial Times to the Present* (New York: H.W. Wilson, 1941).

*Cochran, Alexander Smith, *Sea Call* and *Intrepid* logs, 1915; in ASC's hand. (See Appendix 1.6.)

*———. *Warrior* log, 1916–20; in ASC's hand. Includes his months in British naval service.

*———. *Westward* log, 1910–11; in ASC's hand.

"Cochran, William Francis (1876–1950)," in *National Cyclopedia of American Biography: Being the History of the United States* vol. 39 (New York: James T. White, 1954), p. 225.

*"Cochran Estate Inventory," in *New York Times* (August 6, 1932): 1, 5. Valuation for tax purposes three years post mortem. A very complete assessment of ASC's wealth and possessions at death; includes his houses and apartments, furnishings, securities, provision for Ganna Walska, etc.

Dovkants, Keith, "The Curse of Classic 63m Sailing Yacht *Creole*," *Boat* (December 1, 2015), www.boatinternational.com/yachts/editorial-features/ the-curse-of-classic-63m-sailing-yacht-creole--28755 (retrieved May 18, 2019). ASC's *Vira* was renamed *Creole*. Dovkants is a satisfactory substitute for the vanished Hampton (see below).

*Ewing, Alex C. *Bravura! Lucia Chase and the American Ballet Theater* [Ewing, *Bravura*] (Gainesville, FL: UP of Florida, 2009). ASC's grandnephew celebrates his mother, the widow of Thomas Ewing III, ASC's main heir (d. 1933). (Copy at the Elizabethan Club, gift of the late Chancellor Ewing)

*———. "Ewing Memorandum." Two-page typescript relating ASC's achievements as known to Chancellor Ewing, ASC's grandnephew.

"Ewing, Thomas," by "R. C. M." in *Dictionary of American Biography*, ed. A. Johnson and D. Malone, vol. 3 (New York: Scribner, 1930–31), pp. 238–39. The subject was the distinguished father (Thomas I) of ASC's brother-in-law. (An author's name corresponding to these initials was not included in the list of contributors.)

*Ewing Family Archives [EFA]. These archives descend from ASC's elder sister Anna, who married Thomas Ewing II, and from their eldest son, Thomas III, ASC's main heir. Contains three principal items, detailed below. Each has its own abbreviation.

Ewing 1 [EFA, Ewing 1] (incomplete typescript, 115 pages, pp. 151–58 missing). Anonymous, unpublished essay entitled "Portrait of a Young American." Tracks the Ewing and Cochran families to 1913, at which time Thomas III was 16 years old and a student in Munich.

Ewing 2 [EFA, Ewing 2] (unpublished typescript, 524 pages, by John Williams Andrews). Like Ewing 1, also entitled "Portrait of a Young American," but subtitled "Biography of Thomas Ewing Junior" [Thomas III]. The two biographies appear to have been written by different authors, neither of whom furnishes any indications of sources used.

Scrapbook [EFA, Scrapbook] (55 leaves). Mainly obituaries of ASC; also includes items concerning his civic benefactions and funeral. The identifications (source, date, and page) for many of these clippings have been trimmed away.

*Freeman, James E. *A Revealing Intimacy: A Friend's Tribute to Alexander Smith Cochran* (Washington, DC: [College of Preachers], 1930). Brief and laudatory remembrance, but short on dates and other details. (Gift to the Club by Chancellor Ewing.) EFA contains slim, privately printed memorial volumes of William Francis Cochran and Eva Smith Cochran, also compiled by Freeman; include photographic portraits of William, the Hollywood Inn, and Eva (see fig. 1.3).

———. *In Memoriam Eva Smith Cochran, 1845–1909* ([N.p.], 1911).

French, Robert D., "Cochran, Alexander Smith (February 28, 1874–June 20, 1929)," in *Dictionary of American Biography: Under the Auspices of the American Council of Learned Societies* vol. 2 (New York: Scribner's, 1930), pp. 250–51.

"From Westward to Eleonora. A Noble Legend Sails On." https://www.slideshare.net/losnarejos/westward-eleonora (retrieved May 18, 2019). "Westward to Eleonora: The Revival of Racing Schooner and Big-Class History" is a DVD from the Tom Nitsch Yachting Collection (www.tom-nitsch-images.de/product/westward-to-eleonora-2/). Several films of the replica *Eleonora* may be viewed at: www.youtube.com (search on "Eleonora yacht").

Goffart, Walter. "A. S. Cochran and the Founding of the Club," in Parks I (pp. 133–37). Superseded.

Grant, Stephen H. *Collecting Shakespeare: The Story of Henry and Emily Folger* (Baltimore: Johns Hopkins UP, 2014).

Guiton, Olivier. "*Le Créole*: Yacht de rêve ou bateau maudit?" (film) https://www.youtube.com/watch?v=A9RNTboeQCg (retrieved May 18, 2019). This comprehensive film history of *Creole* (ASC's renamed *Vira*) is more than an hour long. Many beautiful photos of the yacht; rare portrait of ASC on the eve of his death (3.8 min into the film).

Hall, Clayton Colman, ed. *Baltimore: Its History and Its People,* vol. 3, *Biography* (New York: Lewis Historical, 1912), pp. 889–91. About ASC's brother William, with information about other Cochrans.

Hamilton-Adams, C. P. *The Racing Schooner* Westward (New York: Van Nostrand Reinhold, 1977). (At the Club, gift of Alexander Smith Cochran, Baltimore nephew of ASC.)

Hampton, Kim, "Gucci's *Creole*: The Largest Wood Sailing Yacht in the World," in *Boating and Sailing News* (July 1, 2010). Retrieved on internet May 27, 2017, but has since vanished into cyberspace. As substitute, see Dovkants. See also Guiton for a film account of *Creole.*

Hotchkiss, Valerie, and Fred C. Robinson. *English in Print from Caxton to Shakespeare to Milton* (Urbana: University of Illinois Press, 2008). Concerns many Elizabethan Club books.

*Jackson, Abraham Valentine Williams. *From Constantinople to the Home of Omar Khayyam: Travels in Transcaucasia and Northern Persia for Historic and Literary Research* (New York: Macmillan, 1911). https://archive.org/stream/fromconstantinopoojackuoft/fromconstantinopoojackuoft_djvu.txt (retrieved May 5, 2019). Account of the author's voyage in 1907 with ASC, to whom the book is dedicated.

Jordan, Joseph S. "The Baton of a Boss in Every Lunch Basket." *Liberty* (March 7, 1925): 32–34. In EFA, Scrapbook.

Lazarovich Hrebelianovlch, Eleanor Hulda Calhoun. *Pleasures and Palaces: The Memoirs of Princess Lazarovich-Hrebelianovich (Eleanor Calhoun)* (New York: Century, 1915).

*Lewis, Wilmarth Sheldon ("Lefty"). *One Man's Education* (New York: Knopf, 1967). Insider's comments on the early Elizabethan Club by a major figure in Yale history.

*Masefield, John. *In the Mill* (New York: Macmillan, 1941). See Appendix 1.9.

Mays, Andrea E. *The Millionaire and the Bard: Henry Folger's Obsessive Hunt for Shakespeare's First Folio* (New York: Simon & Schuster, 2015).

Mencken, H. L. *Thirty-Five Years of Newspaper Work: A Memoir,* ed. Fred Hobson et al. (Baltimore: Johns Hopkins UP, 1994)

Metcalfe, Nick. "HMS *Warrior,*" *Sacrifice* (February 17, 2015), https://ww1sacrifice.com/2015/02/17/hms-warrior/ (accessed June 19, 2017). *Warrior* in World War I.

*Metropolitan Museum of Art. *A Catalogue of the Collection of Persian Manuscripts, Including Also Some Turkish and Arabic, Presented to the Metropolitan Museum of Art, New York, by Alexander Smith Cochran,* ed. A. V. Williams Jackson and Abraham Yohannan (New York: Columbia UP, 1914). www.metmuseum.org/art/metpublications/A_Catalogue_of_the_Collection_of_Persian_Manuscripts (retrieved May 5, 2018).

Nelson, William H. *The American Tory* (Oxford: Clarendon Press, 1961; also Boston: Beacon Press, 1964).

*Parks, Stephen, ed. *The Elizabethan Club of Yale University, 1911–2011: A Centenary Album* [Parks I] (New Haven: [n.p.], 2011). The Club in documents, reminiscences, and essays. Lacks indication of sources.

*———. *The Elizabethan Club of Yale University and Its Library* [Parks II]; intro. by Alan Bell (New Haven: Yale UP, 1986); 2d edition (New Haven: Yale UP, 2011). Catalogue of the Club library.

———. "Origins of 'the Lizzie': Bibliophilic Dainties, Tea and Talk." Second augmented reprint (New Haven, [n.p.], 2010); originally in *Yale Alumni Magazine* (December 1986). Addresses especially the descent of many Club books, both those given by ASC and additions.

*Phelps, William Lyon, *Autobiography, with Letters* (New York: Oxford UP, 1939).

*———. "William Lyon Phelps on a Good Rich Man" [Phelps Laudation] in *Hartford Courant* (August 4, 1929): F5. (Also in *Washington Post* [August 4, 1929]: SM16; *New York Post* [August 3, 1929]). See Appendix 1.1 for the various states of this commemoration of ASC, the first account of ASC's book collection and the Club's foundation.

*Piwinski, Bob. "A History of the Alexander Smith and Sons' Carpet Company, the Moquette Rows, and the Contributions of the Smith and Cochran Families to the City of Yonkers and Its People." www. victoriansource.com/id41.html/ (retrieved May 3, 2017).

*Plainfield Garden Club. "Member: Stewart, Mrs. Percy Hamilton (Elinor DeWitt Cochran)," http://andyswebtools.com/cgi-bin/p/awtp-pa. cgi?d=plainfield-garden-club&type=4427 (retrieved April 12, 2017). This web page about ASC's second sister is a collection of ASC-related material, mostly reprints of articles separately cited here. The collection lacks an obituary or other biographical article about Mrs. Stewart herself.

*ProQuest (www.proquest.com) "News and Newspapers." Database accessible to Yale readers and others affiliated with selected libraries. My main source for newspaper citations. Also used for newspapers and other periodicals are HathiTrust (accessible via participating libraries) and Library of Congress, Chronicling America (https://chroniclingamerica.loc.gov).

*Selzer, Richard. "Alexander Smith Cochran," in *Yale University Library Gazette,* vol. 73, no.1/2 (October 1998): 47–55. https://www.jstor.org/stable/40859804 (retrieved May 5, 2019). Selzer, a surgeon and novelist, was long an Incorporator of the Club.

Smith, Constance Babington. *John Masefield: A Life* (Oxford: Oxford UP, 1978).

Smith, Robert M. "The Formation of Shakespeare Libraries in America," in *The Shakespeare Association Bulletin,* vol. 4, no. 3 (July 1929): 65–74.

Strachey, John St. Loe. *American Soundings Etc* (London: Hodder & Stoughton, 1926).

*Troxell, Gilbert McCoy. "The Elizabethan Club of Yale University" [Troxell I], in *The Papers of the Bibliographical Society of America,* vol. 27, no. 2 (1933): 83–88. https://www.jstor.org/stable/24293013 (retrieved May 5, 2019). Extract in Appendix 1.2. Troxell was one of the early undergraduate members of the Club, its second librarian and first historian.

*———. "The Elizabethan Club: Its Origins and Its Books" [Troxell II], in *Yale University Library Gazette,* vol. 27, no. 1 (July 1952): 19–28. Has some overlap with the foregoing, but is an indispensable complement. https://www.jstor.org/stable/40857562 (retrieved May 5, 2019). Extract in Appendix 1.2.

*Walska, Ganna. *Always Room at the Top* [ART] (New York: Smith, 1943). See Appendix 2.4 (my review) and the Part 2 bibliography. (The Elizabethan Club has two copies.)

*[Ganna] Walska Archives, Lotusland [GWA] (see Appendix 2.5 and the Part 2 bibliography). Many autograph letters from ASC to his wife. Not seen by me except for one.

*Weeks, Christopher. *Alexander Smith Cochran: Modernist Architect in Traditional Baltimore* (Baltimore: Maryland Historical Society, 1995). Good source for this side of the family and ASC.

West, Anthony James. *The Shakespeare First Folio.* The History of the Book 108, 2 vols (Oxford: Oxford UP, 2001–2003).

*Wrench, John Evelyn. *Struggle, 1914–1920* (London: Ivor Nicholson and Watson, 1935). Part of the autobiography of the founder of the English Speaking Union, to which ASC was an early benefactor and of which he is sometimes regarded as cofounder.

Yale Alumni Weekly. Available on microfilm through Yale University Library, Manuscripts and Archives division (MSSA).

*Yale University, Class of 1896 (at Yale University Library, Manuscripts and Archives [MSSA]), listed chronologically by date of publication:

> *The 1896 Senior Class Book,* ed. Philip Ray Allen and Frederick Whitney Mathews (New Haven: Yale University, 1896).

> *Triennial Record of the Class of 1896 in Yale College,* ed. George Henry Nettleton (New Haven: Yale University, 1899).

> *Sexennial Record, Class of 1896, Yale College,* ed. Clarence S. Day, Jr. (New York: Irving Press, 1902).

> *Decennial Record of the Class of 1896, Yale College,* comp. Clarence S. Day, Jr. (New York: [n.p.], 1907). https://archive.org/details/cu31924030632594/page/n14 (retrieved May 21, 2019).

> *'96 Half-way Book,* by Clarence Day, Jr. (New Haven: Yale College, 1915), pp. 84–86. Famed as a "volume of extraordinary portraits" by the class secretary, Clarence Day, Jr. (see Lewis, p. 157). One of the pen portraits is of ASC; partly reproduced in Parks I, p. 24; see p. 61 above.

> *Quarter-Century Record of the Class of 1896, Yale College,* ed. Dudley L. Vaill (New Haven: [n.p.], 1924). Statistics, including war service; presumably, ASC supplied the details in his entry.

> *Thirty-Five Year Record of the Class of 1896, Yale College* (New Haven: [n.p.], 1932). Obituary.

*Yale University, Elizabethan Club (listed alphabetically)

> *The Book of the Yale Elizabethan Club 1912* ([New Haven]: Yale UP, [n.d.]). https://catalog.hathitrust.org/Record/007687320/Home/ (retrieved July 9, 2017).

> *The Book of the Yale Elizabethan Club 1913* ([New Haven]: Yale UP, [n.d.]). https://catalog.hathitrust.org/Record/008399952 (retrieved April 22, 2019).

> "The Elizabethan Club," Kenneth Borson Architects. www.kbarch.com/higher-ed-elizabethan-club (retrieved July 2, 2017). Record of the Lizzie's renovation and enlargement in 1996.

The Elizabethan Club: Constitution, List of Members, Books in the Library (New Haven: The Club, 1958).

"Opening of the Elizabethan Club of Yale University, Sixth of December, Nineteen Hundred and Eleven" (New Haven: [n.p.], 1911).

The Year Book of the Elizabethan Club (New Haven: Elizabethan Club, 1933)

*Year Books, 1912–1958.

*Yale University Library, Manuscripts and Archives division [MSSA]. The archives of the Elizabethan Club, which were recently transferred to the library, are at call number RU36. As this collection is not abundant, it leaves questions unanswered (see Appendixes 1.2 and 1.3). Some of these documents are reprinted in Parks I, but the Club's "President's Reports" are regrettably incomplete.

Tuberculosis (works consulted)

Dubos, René, and Jean Dubos. *The White Plague: Tuberculosis, Man, and Society* (Boston: Little, Brown, 1952).

Hutcheon, Linda, and Michael Hutcheon. *Opera: Desire, Disease, Death* (Lincoln: University of Nebraska Press, 1996).

Mann, Thomas. *The Magic Mountain*, tr. H.T. Lowe-Porter (many editions).

Ott, Katherine. *Fevered Lives: Tuberculosis in American Culture since 1870* (Cambridge: Harvard UP, 1996).

Rothman, Sheila M. *Living in the Shadow of Death: Tuberculosis and the Social Experience of Illness in American History* (New York: Basic Books, 1994).

Smith, F. B. *The Retreat of Tuberculosis, 1850–1950* (London: Croom Helm, 1988).

Williams, Harley. *Requiem for a Great Killer: The Story of Tuberculosis* (London: Heath Horizon, 1973).

PART TWO

Fig. 2.1. Madame Ganna Walska, ca. 1921. This date suggests
it was taken during Walska's brief marriage to Cochran.
She mentions a fondness for cats only once in her memoirs,
in connection with Grindell Matthews, her fifth husband.
Wisconsin Historical Society

MADAME GANNA WALSKA
(1887–1984)

The Elizabethan Club of Yale University celebrated its centenary in 2011. Its founder, Alexander Smith Cochran, had one wife, Ganna Walska, a Polish would-be opera singer, who lived a long and engaging life. This brief essay is about her.

The Yonkers carpet heir Alexander Smith Cochran was 46 years old and reputedly America's richest bachelor when he traveled to England aboard the *Aquitania* in July 1920.[1] He was deeply disappointed that his racing yacht *Vanitie* failed to win the trials for the defense of the America's Cup and, angrily, was turning his back on the New World.[2] Near the last day of the voyage, he was introduced to the beautiful Madame Ganna Walska (fig. 2.1), a recently widowed opera diva, who was en route to Paris to recuperate from the death of her husband.[3] Cochran saw her several times that day, and he twice proposed marriage. Although refused, he evidently was not discouraged.[4] During the following weeks, he flew from London to Paris to continue his courtship. Weeks of wooing passed, bringing them into September.[5] Two days before Madame Walska was to embark for America to assume the title role in the Chicago Opera Company's production of Leoncavallo's *Zaza*, she relented and accepted Cochran's proposal. By heroic exertion and great expense on his part, they achieved the unheard-of feat of being married in Paris on the same day they became betrothed.[6] Cochran became Walska's third husband.[7]

The prelude was seemingly ardent, but the marriage was not. In her memoirs, *Always Room at the Top* (ART), Walska says that "we were divorced from the moment of our wedding." Her account of the wedding night, centering on Cochran's after-dinner stroll, offers evidence of their incompatibility. Cochran's normal evening constitutional gave Walska, who had just moved from her hotel to his, time to arrange her wardrobe. The walk took an hour. Cochran returned with a story that, when a prostitute approached him invitingly, he had replied to her, "Not tonight, my dear. Tonight I am married!" Laughing uproariously, unable to stop, he reported this encounter to a disgusted Walska. Not every bride need have recoiled at Cochran's story or failed to join his laughter, but for this bride it was an inauspicious beginning. The next morning, while Cochran was sleeping off the wedding night, Walska was pouring coffee next door for her disappointed suitor, Harold McCormick, who had just flown in from Zurich. He announced "in a businesslike way, quite naturally," that his wife had agreed to a divorce and Walska must now divorce Cochran and marry him. She demurred. This scenario of divorces and remarriage, in fact, played out in the next two years.[8]

Six months passed before Cochran walked out. Walska and Cochran returned to New York on October 9, 1920. They were greeted the next day by a long syndicated article headlined "Surprising Romance of America's $100,000,000 Bachelor." The article surveys both Cochran's and Walska's backgrounds, contrasting their very different beginnings. Perhaps the most important part concerns Walska's "[essaying] to be a grand opera prima donna." It said, "she had been moderately successful on the stage in Europe," endorsing the rumor of a Kiev debut in *The Merry Widow.* Next came a Havana engagement, which went badly: "She did not in the least appeal to the taste of the Cubans.... The manager had to return their money to the seat buyers." Walska was not discouraged: "Mrs. Cochran is so devoted to the musical art that she is still likely to make another plunge into grand opera, but this seems too improbable to be believed." The New York articles from which these reports came were important for Walska's reputation. The feature article of October 10 demonstrates awareness of her somewhat loose New York past among entertainers and, notably, of the reception of her operatic performance in Havana, and it speculates about her future in opera with the expectation of renewed failure. This evocation of the Havana misadventure may be the point of departure for Walska's negative musical reputation.

Walska and Cochran spent the six or seven weeks before her Chicago engagement together in New York, probably at Walska's house on 94th

Street. (Cochran had no New York house.) During their residence in the city, from September to November 1920, the house she had inherited from her second husband, Dr. Joseph Fraenkel, was fully redecorated at Cochran's expense. These weeks were when Walska met Cochran's family and friends. She mentions a meal with sister-in-law Elinor and another attended by brother-in-law Gifford, whom she refers to as "dear Gifford." Also mentioned is an unpleasant lunch at her home at which Walska met Robert Perkins, president of Smith Carpet's rival company and Cochran's inseparable friend. On this occasion, Cochran committed the blunder of treating his spouse as though she were a stranger. With a view to the *Zaza* performance, Walska reached Chicago toward the end of November.[9]

Upon marrying, it had been understood that Walska would continue her operatic singing, as she "was not the kind of person who would be happy living as a decorative mannequin in this futile world." Indeed, in a news item from late November 1920, Cochran says he has no objection to her continuing her career. During the time before Walska's Chicago première, he was fox hunting in South Carolina. When joining her in Chicago, he was enraged to find that she had registered at her hotel under her professional, rather than married, name. He stormed back to New York, and they exchanged telegrams about her position, Cochran now demanding that she choose between domesticity and opera. Walska claims that she was torn, but her career was frail: she had no record of success and only this single booking; as she saw it, she had no choice. She walked out of the Chicago Opera and *Zaza,* fueling speculations about her singing and making headlines.

The first interpretations of Walska's abandoning *Zaza* were restrained. One was given by Edward Colman Moore, another in the magazine *Le Ménestrel:* "At the Chicago Auditorium, the showing of *Zaza,* by Leoncavallo, has been postponed. Mme Ganna Walska, who was to have made her debut, withdrew, it seems, after the first rehearsal, either because she had a cold, or that she was inadequate, or that her husband did not wish her to continue in the theatre. People are speculating." The first newspaper notice, in the *Chicago Tribune,* was noncommittal: "'Richest Singer in World' Flees on Eve of Debut"; the *New York Tribune* (December 22) had the headline "Mme. Walska Had Vocal Trouble, Is Latest Report" (the possibility was raised that Cochran had a part in the incident). The first developed explanation is in the *New York Tribune* (December 30): "Opera Conductor Protested after Hearing Walska Sing. Marinuzzi, in Terse Phrases, Said It Would Be Impossible to Produce 'Zaza' with Much Heralded Diva in the Leading Role. Accompanied only by her maid, she slipped away." (Notice that here she is "much heralded"; even though she had no record of successes, she had accumulated publicity.) The Marinuzzi story, published just after the Cochrans had sailed for Europe, has variants, only one of which, in later writings, is cited here: early in rehearsals Marinuzzi could no longer work with Walska, and he turned the task over to Pietro Cimini. During a rehearsal, Cimini asked Walska to sing in "her natural voice." She stalked out, went to the opera's managers, told them she was packing her bags and that they soon would be packing theirs, too; that proved true. However the story was told, the Chicago fiasco solidified Walska's fame as a failed singer.[10]

Once she was back in New York with Cochran, the family crisis was over: "As soon as he had his own way," Walska recalled, "he forgot that I had abandoned my singing for his sake." Nevertheless, in the days following, she appears to have written to the artist Erté and ordered costumes for the soprano leads in 14 operas, notably: *Faust, Louise, Manon, Rigoletto, Pagliacci, Zaza, La Bohème, Madama Butterfly, Tosca,* and *Fedora.* She had engagements for none of them but, despite recent events, she seemed to believe she had an operatic future. Erté adds: "She very rarely performed the parts for which [the costumes] were designed."[11]

Soon after, the couple was again in France.[12] Cochran had bought Walska a magnificent town house in the best district of Paris.[13] He had his own Paris house on rue de l'Élysée, but considered it too small for a couple. He wanted to go back to England for fox hunting and so sent Walska to Cannes by herself for the winter season, securing half a floor at the resplendent Carlton Hotel for her and six servants. Scorning the season, she returned to Paris after five days. Cochran further plied her with a chauffeured Rolls Royce, a million-franc sable coat, whatever jewel she might care to buy at Cartier, and the guarantee of $100,000 a year in pin money. His idea of marriage was to bury his bride in gold, but not even an extravagant "morning gift" could mend their union.[14] Cochran rejoined Walska in Paris in January, and the couple then entertained and engaged in redecorating the house, but in March 1921, weary of married life, Cochran returned to England. He was expected to come back, but within a week his things were packed by his valet and cleared out of the house. Soon Cochran would attempt to seize it from beneath his abandoned wife.[15]

The Elizabethan Club had no part in all this. Cochran founded it nine years before he met Walska, and since 1911 his concern for it had diminished, crowded out by other interests. Although he was one of the Club's original Incorporators, he was notably absent from their meetings and from the Club itself. He took Walska to Yonkers to be cheered by the carpet workers, but she never saw New Haven.[16]

Hammering out the Cochran divorce lasted twice as long as the six months that they cohabited. Walska was represented by Dudley Field Malone, a specialist in transatlantic divorces. Cochran's lawyer was Samuel Untermyer, a very distinguished jurist, who would include the Cochran divorce in the list of his celebrated cases. Cochran was in the perilous position of trying to discard his wife without having any grounds for doing so.[17] To compensate for this flaw, early in the dispute, the legality of the Cochran marriage was contested: it seemed that Walska's union with her first husband, Arcadie Eingorn, had not been properly ended, and that he might still be alive. The divorce from Eingorn attracted press attention. It and Eingorn himself faded from the proceedings, but not without affecting the outcome.[18] In the 1930s, it became an accepted fact in the press that the now-deceased Cochran had left Walska $3 million in his will, but this was an invention related to a later divorce. In the case of the Cochran divorce, the reality was more modest. Walska ended up obtaining a trust fund of $300,000 that yielded an annual income of $20,000 when topped up to the target sum—not bad, but small in light of what could have been expected from a man of Cochran's wealth.[19] Fortunately for Walska, the Cochran settlement was outdone by what came soon after. Within days of the final divorce decree, still in Paris, Walska married Harold McCormick, grand patron of the Chicago Opera and ex-president of the vast family

firm International Harvester (IH). What he would lavish on Walska made
Cochran look stingy. For a start, in a *pre-nuptial* provision, he settled a large
block of IH stock in her name, guaranteeing an annual return of $100,000.
(It seems more than coincidental that this sum matched the pin money
promised by Cochran.) By the time her third husband was jettisoned in
1922, Walska had become a rich woman.[20]

❖ ❖ ❖

Ganna Walska was Polish, born in 1887 into a middle-class family named
Puacz who baptized her Hanna. The family lived in Brest-Litovsk, on
Poland's Russian frontier. (An alternative account places her birth and family
home in Siedlce, a smaller town between Brest and Warsaw.) Blessed with a
strong constitution and enviable good health, she is later seen traveling in an
open limousine, impervious to heat and cold. In her extraordinarily long life,
she is not recorded as ever having had a serious illness until afflicted by late-
onset breast cancer and the various infirmities of extreme old age.[21]

Walska, at age 19, eloped to St. Petersburg with a Russian army officer,
Arcadie Eingorn, whom she met in her hometown. Her elopement to St.
Petersburg resulted in temporary ostracism. Reconciled, the couple then
visited Brest-Litovsk to introduce Arcadie to her family.[22] Rare reports of
their life together show the pair in the Paris neighborhood of Montmartre
and, again, skating in Dorpat (now Tartu, Estonia). But the marriage
broke down, and they separated.[23] She found she had an appealing voice
and turned to the stage for a living. The professional name she adopted
was Ganna Walska, simply changing her first name to its Russian form;
the prefix "Madame" came later. When Nicholas, the partner of the artist
Erté, was shown a photograph of her, he remembered having seen her
performing in a Russian *café chantant.* Arcadie and she came face to face
again in Kiev, where she had a theatrical engagement, but never again.

In 1912, in St. Petersburg, the noted painter Victor Stember glimpsed
Ganna Walska at the theatre and was entranced by her great beauty. He and
his wife invited her to sit for a portrait. At the time, she was working "in
one of the dashing night clubs"; she came to sittings "sleepy and sometimes

not too sober." "Mlle Walska" was a star of St. Petersburg music halls, according to an October 1913 Paris press item hailing her coming to Paris for an engagement to sing Russian songs in a revue; her "*jolie voix*" and "*rare beauté*" were advertised as having aroused enthusiasm in the Paris audience.[24] She may have decided to change from a popular-music singer to a soprano in opera, as she maintains in her memoirs, prompting her to go to Paris to study with Jean de Reszke, a famed teacher. Meanwhile, she earned her keep as she had in St. Petersburg, as a music-hall singer. Writing to the painter Stember, she induced him to send her his portrait of her so that she might display it at the Paris Salon. Beauty continued to be her main recommendation, as seen in a listing of the Paris revue cast in which she appears as "la belle Walska," the only qualifier in the list; she appears continually in cast lists of 1913 and 1914. In the first months of World War I, she came to the attention of Broadway impresario Lee Shubert, who invited her to America. She extricated herself from wartime Paris, made her way to Liverpool, and took the White Star liner *Arabic* in December 1914.[25]

On the playbill of a Christmas concert aboard the *Arabic,* in which she performed two songs, Walska's name is recorded for the first time with the prefix "Madame," which normally was reserved for accomplished and celebrated singers with international careers. This assumed title confirmed her vocation as an opera prima donna, a distinction she had yet to acquire. "Madame" was an agenda for her life. It may be at this time, if not before, that she swore off smoking, drinking, and dancing.[26]

The central fact about Walska is that she was self-made. She alone was in charge of herself, and she made the most of her strengths. No family or riches or special skill and training assisted in her progress. During her twenties and later, her main asset was great beauty, which all observers emphatically affirm—that and, in her own words, "unshakable tenacity and a very strong will." She overcame great odds to become a celebrity.[27]

Landing in New York on January 3, 1915, she was slated to give her first American performance a month later in the vaudeville sketch "Before the Play" at the Shuberts' Victoria Theatre. Just then, however, word came that her (unnamed) husband, a captain in the Russian army, had been killed in the war; she was "prostrated," and her first stage appearance postponed. The delayed debut took place in April in *Mlle Nitouche,* an operetta performed by a French company. In the intermission between the second and third acts, Mme Ganna Walska sang a repertoire of Russian, Polish, and French songs. At her first appearance, inspired by the European war, she was draped in a French flag and sang "La Marseillaise," with the audience standing and joining in. In May, Mme Walska, "the beautiful Petrograd prima donna," (fig. 2.2) was cast in the Shubert production of the musical *Hands Up.* Also in the prospective cast was Fanny Brice, but neither she nor Walska was in the play when it finally opened in July.[28]

On August 12, an announcement appeared of the engagement of Mme Ganna Walska, prima donna of Paris and Warsaw, to Lowell Palmer, Jr., scion of a very rich Brooklyn family. The announcement filled in the prospective bride's past: born in Warsaw into the Polish royal family of Leszsynska and widow of Baron Arcadie Eingorn, who was killed with the Russian army in Poland; his death was not "absolutely confirmed." Later in August, Walska was among four "superbeauties" in the studio of the noted illustrator Coles Phillips; she was again identified as a Leszsynska, associated with a Polish royal house. (Phillips's portrait of her survives.)[29] In February 1916, Mme Walska, now heralded as a "Polish prima donna of the Metropolitan Opera," broke her engagement with Palmer so she could continue her singing career. A newspaper photograph dated June 18, 1916, shows her standing with the Stember portrait (fig. 2.3), which had come to New York. In the summer, "Mme. Ganna Walska, the noted Polish grand opera singer, who [has] recently lost her singing voice," appeared in the movie *The Child of Destiny,* playing the heroine's mother. Later in the summer, on the advice of financier and opera patron Otto Kahn, Walska took her still ailing voice to Dr. Joseph Fraenkel, a celebrated neurologist and diagnostician. On September 7, 1916, ten days after the first consultation, the widow Walska and Dr. Fraenkel were married.[30]

Fraenkel had learned medicine at the University of Vienna. He moved to the United States to escape anti-Semitism. In New York, he had a large practice among poor Jews as well as New York's Jewish aristocracy and other rich patients. Cofounder of the New York Neurological Society, he was the most estimable of Walska's six husbands.[31] From 1909 to 1911, he was fast

Fig. 2.2. One of Walska's New York publicity portraits by
Mishkin, ca. 1915. The diva sat for many portrait photographs
by the prominent Russian-born New York photographer
Mishkin, who also did work for the Metropolitan Opera.
This pose is the most seductive among them. Archive of
the Anna and Jarosław Iwaszkiewicz in Stawisko Museum
archive / FOTONOVA (archiwum Muzeum Anny i Jarosława
Iwaszkiewiczów w Stawisku / FOTONOVA)

Fig. 2.3. This newspaper photograph, here from a later
printing, was first published in the *New York Sun* on June 18,
1916. It documents Walska's being in possession of her
portrait by Victor Stember earlier than is generally claimed.
(See Appendix L.1, "The Stember Portrait.") Courtesy of the
New York Public Library

friends with Gustav Mahler and his stunning, accomplished wife Alma, a noted beauty. He fell in love with Alma and, after Mahler's early death, tried to convince her to marry him, but she firmly refused. Now, a few years after this disappointment, Fraenkel saw an image of Alma in Walska's beauty. His good friend Otto Kahn, who had sent Walska to him and also knew the Mahlers, may have urged him to seize the opportunity. Walska did not resist Fraenkel's proposal of an instant wedding.[32]

Walska deprecates the marriage in her memoirs: "In my life with him there was no day, no hour of simple happiness, of beneficial, carefree joy." To hear her tell it, Fraenkel, who was 49 years old to her 29, called her "Baby" and treated her more like a daughter than a wife. She is playful with her age. At one point, she claims to be younger than Fraenkel by 30 or perhaps even more years (i.e., about 20 years old). Elsewhere, she says that he was near 60 when, in fact, he died at age 54; she also credits him with having studied for "fifty years." She wished "to participate with the full enthusiasm of her juvenile heart" in the doctor's talks—in this case "juvenile" means 29 and older. Walska's comments about Fraenkel reveal her ambivalence toward him. She considers him a great man and says his death broke her heart and "blackened my soul," assuring us that his death was a terrible loss. He "changed me from an undisciplined, rich Slavic nature into a person morally and intellectually worthy of being the companion of such an exceptionally-minded creature [as he was]." But in making such changes, she "sacrificed her soul to Dr. Fraenkel's intellectuality" and lost her personality. Fraenkel's difficult beginnings and the great pain he experienced from a chronic illness "diminished the greatness of his soul" and caused him to lack goodness.[33]

Her complaints about Fraenkel were not wholly unfounded. Alma Mahler once wrote to him that, "when it comes to living you're a miserable failure." She said he strove "for consummate dematerialization" and had a "cerebral makeup"; he was not earthy. An underlying issue in Fraenkel's union with Walska explained "his rather sudden proposal of marriage. The explanation was simple, if cruel to me—I looked very much like Frau Mahler, and the resemblance made him believe he loved me. I realized that fact, alas, too late—when we were united." It sounds as though Fraenkel

forgot that he loved Alma Mahler for more than her looks: Walska's resemblance to the very accomplished Alma was only skin deep.[34]

It was with Fraenkel's support that Madame Walska, the prima donna,
at last began major musical study and obtained her inaugural dates in
serious singing. How she managed her studies during the Fraenkel years is
not spelled out in ART. She had been taking profitless lessons in the spring
of 1915. Even if her claims about earlier study with Tartakov and de Reszke
are credited, she needed further training. Two newspaper photographs show
her at singing lessons with a teacher, Will Thorner. Her participation in a
scattering of minor concerts suggests the context of a music teacher taking
his students on trial outings. By 1917, Walska had a manager, R.E. Johnston,
who issued a noteworthy publicity circular, cited here as Biographical
Document 1917. Because of its part in inspiring the Walska legend (notably
of her court life) in earlier biographies, this summary warrants paraphrasing. Johnston affirms that Walska was a descendant of the Polish royal
Leszczynski line and became the wife of a nobleman (Eingorn) at 17. She
experienced court life in St. Petersburg and discovered she had an appealing
voice, which aroused her musical ambition. She changed her name to
Ganna Walska. When she attempted to perform incognito in Kiev, her
identity was revealed by the local press, and the two noble families whose
name she bore were horrified. Renouncing the "entire social fabric" in
which she had been, Walska gave up husband and home and went to Paris
to study opera. There she was a pupil of Édouard de Reszke, with whom
she had already studied in Warsaw. They developed a repertoire suitable
for the Paris Opéra-comique. All was arranged for her debut in *Tosca,* but
the engagement was cancelled when war broke out. She followed the lead
of other European artists and went to America, where she continued her
operatic studies as well as developed as a concert artist, able to present rare
Russian songs. Her operatic roles included Thaïs, Tosca, both Manons,
Butterfly, Mimi, Marguerite, and Louise. Her voice went with "extraordinary physical beauty." Johnston's circular credited her with glittering
social beginnings and a sturdy musical past. The musical-hall artiste of St.
Petersburg, Paris, and New York was suitably disguised.[35]

More than a full year elapsed between Walska's marriage to Fraenkel and her first publicized concert, a morning musicale in February 1918 at the Biltmore Hotel. It consisted of three simple songs followed by a duet from Bizet's *Pearl Fishers* with none other than Enrico Caruso. It was related that Caruso generously sang especially soft in order to let Walska's voice ring out more fully.[36]

Next came Walska's debut in grand opera. A Ouija board urged her to study Giordano's opera *Fedora*. Providentially, the Italian impresario Bracale offered her the lead in a Havana production of *Fedora* if she guaranteed to compensate him financially for seats that remained unsold. Also on the bill was the great ballerina Pavlova, so there was no risk, Bracale assured her. The Fraenkels were friends with Elsa Schiaparelli (later a famous couturière), whom Fraenkel asked to chaperone his wife in Havana. The omens were poor. The rehearsal with orchestra was cancelled because of mourning for the death of Theodore Roosevelt, who died on January 6, 1919, and Walska complained that she had never sung with an orchestra before. At the performance, she had her initial experience of paralyzing stage fright, which would be the nemesis of her career. Schiaparelli reported the events light-heartedly in her memoirs: "[Ganna] sang until the noise became deafening." Faced with the spectators' clamor for refunds, the theatre manager demanded that the diva pay a large sum in compensation. Walska, lacking ready money and not wishing to wait until funds came from New York, gave him a rare pearl as restitution. Two years later, when Walska's marriage to Cochran came to the attention of the press (as seen above), the Havana fiasco was recalled and supplied the grounding for her fame as a failed singer.[37]

Untroubled, Dr. Fraenkel continued to encourage her musical training. She was auditioned in New York by Cleofonte Campanini, director of the Chicago Opera, who declared that she was well suited for the title roles in both *Fedora* and *Thaïs*. In 1919, Walska contrived a meeting in the lobby of New York's Plaza Hotel with Harold McCormick, president of the Chicago Opera. It was the turning point of her life, but at the time it led only to innocent socializing at the Fraenkel house. McCormick had long been married to John D. Rockefeller's daughter Edith. Now enamored of

Walska, he used his presidency of the Chicago Opera to have her engaged as the lead in Leoncavallo's opera *Zaza,* which was on the bill in Chicago for December 1920. Madame had no singing dates in the months until then.[38]

A chronic intestinal disorder nightly tore Fraenkel with pain. Walska describes herself nursing him, complaining that she "learned about his great illness only after our marriage." On April 24, 1920, the doctor died. He left Walska their house at the corner of Park Avenue and 94th Street, which remained her New York base until she sold it in 1965.[39] She also had first claim to his net inheritance of $162,866, of which she received $113,148 ($1,384,852 in 2017 dollars). The legacy was contested by the blood heirs and would be secured only 19 months later.[40] Fraenkel had provided Walska with a fine standard of living. In the early days of widowhood, when the inheritance had yet to be sorted out, she had reason to think that her financial future was bleak.[41]

In July 1920, Walska's admirer Harold McCormick boarded the *Aquitania* for Europe. His destination was Zurich, where his wife had resided with their children since 1913. He was, it seems, going to ask her for a divorce. Walska was aboard, bound for Paris, and so was Alexander Smith Cochran, who had the crucial asset of bachelorhood as well as great wealth. Walska's memoirs describe her shadowing Cochran in New York and trying to arrange for them to cross paths while Fraenkel was still alive. On the *Aquitania,* they were about to meet. The Widow Fraenkel, although much comforted by McCormick when her husband died, did not have the leisure to await Edith McCormick's pleasure.[42]

Cochran may have been a brief link between more important husbands in Walska's life, but he had a decisive part in her history. She loathed him. He had, she says, "insane selfishness," "limitless egoism," a "morbid desire to hurt." She avers that "he was the most miserable man I have ever met." But because of his fame as one of America's very rich men, he put the name of Madame Walska, the would-be singer, up in lights. As his present or former wife, regardless of any vocal performances, she became an operatic celebrity. Her fame would further swell upon union with a larger fortune.[43]

Harold McCormick was the second of three sons born to the reaper-inventor Cyrus. Harold was high up at the International Harvester

Company of Chicago, which was at the heart of the agricultural machinery industry at a time when agriculture was foremost in the U.S. economy.[44] He was an affable, good natured, fun-loving, and well-liked man— a peacemaker, about whose personal charm everyone agreed. Dutifully he went to Princeton, married the younger Rockefeller daughter, lived long with this difficult woman, and had five children by her. Also dutifully he took his place in the family firm. He was a talented whistler and held public whistling concerts.[45] His suspected womanizing reputedly prompted Edith's departure for Zurich to undergo analysis with the celebrated Carl Jung.[46] Edith and Harold loved opera, which they amply subsidized in Chicago, and of course it was opera that brought Harold within Ganna Walska's orbit.[47] Aboard the *Aquitania,* Walska had not been wrong to prefer a bird in the hand, Cochran, to his richer but married rival. Edith was not about to be speedily divorced. But both divorces—Harold's from Edith, Cochran's from Walska—eventually came through.[48] McCormick and Walska were wed in Paris on August 11, 1922, and they honeymooned at the Salzburg Music Festival, then at Karlsbad, the famous Bohemian spa.[49]

McCormick was the prince among Walska's husbands. Their marriage was Walska's longest lasting; they had known each other for three years before being married, and they stayed on good terms after divorcing in 1931. Much the largest part of her singing career took place in the McCormick years, and much the largest share of her wealth came from him. We have already seen her receiving a huge provision from him even before marriage. He was the only one of her husbands whom she took to Poland to meet her family. Her memoirs speak at great length, scathingly, about Cochran, but we learn little more about the "charming" McCormick than that he had "wonderful boyish blue-eyes … the reflection of his beautiful soul." Her other main benefactor, a French musician, receives little mention in *Always Room at the Top,* neglected along with her family and near friends. She evidently believed in leaving those whom she cherished out of the account of her inner life.[50]

Still, her union to McCormick had its downside. Walska plainly says that the 51-year-old McCormick was too old for sex. A devotee of physical fitness, he had had a rejuvenating gland-grafting operation to prepare for the wedding. According to the *St. Louis Post-Dispatch,* he sailed to Europe in high spirits. On arrival, for discretion's sake, he stayed at the Hotel Princesse (Caroline), near the Étoile, which also was near Walska's house on the rue de Lübeck, rather than at a more majestic hotel, such as the Crillon. McCormick's attempted rejuvenation evidently did not impress Walska. She calls him a hypochondriac, whose pockets were always full of pills. That the marriage was not consummated is implied by a passage in her memoirs:

> Unfortunately the same idiosyncrasy led [Harold] to idolize the physical expression of love and he became insatiable in his search for the realization of the physical demands—insatiable because they were unattainable for him any more. [After nature had given him many children, he chose] for his second wife an idealist who was able to put so much value on the richness of his soul that she could not even imagine the possibility of his preferring to seek further for a gross and limited pleasure rather than being satisfied with the divine companionship of the spiritual love she was willing to share with him.[51]

Because of their different occupations, she lived in Paris and he in Chicago. During their marriage, she came to America three times for musical tours; Harold also joined her in Paris, but how often or for how long is hard to tell.[52] Despite their separate residences and only intermittent cohabitation, their relationship seems to have held firm, even after divorce.[53]

McCormick lavished a fortune on her. For a start, he paid her lawyer for the Cochran divorce. Shortly after marriage, he helped her to buy one of the architectural treasures of Paris, the financially distressed Théâtre des Champs-Élysées (fig. 2.4), a superb three-theatre complex in need of a cash infusion. Walska's prized singing teacher—the conductor Walther Straram—arranged the purchase. She remained proprietor of the TCE until 1970, and for a time she financed its deficits out of McCormick's pocket.[54] Malicious tongues claimed that McCormick bought the theatre so that Walska might stage her otherwise despised performances there, but this was unfair: the purchase made her owner of only the physical structure of the TCE; she had no say in the playbills until the long term leases ran out, five

Fig. 2.4. The Théâtre des Champs-Élysées, Paris, opened
in 1913, and its architecture inside and out is world famous.
Walska's acquisition of the theatre in 1923 was of only its "fabric"
(i.e., walls, floor, roof). She sold the theatre in the early 1970s
to an organ of the French government. A suite of rooms went
with ownership, and under Walska's auspices during the 1920s
and early 1930s, many fashionable receptions were held there.
Coldcreation / Wikipedia CC 3.0

years after the purchase, and even after 1928 she did not abuse her position.[55] Straram did engage her to perform in various concerts he organized at the TCE. She sang the role of the Countess in *The Marriage of Figaro* at a Mozart festival in 1924 and was soprano soloist in Beethoven's Ninth Symphony and Mozart's Requiem. She also participated in a modest string of concerts, not all at the TCE, during 1927, 1928, and 1930. Straram was her accompanist on a German recital tour culminating unhappily with a poor performance in Berlin. Straram had experience as a vocal coach; according to Erté, his teaching improved Walska's singing. But the importance of her acquisition of the TCE was elsewhere. Instantly, Madame Walska McCormick became a star in Paris society; her theatre box and reception salon glittered with dignitaries. The orchestra organized and led by Straram and subsidized by her was considered the best in Paris. Not yet 35, she had found room at the top.[56]

The theatre and the payment of its deficits were only the start of McCormick's generosity. The prenuptial gift of IH stock yielding an annual $100,000 was mentioned above. There also was an open charge account for her at Cartier. She bought masses of jewelry, much of it from distressed Russian noble refugees; they included an authentic Fabergé egg. Her pearls were fabled.[57] When sold at auction in New York in 1971, the bulk of her jewels fetched more than $900,000 (roughly $5.5 million in 2017).[58] Although later denied, a rumor in the 1930s had her selling a precious necklace to Barbara Hutton for more than $1 million.[59] Also acquired were opera costumes, almost all designed by Erté (now at LACMA).[60] She was famous for her clothes, both on stage and off. Her concerts were virtual fashion shows as they involved costume changes between numbers; she traveled to America with as many as 15 trunks.[61] McCormick gave her a new Rolls Royce limousine in 1926.[62] She also had the means to buy for herself. In 1927, she opened a perfume shop on the rue de la Paix in Paris, and a New York branch followed the next year. (Her first perfume was daringly called "Divorçons"—Let's divorce.)[63] Not the least of her purchases came in 1928 in the form of the small Chateau de Galluis, 25 miles from Paris, which became Walska's dearest possession "the only place in which I feel … less unhappy." To celebrate her birthday in 1930, McCormick covered the lawns at Galluis with one specimen of each kind of farm machinery made by the McCormick factories in France; she was delighted by Harold's show of attention, "sweet as only he can be." Finally, there were Walska's American concert tours and European operas: someone had to make up for the fact that the audiences were thin or had to be encouraged to attend.[64]

By the time Walska turned 40, she had sufficient wealth to support her social standing. She had town houses in Paris and New York and a chateau in the French countryside, and she had the wherewithal to maintain and staff them and to entertain in style. Adding the $20,000 per year from Cochran to the annual $100,000 from McCormick shows that, as early as 1923, her monthly income was $10,000 ($142,000 in 2017 dollars). Per year, she pocketed well over $2.4 million at today's value. Without exaggeration, in 1928 she characterized herself as having a "comfortable (or even call it luxurious) income."[65] And she was tightfisted. So what did it matter that her voice repeatedly betrayed her?[66]

Ganna Walska had a voice and, intermittently, it was acknowledged by judicious critics: "a pleasing, natural voice" (Olin Downes, 1929); "a voice naturally of unusual power and beauty" (*Boston Globe,* 1923); *Le Ménestrel* (1922) referred to her voice in Beethoven's Ninth Symphony as "*un soprano très pur.*" Concert manager Charles Wagner was surprised: "Could Walska sing or couldn't she? … [Attending] a full recital in her home … I was surprised to find a beautiful voice, fine musicianship and rare musical intelligence. Her trouble had always been nervousness; if she could conquer stage fright she might be a fine concert artist."[67]

There was dissent. Conductor Walter Damrosch reported to Harold's sister Anita Blaine that "my musician friends who have heard her [observe that] her voice is absolutely devoid of charm." Many newspapers affirmed that she had no voice. Although recitals were better suited to her abilities, she did not always break down on the opera stage. Her musical career appears to have suffered from two main problems: she was inadequately trained, never fully outgrowing her music-hall origins; and apparently she was incapable of learning from even the ablest and costliest teachers. (She resorted in vain to spiritualism to make up for that.) Only at rare intervals did she master stage fright, to which she was subject to an alarming degree, especially in opera performances. Also, she was reputed to have "the compulsion of nonappearance ... that made [her] back out of her concerts." It was the luxury of being rich.[68]

She was a butt of humor; newspaper critics knew what to expect. But there was a silver lining: her fame came precisely from her salient traits—she was the singer who couldn't sing and who kept having rich husbands. Owning a famous theatre also did not hurt. In 1931, the Polish government decorated her for service to the arts, and in 1934 the French government elevated her to the Légion d'honneur for the same reason.[69] Her musical career was secondary to her place in the Paris musical scene. She gained headlines for incompetence—but headlines all the same—and, in the words Walska attributes to Sarah Bernhardt, "it is better to be spoken of badly than not at all." To the luminaries whom she fêted at the theatre and in her grand house or chateau, she was renowned as Madame Ganna Walska, the bejeweled opera diva; it did not matter to society that her voice often failed her or that she rarely performed in operas. We learn from a press report that she welcomed the chancellor of Austria at a fashionable reception at the TCE; only afterwards came his call on the president of France. Another report involves Marshall Lyautey, a French imperial proconsul and member of the Académie française; we glimpse the celebrated warrior going to Walska's table to kiss her hand.[70]

When Mme Ganna Walska married opera-lover Harold McCormick (fig. 2.5), she still had performed only once on an opera stage, and abjectly so at that. Her archives record where and when she had recitals on the Continent and in the United States; they would require painstaking combing to arrive at an accurate count. The operatic roles for which she bought costumes, such as Verdi's Violetta (*La traviata*), the two Manons, and Charpentier's Louise, must be sorted from roles for which she commissioned costumes and in which she actually sang. She had about eight operatic roles in a lifetime, performing each a modest number of times.[71] Walska's greatest disaster was in 1923, when she played Gilda in Verdi's *Rigoletto* for a very select audience at a special benefit performance at the Paris Opéra. The good news was that, thanks to an able conductor, she

Fig. 2.5. Walska's married-name signature on this passport
portrait from 1922 is noteworthy. The passport was issued
in Paris in anticipation of her visit to the U.S., when Harold
McCormick took his bride home to meet his family in Chicago
and his mother in California. History and Art Collection /
Alamy Stock Photo

actually finished the performance; the bad news was that the audience
tittered and laughed. *Time* magazine had a field day: Madame Walska
McCormick has no voice. Our heroine was not disheartened; the *Rigoletto*
disturbance, she said, was the doing of personal enemies.[72] She forged
ahead with a performance here and there, such as at Nice and Belgrade, and,
under a pseudonym, in the French provinces.[73] Her attempts to sing opera
in America were thwarted, she claimed, by the machinations of the repudi-
ated Edith Rockefeller McCormick. A role that Walska performed several
times, including at the Vienna Volksoper, was Cio-Cio San in *Madama
Butterfly*; her costumes were admired more than her singing. As she saw it,
her operatic apotheosis came in 1933 when she sang Debussy's Mélisande at
her own theatre (and expense). It also marked her unannounced retirement
from opera, though not from the concert stage, to which she occasionally
returned, including for a U.S. tour in 1934. One performance, in Chicago,
was enlivened by loud applause from her ex-husband.[74] Despite this limited
and dispiriting career, perhaps because of it, her claim to being a diva
and prima donna became affirmed; in America she was referred to as "the
famous Polish opera singer," with suitable variations. One publication went
so far as to dub her *"stella della lirica."*[75] She kept up her side into the 1940s,
not by performing, but by continually taking singing lessons, practicing
long hours, and devotedly attending the opera. Against all reason, she was
one of the noted singers of her generation.[76]

Off the musical stage, Walska reached her high point as a career
woman when she became a champion of women's rights and brought
about a strengthening of women's independence from their husbands. On
September 19, 1928, accompanied by 15 trunks of personal effects, she
arrived aboard the SS *Paris* at New York, where McCormick greeted her.[77]
Her belongings, duly declared and unofficially valued at $2,500,000, were
treated as the foreign-acquired property of a U.S. resident. Evaluated at the
enormous rates applicable to foreign jewelry and luxury fabrics, the duty
charged was about $1 million. Walska rejected the claim, saying that she
lived in Paris and should be treated as a visitor who would take her possessions away when she returned home. Her lawyer set out the principle at
issue: "recognition of a woman's right to maintain a separate residence while

remaining on amicable terms with her husband."[78] Enforcing then-current law, Customs ruled that, because her husband lived in Chicago, so did she, which made her a returning resident. In reply Walska contended that her base was Paris, where she owned a house, a theatre, a beauty shop, and a perfume factory; she was visiting her husband, as she had twice before during their marriage. McCormick filed an affidavit declaring his agreement with Walska about their separate homes.[79] Two weeks after the initial ruling, the case reached the U.S. Secretary of the Treasury, Andrew Mellon, who decided in favor of the Customs Department's interpretation.[80] Walska appealed again, this time to the U.S. Customs Court, to which the first woman to be made a federal judge had recently been appointed. Walska had joined the National Women's Party in 1922, and now she allied with it in reviving a New York State bill on women's residence that had long languished in the legislature.[81] She went to Albany and testified before a legislative committee to urge passage. Her plea succeeded. On April 10, 1929, a woman's right to have a separate residence from her spouse was signed into New York State law by Governor Franklin Delano Roosevelt.[82] As for the court case, it was unanimously decided in Walska's favor on January 17, 1930, adding to U.S. law the rule that women might have domiciles separate from their husbands. Unlike earlier steps in the suit, Walska's victories for women earned perfunctory notices in the American press, but *Time* did proclaim: "Walska Triumphant."[83]

Harold McCormick divorced Walska for desertion in 1931, to qualify for which the couple had had to remain apart for two years. The divorce was amicable and unopposed, and it occasioned an exceptionally rich financial settlement, starting with one-quarter of McCormick's stock in IH. Amazingly, McCormick's lawyer succeeded in keeping this coup out of the papers. What the press learned was that no property was involved. This absence of a financial settlement went with the false but often repeated assertion that the recently deceased Alexander Smith Cochran left Walska $3 million in his will.[84] Newspapers had suggested an impending McCormick divorce in 1924, 1927, and 1928, but all such rumors were denied, and they died down. The puzzle is, why did McCormick divorce her?[85] Contemporaries were surprised. An unnamed gossip columnist wrote,

Fig. 2.6. This photograph of Mr. and Mrs. Harold McCormick, ca. 1925, is a rare document of Walska in company with one of her spouses. It is impossible to tell whether it was taken in France or the U.S. Walska and McCormick are dressed to the nines, not for a strenuous hike. Wisconsin Historical Society

"I thought the McCormicks were so happy together" (fig. 2.6). He had given her all that agricultural machinery just the year before. It looks as though nothing had changed in their relationship, but they divorced all the same and stayed friends. He conspicuously applauded her Chicago concert of 1934 and sent her flowers when she sailed back to France.[86]

After the McCormick divorce, Walska continued to be based in Paris but periodically traveled to the U.S. and elsewhere. She even slipped from Paris to New York for a mere week to supervise a needed repair to her house. The soprano Frances Alda, a guest at Galluis in 1932, left disobliging memories of her quarters:

> I had more doubts when I saw the chateau, which was old enough to antedate the kind of plumbing the American Radiator Company would have approved, and which had successfully resisted any efforts to bring it up to date in that direction. Its windows looked sadly out across untidy lawns and shrubberies that made my fingers itch for a pair of gardening shears, and a drive in which weeds were more apparent than gravel. An odd assortment of servants whisked in and out around corners and up and down the crooked stairs. Its mistress had filled the place with the exotic, untidy, confused atmosphere of Poland, which Poles seem to carry with them wherever they go.

Walska had hired Alda to teach her to sing during a six-week residence. Alda thought she had had no success. Contrary to her guest's opinion about Galluis, Walska rejoiced in her country house and took pains to update and decorate it.[87]

Walska's penultimate marriage—to the English inventor Harry Grindell Matthews—is less weird than it first appears. In May 1937 Walska was in London for the coronation of George VI. A friend brought her together with Grindell Matthews, a fellow opera lover. The subject of two biographies, Grindell Matthews had had an up-and-down life, continually being on the verge of inventing an earth-shaking military product. His most notorious almost-invention was a death ray. When Walska met him he had *almost* completed a sort of sonar for detecting submarines, in which the British government took an interest. Its success, it was claimed, would wholly prevent war. Grindell Matthews said he needed only two months, then fame and riches would be in his grasp.[88] His invention, with its promise of ending war, seemed to be a cause to which Walska would gladly apply her wealth. Grindell Matthews was tall and presentable; Walska describes him as "poor human wreckage with divine possibilities." They even were near in age. Her involvement was not wholly disinterested. Rearmament was in the air and, she says, "I needed an investment that would bring me enormous and quick returns." She sensed that he was something of a fraud, content to take her money and anyone else's, but she decided to gamble that his invention would succeed, make war impossible, bring her a fortune and even, as he claimed, a peerage. She protested that she did not want another marriage but yielded to his fervent entreaties.[89]

Walska did Grindell Matthews some favors, such as paying for an operation that saved his eyesight and setting up working space for him at Galluis, which he visited for just one week. Her subsidies financed his research and living expenses; she even bought him a new car.[90] They were married in London in January 1938. No sooner were they wed than he returned to his laboratory in Wales, and she to Paris.[91] The next year, a biographer claims, she visited Grindell Matthews's Welsh retreat, then stepped into a car and drove out of his life.[92] World War II broke out in September 1939, and Walska was not going to wait around in Europe. Her chauffeur was ordered to stash her two Rolls Royces at Galluis and disable them; her valuables were crated and buried in the chateau grounds.[93] She herself boarded the ultra-luxurious Pan American clipper in Lisbon and landed in New York on October 10. The *New York Times* billed her as an arriving celebrity, and Dr. Fraenkel's house on 94th Street welcomed her.[94]

We've come to Walska's sixth—and final—husband: Theos Bernard. Bernard was a semi-charlatan, but also a man distinguished enough to earn a Ph.D. at Columbia, have seven titles in Yale's library, and warrant being, like Grindell Matthews, the subject of two individual biographies. Bernard's claim to fame was that, in 1936–37, when he was in his late twenties, he had been an early visitor to Tibet, where he spent many months frequenting monasteries. He came back to America with a trove of art works, artifacts, rare books, photographs, and films, much of which has yet to be explored. Bernard's papers fill 30 shelf-feet at the Bancroft Library of the University of California at Berkeley, and other institutions at the university hold additional parts of his vast accumulation. Many of the hundreds of wood-cut-printed books he brought from Tibet are in Yale's Beinecke Rare Book and Manuscript Library, while smaller hoards are at Harvard and the Deutsche Staatsbibliothek Preussicher Kulturbesitz in Berlin.[95] He was an extraordinary and discriminating collector, who assembled a priceless legacy for Tibetan studies that has more recently gained further value in light of Chinese efforts to efface Tibetan culture. The reverse side of the coin is that Bernard's months in Tibet were more acquisitive than learned; his scholar-ship was derivative and superficial; his doctorate was awarded by professors holding their noses; his teaching was oriented to rich seekers after spiritual light; and he lived off women. Bernard vanished in the Punjab in 1947, a year after he and Walska divorced.

Readers of *Always Room at the Top* understand how Walska came into Bernard's orbit. Ever since the days of her marriage to Fraenkel, she had sought metaphysical and spiritual assistance and enlightenment. One goal of hers was to gain help for her voice, which stubbornly resisted improve-ment through conventional means. Interminable portions of her memoirs concern efforts with changing mentors to achieve a metaphysical break-through for her singing and to learn the meaning of life. For her, Eastern wisdom was a potent draw. Shortly after her 1939 arrival in New York, a friend took her to the yoga classes that Bernard held at the Hotel Pierre. She soon returned on her own and also started to attend his Wednesday-evening seminars. A nearer relationship developed in the summer of 1941 when Bernard came to her declaring that he had loved her at first sight and wanted to marry her the next day.[96] She was 54 to his 33, but infatuated with the "California prodigy … possessor of great undying Truth." When told that she was still married, he furiously replied that she must get a divorce. They drew much closer. She was finishing her memoirs, in which she wrote, "It was only last winter … that I learned and understood, again thanks to my youthful teacher, for the first time the actual value of our physical body, the dwelling place of our spiritual being!"[97]

Information about this part of Walska's life is more abundant
than for any other; there is even an unpublished continuation of her
memoirs—"My Life with Yogi"—to which access is restricted.[98] In 1941,
Grindell Matthews died, freeing Walska.[99] The year after, she and Bernard
married in secret in Las Vegas, she having imposed a strict prenuptial
agreement. As was her custom, the marriage was not consummated.[100]
What is lasting about this part of her life is that Bernard transposed her to
California and convinced her to buy the 37-acre property called Cuesta
Linda in the ultra-chic Montecito section of Santa Barbara.[101] The plan at
the time was that this estate, renamed Tibetland, would be the home of an
academy of Tibetan literature, at which the corpus of Tibetan Buddhist
scriptures would be translated. But war got in the way; Tibetan scholars
could not be brought to America.[102] An idea had been floated, perhaps
by Bernard, to plant Tibetland with lemon trees and thus support the
academy. Walska was ostensibly in favor of this money-making project,
but immediately turned Tibetland in a different direction. She had done
much to improve the garden of her French chateau. Now she engaged a
Santa Barbara landscape architect, the aptly named Lockwood de Forest, Jr.,
and started "an ambitious project for replanting the estate's gardens." She
was launching the work of her next decades—the creation that gradually
became Lotusland, her enduring and flourishing monument.[103]

Meanwhile, she had Bernard to worry about. Walska divided her
time between California and New York, where she lived especially for the
Metropolitan Opera season. Bernard's doctoral studies at Columbia were
financed, and a floor of the 94th Street house was decorated for his use and
public seminars. With their marriage still secret, Walska showed off her
young escort at the Met, where she had an established box.[104] But relations
soured. Bernard was cheating on her with another disciple. (Despite an
indiscretion, this adultery was hidden from Walska until after the divorce.)
He also wanted too much of Walska's money.[105] In California, he lived with
his father, who was in fact the main source of Bernard's Eastern philosophy.
They shared a spectacular mountain retreat 20 miles from Santa Barbara,
which Walska had bought to be Bernard's study refuge.[106]

When Walska flew in from New York and got off the plane at Burbank
Airport in May 1946, she expected to find Bernard with her Cadillac.

A process server met her instead, with the papers of a suit in which Bernard sought separation from her. Pleading poverty and inability to work because of the heart complaint that had kept him out of the war, Bernard asked both that he be given permanent alimony of $1,500 a month and that, because Walska had failed to fulfill financial commitments to his enterprises, the two estates be turned over to him with all their contents. But Bernard had overreached himself. At the divorce trial, Walska's lawyer extracted an admission that Bernard had lied about his indigence; he actually had sizable means and had no right to the properties.[107] Walska was rid of him with a payment of $5,000 for his lawyer and a single $1,500 for him. Bernard and his father had already cleaned out all his papers, books, art works, and artifacts from both estates and hidden them away. Some stayed in the father's care and were partly disposed of to libraries; others were uncovered decades later in four self-storage units in Upland, California, and pressed on the University of California at Berkeley.[108]

After routing Bernard, Walska lived almost 40 more years, and she did so vigorously, confidently, and with much greater success than she could claim for her musical career. "Perhaps one day," she said, "[the forces in me] may be sufficiently concentrated to crystalize in some individual creative manner." That day had come. She did without spiritual mentors and stopped looking for the meaning of life; singing lessons ceased and so did the hours of practice. She never married again; the New York visits tapered off; and she gained a place in Santa Barbara society, fostering its musical life and entertaining in her continually improving gardens.[109] "After dispatching [Bernard]," a journalist wrote, "she settled into the longest relationship of her life—the love affair with the Lotusland garden."[110] Intermittently, she boarded a station wagon with her handyman and was driven to Los Angeles nurseries to return with a full load of new plants. She kept gardeners busy, and with professional help shaped her acres in accord with her vision.[111] Even vocally she had the last laugh. When the renowned Lotte Lehmann died in 1976, her New York Times obituary said, "Mme. Lehmann appeared with virtually all the great singers of her era." Ganna Walska's name came first in that distinguished list.[112]

Notes

1 The *Aquitania,* a Cunarder, was among the most popular liners of the time. See "RMS *Aquitania,*" https://en.wikipedia.org/wiki/RMS_Aquitania. Another passenger on that crossing was Harold McCormick, president of IH, who was in love with Walska.

2 ART (pp. 63–75, 81–91) is the source for all the details of Walska's shipboard meeting with Cochran, their courtship, and their marriage. It is there that she mentions his deep disappointment, saying he even ceased believing in God (ART, p. 66).

3 Walska was very conscious of Cochran before being introduced on shipboard (ART, pp. 190, 192, 193; 59, 60, 63). The whole of Walska's diva-hood stemmed from her having sung in Havana in one opera (1919), which was poorly received, and she had only a single future engagement, for Chicago in December of the same year. In her case, the claim to being a prima donna went with the honorific "Madame."

4 For Cochran's proposal of marriage, see ART (p. 66). Walska repeatedly insisted that the men in her life were instantly smitten with her and demanded that they immediately marry them. A fuller discussion of this theme is given in connection with Joseph Fraenkel (see note 31, below). A newspaper article contemporary with Walska's marriage to Harold McCormick reports that she was engaged to Cochran by the time they disembarked in Europe (*New York Evening World* [August 12, 1922]: 3). While Walska says differently in ART, there is no reason to prefer her account to the newspaper's. Whether one way or the other matters little to the general course of events.

5 Cochran made numerous trips to Paris by air. Regular England–France air service had just begun in 1919, and by 1920 one French and three English companies were flying very small-capacity airplanes. For details, see Evangeline Holland, "Traveling by Air in Early 1920s England," Edwardian Promenade (August 16, 2013): www.edwardianpromenade.com/travel/traveling-by-air-in-early-1920s-england. Walska claims that Cochran took time off wooing so as to go fox hunting in England as well as in Pau in southwest France (ART, p. 66). Cochran was a keen fox hunter, but his doing so as Walska relates is impossible. The hunting season runs from November to April; midsummer fox hunting (in France or England) is out of the question, as it would disturb the growing crops. This glaring error shows that Walska's account of the courtship needs cautious handling.

6 Cochran arranged the marriage on September 15, 1920 (ART, pp. 67, 73, 209–10). (A copy of the Paris church-wedding certificate is in GWA.) Walska's *Zaza* performance in Chicago was slated for December 21, which makes her assertion that her departure for America was a mere two days away seem faulty. She and Cochran arrived in New York on October 9, three and a half weeks after their wedding (*Washington Post* [October 10, 1920]: 64). Allowing a week for the transatlantic crossing, their post-nuptial Paris stay would appear to have lasted about two weeks. According to ART (p. 199), in two days in Paris, Cochran bought her a magnificent house and a Rolls Royce Silver Ghost. This speed in making the purchases is not wholly impossible, but the time between wedding and sailing seems to need adjustment. (Cochran definitely purchased the Paris house only in December, while they were in New York; see below.) For their voyage to New York, he was only able to secure himself a stateroom on a different deck from hers [ART, p. 73]. Storms kept Walska confined to her cabin during the crossing.

7 Perhaps more remarkable than Walska's having a total of six husbands is that four of them occupied the ten-year period from 1913 to 1923. Walska's time with Cochran, from first meeting to separation, was short (July 1920–April 1921), but she writes more, and more scathingly, about him than about any of her other husbands (see ART, pp. 67, 189–90, 192). I don't believe he receives a single positive comment from her. Walska accepted his suit only because he pleaded abjectly to be saved (ART, p. 67), and though not loving him, she married Cochran because she loved "the ideal [of him], which I had created myself" (ART, p. 192). Bitterness about the financial aspect of their divorce (see Appendix 2.2, "Arcadie Eingorn and the Cochran Divorce") may have slanted her account. Much of her disparagement needs qualification. A seven-week courtship is short, but long enough to reveal salient incompatibilities between the two parties. For example, Cochran was not an opera lover and was old for a first marriage; Walska did not care for fox hunting or yachting. Walska could not have been wholly surprised on the morrow of the wedding. The issue may have been how much incompatibility a multimillionaire was worth. Cochran did not stand in the way of Walska's singing (ART, p. 72; *Baltimore Sun* [November 29, 1920]: 3). What she refers to as his "selfishness" in marriage may have had to do with how little time he spent in her company. In ART (p. 195), Walska rejoices when hearing that Cochran's fortune had passed to his widowed niece-in-law in 1933, thus, finally, it was placed at the disposal of art, in this case ballet (see Ewing, *Bravura,* Part 1 bibliography). In life, although not on paper, Walska seems not to have held a grudge. GWA has a letter dated September 21, 1926, that Cochran sent from the Claridge Hotel, London, replying to correspondence from her. He indicates that hers was a letter of "friendliness and generosity," assuring him that when they meet "there will be no bitter feelings between us." Cochran replied that it was "good to know" this was the case.

8 Did Walska love Cochran? ART does not say she loved any of her other husbands. (The tale about the tubercular Arcadie Eingorn implies that she loved him, but the whole story looks like fiction [ART, pp. 313, 325, 328]). In the case of Cochran, her claim was, "we were divorced from the moment of our wedding" (ART, pp. 70–71, 90). Cochran's after-dinner stroll has nourished the mistaken claim that he roamed the streets of Paris on his wedding night (Selzer, p. 52; Veenhof, p. 304). Walska's version (ART, pp. 70–71) sets matters straight. Walska on McCormick's intrusion: ART, p. 197.

9 Arrival in New York: ART (p. 74); syndicated article, "Surprising Romance of America's $100,000,000 Bachelor" (*Washington Post* [October 10, 1920]: 64; also in the *Detroit Free Press* and, probably, elsewhere). Kiev debut probably from the Biographical Document 1915. I have not found a newspaper report of the Havana incident. One must exist. For a fuller account, with documentation, see note 37, below. Redecoration of Fraenkel house implied by *New York Times* (September 29, 1921): 21. Socializing in New York: ART (pp. 74–77); with Cochran's family, ART (pp. 68-69); Cochran's clumsiness at Walska's home, ART (pp. 61, 75). To Chicago: *New York Tribune* (December 30, 1920): 9; *Chicago Tribune* (December 2, 1920): 21: Mme Ganna Walska-Cochran is at a benefit concert.

10 Harold McCormick had been responsible for the Chicago engagement; where he was at this time is uncertain. The *Baltimore Sun* (December 22, 1920: 3) is the sole source that reports his escorting Walska on one occasion during these Chicago weeks, and the report dates from after her return to New York. Surprisingly, McCormick has no place in accounts of the abortive *Zaza* performance. With Cochran she had been adamant about her career: ART (p. 72). Initially, Cochran did not object to her continuing on the stage: *Baltimore Sun* (November 29, 1920): 3). It had been with this understanding that Walska entered into the marriage. Now, however, possibly set off by her registering under her stage name at the hotel, Cochran was changing the terms. In Walska's version of how she broke her Chicago opera date (ART, pp. 81–84, 191), she debates inwardly for two days and also seeks advice from friends. Finally, accepting the counsel of a trusted confidante that she must follow Cochran to New York, Walska left Chicago. This began the *Zaza* crisis.

11 Edward Colman Moore, *Forty Years of Opera in Chicago* (pp. 214–15); *Le Ménestrel* 83 (1921): 47 (my translation). Newspapers: *Chicago Tribune* (December 20, 1920: 1) " 'Richest Singer in World' Flees on Eve of Debut"; *New York Tribune* (December 22, 1920: 11). Developed explanation: *New York Tribune* (December 30, 1920: 9), "Opera Conductor Protested after Hearing Walska Sing. Marinuzzi, in Terse Phrases, Said It Would Be Impossible to Produce 'Zaza' with Much Heralded Diva in the Leading Role. Accompanied only by her maid, she slipped away." Later accounts: Erté, *Things I Remember* (p. 54); also a detached observer (Mintzer, p. 73). The firing of the managers proved true (cf. ART, p. 84). Later versions wrongly introduce into the story the star soprano Mary Garden, who was newly appointed director of the Chicago Opera Association: "Chicago Opera Troubles Told by Sopranos," *San Francisco Chronicle* (January 10, 1921: 2); Jane Dixon, "Romance and Scandal Run Riot with Second Husband's Ghost in Mme Walska's Life," *New York Evening Telegram* (October 4, 1921: 3). In fact, Garden was not involved. She did not become the company's director until 1921, some time after the *Zaza* problem (*Time* [November 5, 1923]: 17) After Walska's return from Chicago, she and Cochran stayed in New York about a week, during which Cochran lodged at one of his many clubs. Walska celebrated Christmas at home, receiving precious, but perfunctorily given, jewels from Cochran (ART, p. 88). Crisis over: ART (p. 89). Commissioning of costumes:

Erté, *Things I Remember* (p. 53). The Paris dressmaker Redfern produced the costumes after Erté's designs, and Erté's renderings were later hung in Walska's Paris house. The costumes survive, together with Erté's painted designs, at LACMA. Some are also in New York at the MMA. Although Erté says the costumes were for performances at the Chicago Opera, the fact of Walska's no longer having Chicago engagements and her not performing these roles suggests that the costumes were mainly for display. Singers do not normally appear at operatic productions with their self-supplied costumes.

12 Rumor had it that Cochran's Colorado estate Glen Eyrie was being readied for a visit (*New York Tribune* [December 23, 1920]: 8). ASC and she originally planned to return to Europe in March; instead, they sailed aboard the White Star's *Olympic* on December 29, 1920 (ART, p. 88), refusing to speak to the press (*New York Times* [December 30, 1920]: 12): "Mrs. Alexander Smith Cochran (Mme Ganna Walska) sailed last week on the *Olympic* with her husband for London, where they will spend four days and then go to Paris and later to Pau." Only Cochran was interested in the winter resort of Pau, where there was fox hunting. The RMS *Olympic* was the sister ship of the *Titanic* and the largest ship on the North Atlantic run.

13 Cochran bought Walska's Paris house by cable from New York (*Washington Times*, December 28, 1920: 4). It was at 14, rue de Lübeck, in the 16e arrondissement. This is close to the Étoile and the Champs-Élysées, which eventually made it very convenient to Walska's TCE. This large *hôtel particulier*, four bays wide, had belonged to James Gordon Bennett Jr. (d. 1918), who was publisher of the *New York Herald* before relocating to Paris as an American expatriate. It remains in excellent condition and is currently occupied by a professional association.

14 Cochran's Paris house, ART (p. 199). Walska at Ritz Hotel: ART (p. 89). Gifts: car and fur coat: ART (p. 89); carte blanche at Cartier and pin money: ART (p. 199). The carte blanche was for a single item, a wedding gift. A morning gift to the bride on the morrow of their marriage, symbolic as the price of her virginity, is a custom followed by some cultures, notably the early Germans' *Morgengabe*.

15 Walska and Cochran in Paris: ART (p. 68). Cochran departs: ART (pp. 90–91). Officially, April was the month of the couple's separation (*New York Tribune* [May 2, 1922]: 1). A "for sale" sign appeared on the house almost on the morrow of Cochran's departure (ART, p. 91). An attempt to lock out Walska was foiled: *New York Times* (October 8, 1921: 14). Her lawyer, Dudley Field Malone, played a heroic part in retaining the house before it could be seized. At the time of the separation and divorce, Cochran owned the house, which is why he could put it on sale. It is generally understood that McCormick later bought it from him and gave it to Walska (*Chicago Daily Tribune* [May 4, 1922]: 21; Erté, *Things I Remember,* pp. 53–54). Ganna Walska Lotusland, the nonprofit organization of Walska's garden, sold this house in 1988 for $2 million (Gardner, p. 115; this is perhaps an unreliable source for the sale price). Complementing the Biographical Document 1921 (September 27, 1921), the opening salvo for the divorce—Cochran was suing—occurred on September 28: "Cochran Gets Writ for $25,000 of Art Pieces Taken from Home of Mme Walska, His Wife" (*New York Times* [September 29, 1921]: 21); a more complete account is in *Philadelphia Inquirer* (September 29, 1921): 4.

16 See Appendixes 1.1 and 1.2. Between 1911 and 1920, Cochran engaged in competitive sailing, politics, thoroughbred racing, fox hunting, flying, polo, ocean cruising, and service in the British Navy. On his diminishing interest in the Club, see Appendix 1.4; on the couple's visit to Yonkers, see Part 1, note 113.

17 On the Cochran divorce: see Appendix 2.2. The struggle over a settlement left traces in the press; e.g., *San Francisco Chronicle* (October 17, 1921: 1): "Diva Increases Divorce Price. Wants $500,000 if Millionaire Is to Have Freedom"; *New York Times* (October 23, 1921: 13): "Defies Cochran to Sue for a Divorce"; *New York Times* (March 30, 1922: 5): "Mme. Walska to Accuse Society Woman in Suit"; *Chicago Tribune* (May 2, 1922: 1): "Golden Path to Freedom for Mme. Walska." For the offensive on Cochran's behalf in autumn 1921, see Appendix 2.2.

18 Just over one year elapsed from the separation to the divorce (April 1921–May 1922), but the divorce proceedings began in September or October 1921. Part of the delay included two months that Walska's lawyer insisted on, but that is still only a small part of the hiatus between October and April. I cannot explain.

19 The financial agreement is dated May 1, 1922. Contemporary reports of the divorce settlement are not consistent, with some being extravagantly wrong, such as the report in the May 10, 1922, issue of the *Pittsburgh Gazette Times,* which had Walska receiving $1 million cash. More credible is the *Baltimore Sun* (May 4, 1922: 1), datelined New York: the end of the marriage "was settled on a basis of investment of a trust fund of $300,000, the income of which goes to Mrs. Cochran." *The Jewelers' Circular* 85, no. 1 (August–October 1922): 86: "Instead of millions in cash the Polish singer gets only $20,000 a year for life, possession of the home in the Rue de Lubeck [*sic*], bought by Mr. Cochran when he married her, and she keeps jewels worth not more than $100,000." Later, the details would be recalled when Cochran's estate was settled: *New York Times* (August 6, 1932): 1; *Chicago Daily Tribune* (August 6, 1932): 8. Cochran's will wholly excluded Walska; see "Cochran Will Lists $16,255,000" (*New York Times* [June 26, 1929]: 21): "Having heretofore by

written agreement made provision for the
support, maintenance and benefit of my
former wife, now known as Ganna Walska
McCormick, by the terms of which agreement
she relinquished any rights to my estate to
which she might have otherwise been entitled
by law, I therefore make no provision for her
in this, my will, and I direct that she shall not
share in any part of my estate." A clear sign
of Walska's fame is that newspaper accounts
of Cochran's will and estate conspicuously
mention her exclusion; see *Washington Post*
(August 4, 1932): 2, "Cochran Will Bars Sharing
by Walska: Opera Singer, Former Wife, Has
Trust Fund"; *Chicago Tribune,* August 6, 1932):
8, "Cochran, Ex-Husband of Ganna Walska,
Cut Her Off in Will." It seems implied that he
should have left her something. In fact, she
was not totally excluded. Cochran's divorce
settlement obliged him to top up the proceeds
of her trust fund so that it would provide
$20,000 per year, and this guarantee did not
lapse upon his death: "Future payments due
to the guarantee are estimated at $133,998":
(*New York Times* [August 6, 1932]: 1). The trust
fund reverted at Walska's death (1984), and
what remained of it passed to the descendants
of Cochran's main heir, Thomas Ewing III
(d. 1933), and in particular to his widow, Lucia
Chase Ewing, who then was on her deathbed. In
correspondence, her son, the late Alex C. Ewing,
kindly informed me that the sum in question
was about $100,000.

20 It was said that McCormick paid Malone.
McCormick's prenuptial settlement is
arresting: "M'Cormick Gives Ganna $100,000
Year and Gems. Singer's Allowance from
Husband [i.e., Cochran] ... $20,000 a Year"
(*Washington Post* [August 17, 1922]: 1).
McCormick signed a contract settling $100,000
per year on Walska for life "on condition that
she abandon her intention of returning to the
stage." He also gave her a $200,000 string of
pearls and an engagement ring worth $40,000.
In 1922, $200,000 for pearls and $40,000 for

a ring were colossal sums, but *The Jewelers'
Circular* 85 no.1 (August–October 1922): 86,
confirms the *Washington Post.* Although
well attested here, the condition to retire
from performing is never found again. (See
Appendix 2.3.) Adams (p. 98) writes that,
before marriage to Walska, McCormick
transferred to her thousands of shares of IH
stock (ordinary and preferred), yielding, in total,
$100,000 per year. (Adams gives the numbers
without indicating his sources.) By late 1922,
McCormick's support was clear: "McCormick
to Act in Role of Angel to Ganna Walska,"
Atlanta Constitution (October 31, 1922): 7.

Newspapers sometimes referred to Walska
familiarly as "Ganna," as in the *Washington
Post* headline above; she had become notorious.

21 There is a semi-official Lotusland version of
Walska's early years (conveyed in, e.g., Adams,
Crawford, or Tentler and Hayes). Most of it is
undocumented, and some of it is plainly the
stuff of legend. Much is not substantiated by
ART and sometimes even contradicts it. My
reconstruction is a radical departure from this
"authorized" version. I have based it on a critical
appraisal of the available, when possible
contemporaneous, sources, including items
(often newspaper clippings) from GWA.

Walska prided herself on being of Polish
origin and was pleased to have "the Slavic
temperament." Her Polishness was emphatic.
After the Nazi conquest of Poland in 1939,
the *Boston Globe* ([February 11, 1940]: B4)
reported that "Poland Is Not Yet Lost....
An imposing sign of the collective quality of
[Polish-blooded] people is the professional
eminence [in America] attained by some of
them," and in the accompanying photo-album
Walska is the sole woman. She consorted
with Polish diplomats and nobility in Paris and
New York; she held annual parties to benefit
Polish orphans in Paris; the Polish government
decorated her in 1931. But in ART, she does
not even allude to the Russo-German rape

of Poland in 1939, an extreme example of her indifference to contemporary events. Walska claims to have had a German governess, which, if true, would suggest a middle-class upbringing (ART, p. 70). For photographs, see ART (opposite p. 232). Her birth certificate (dated October 23, 1887, in Brest-Litovsk) survives in GWA. In ART (p. 37), Walska says she did not know her birth year. The Biographical Document 1921 gives her place of birth as "Siedlec" [for "Siedlce"], a small town west of Brest, but her birth certificate contradicts this. When she first arrived in the U.S. (1915), her age is given as 25, which agrees with her reference to having been 17 when just married to Eingorn (and taking him to Davos) in 1907 (ART, p. 317). She was, in fact, two years older, but 17 was a magic number for her. In the Lotusland-inspired biographies, she is also 17 when she moved from home to live with a painter uncle in St. Petersburg (Adams, pp. 17–18; Crawford, p. 7; but based on what evidence?). The Biographical Document 1915, says that her romance with Eingorn was in Warsaw, from which they eloped to St. Petersburg. Judging from ART, Walska was fascinated by herself at age 17, and she implies her birth year was 1890. She attributes an age of 17 to herself at many moments of her life (e.g., in Montmartre, Davos, and Dorpat, which was Russian until 1917: ART, pp. 218, 239, 312–28. She intermittently lowered her age (e.g., in relation to her second husband, Dr. Fraenkel). Her birthplace gained fame in World War I: Brest-Litovsk was the site of the treaty signing that ended the war between Russia and Germany in 1917. Brest-Litovsk is now Brest, a provincial town in Belarus at its border with Poland. Until 1917, both lands were part of the Russian Empire, although culturally the city was Polish (and Jewish). Erté, *Things I Remember* (p. 56) and ART (p. 166) note her traveling in an open limousine. It had a landaulet body, i.e., the rear of the passenger compartment was convertible. Walska's cancer and decline: Adams (pp. 8, 423–37).

22 ART tells little about her years growing up except for two highly questionable stories: (1) the romantic pursuit of an ultrarich, clean-shaved youth in St. Petersburg (pp. 6–12); and (2) Arcadie at a Davos tuberculosis sanitorium (pp. 320–30). In telling of the fruitless St. Petersburg romance, her goal was to explain how she resolved to become an opera singer. Her first husband is not mentioned before the second half of ART, and nothing in ART or elsewhere substantiates his having tuberculosis. He is not called a baron or count nor is he associated with the czar's court. (Arcadie materializes, as a baron [and war casualty], in the New York report of Walska's engagement to a young man from Brooklyn in 1915 [i.e., the Biographical Document 1915]). The Biographical Document 1921 contests that he was a baron and died in war. The Biographical Document 1915 is a capsule biography with details that necessarily originated from Walska. Intimating that she was of royal blood, it starts when she was 17, with her meeting Arcadie Eingorn, a Russian baron and army officer stationed in Warsaw, and their eloping to St. Petersburg. ART (pp. 219, 398) indicates that she went to St. Petersburg—she was not already there—when she eloped. The couple was ostracized by her family but only temporarily; the spouse was soon taken to meet them (ART, p. 397). Adams's (p. 19) unsubstantiated story about the Eingorns being wealthy landowners and doctors to the czar is impossible.

23 The two scenes of married life reported in ART are the only images of the Eingorn couple together, although they are not explicitly named. Dorpat is not far by rail from St. Petersburg, and the skating story that takes place there is innocent (p. 218). The scene in Montmartre, if true, shows Arcadie in a nasty light (almost a pimp) and presupposes an expensive trip to Paris, without necessarily implying great wealth (a theatrical engage-ment?) (p. 218). It brings Walska into a cabaret setting. The Eingorns' separation is in the Biographical Document 1915. Jane Dixon, *New York Evening Telegram* (October 4, 1921): 3: "Young love died an early death." It's hard to tell whether this was an inspired guess that Dixon inferred from a source or if it was based on testimony. The portrayal of Walska as "a poor, Polish peasant girl" (Blumenthal, p. 249; Harrison, p. 191, reporting the opinion of Harold McCormick's sister) is improbable. It is likely her family was middle class (e.g., Walska took McCormick, her very rich husband, to visit her family). The Biographical Document 1921 refers to them as "an obscure and humble family of Sieldec [*sic*]." Sieldce is disproved by Walska's birth certificate from Brest-Litovsk (GWA), but the 1921 document supplies an authenticating detail, that Walska had a brother named Leon, a name not confirmed anywhere before Adams's biography, where it is in a much later, U.S. setting (p. 342). Walska's divorce from Eingorn is not in the Biographical Document 1915, let alone ART. It is first heard about at the time of the Cochran divorce; see Appendix 2.2.

24 Early career: Biographical Document 1915; for the discovery of her voice, see the Biographical Document 1917 (GWA). The prefix "Madame" was not used when she was named in 1912 St. Petersburg (see Appendix 2.1, "The Stember Portrait," as well as the Biographical Document 1917). She is "Mlle" in the Paris news item, below. The circumstantial explanation of her renaming in ART (p. 6) evidently was made up; it's contradicted by the Biographical Document 1917. The lilt of the new name was an inspiration. Her account of an opera vocation is part of the fable of the clean-shaved billionaire, ART, (pp. 6–12). Nicolas's recollection: Erté, *Things I Remember* (p. 53). To Paris for vocal study, ART (p. 12). Her past and then current music-hall careers are in a Paris news item: *Le Figaro* 302 (October 29, 1913): 5, col. 5; the cast list: *Le Figaro* 333 (November 29, 1913): 6, col. 3.

25 Jean de Reszke and his brother Édouard were famous opera stars who both taught after their retirement from the stage, Jean in Paris, Édouard in London. Walska cannot always remember with which one she worked. She invokes Jean in an article in the *New York Tribune* (April 25, 1915; in GWA) and in ART (p. 12), which Adams cites (p. 34). Édouard is preferred in the Biographical Document 1917 and an article in the November 1924 edition of *Revue internationale des questions politiques, diplomatiques, économiques* (Raffestin-Nadaud). Because Paris was the scene, the teacher had to be Jean. Adams (p. 34) and Crawford (p. 8) claim that studies with de Reszke made it possible for her to have cabaret engagements. On the contrary, the *Figaro* item shows that music hall performance was primary in her Paris stay and continued in 1914. Lee Shubert was the leading member of the legendary New York theatrical family. Jerry Stagg (*The Brothers Shubert* [New York: Random House, 1968], p. 132) confirms that Shubert was in Paris at this time, where he learned of Walska's beauty and music hall talents, which prompted him to persuade her to come to America. Erté (*Things I Remember*, p. 54) says that, soon after her New York arrival, Walska was "firmly ensconced as Shubert's mistress," but this is improbable. Lee Shubert, although highly promiscuous and accustomed to preying on his female employees, is unlikely to have settled with one of them and is not recorded as having done so. (For Shubert's New York sexual boudoir, see Foster Hirsch, *The Boys from Syracuse: The Shuberts' Theatrical Empire* [Carbondale: Southern Illinois UP, 1998], p. 100.) When Walska left Paris, how did she travel to England in December 1914? All the familiar channel ports were in the war zone, and Le Havre was monopolized by military transport. Cherbourg was possible as it had good Paris rail connections and established ferry routes to England. SS *Arabic* returned to service from Liverpool to New York late in

1914; https://en.wikipedia.org/wiki/SS_Arabic_ (1902). Walska's journey may have been on its first run after return to service. She later learned that the ship was sunk on August 19, 1915 (ART, p. 21).

26 The program of the shipboard Christmas concert is in GWA. For usage of the prefix "Madame," see the obituary of Lotte Lehmann (1888–1976), one the foremost singers of her generation: "The great prima donnas were always addressed as 'Madame' " (*New York Times* [August 27, 1976]: A1). Walska claims she took lessons from Joachim Tartakov in St. Petersburg and de Reszke in Paris. Assuming these celebrated teachers actually worked with her, she admits that the lessons were brief and superficial, "taken with the utmost lightness." In ART (p. 13), she contrasts her youthful self to the paragon of hard work at singing she later became.

Her eventual abstinence from smoking, drinking, and dancing is affirmed three times in ART (pp. 89, 178, 413). Abandoning these pleasures, as conjectured here, might have been a sign of her resolve to leave her music-hall days behind. She sets no date on this change, but in ART (p. 6), she writes "I loved to dance"—indeed, she chose the surname *Walska* because the waltz was her favorite— and she danced in Montmartre when Eingorn was present (p. 218). According to Stember, she was tipsy at the painter's studio in 1912 (see Appendix 2.1). A moment of transition was a good opportunity for Walska to bid such dissipations farewell.

27 Abundant testimony about Walska's beauty leaves no room for doubt. In her early years her name is rarely mentioned without reference to her beauty ("la belle Walska"; her "rare beauté") Photographs of her in Lynn Kirst, "Fashion Game" (pp. 28–29), are stunning. The major article of October 10, 1920 (*Washington Post:* 64) says that "her face and figure were an even greater attraction than

her agreeable soprano voice." The quotation about her tenacity and will is from ART (p. 24). These words may sum up her life better than any others, and they help to explain why, in ART, Walska thought of her life as having been a vale of tears (see Appendix 2.4, "The Sorrows of Madame Walska").

28 U.S. immigration records show Walska listed as being age 25 when she arrived in New York in 1915, thus she would have been born in 1890 (instead of, correctly, 1887). In a clipping from the *Morning Telegraph* in the GWA, dated "…ary [probably February] 27, 1915," she is called a "Shubert foreign importation." Walska's first New York appearance was covered by the *New York Tribune* (April 25, 1915; in GWA). In summary (and paraphrased), her initial publicity release informed about the revival of *Mlle Nitouche* at the Century Theatre, maintaining that Mme Ganna Walska sang at the leading theatres of Petrograd, Paris, and other continental cities; that she was a pupil of Jean de Reszke and that her operatic debut at the Paris Opéra-comique was postponed because of the war. The article also claims that Mme Walska was engaged to come to the United States for an important production, but that fell through, so she was making her first New York appearance at the Century. Much of this was invention and is unverifiable. The diminuendo is noteworthy, but the press accepted it. Her widowhood was not mentioned. An unidentified 1915 press clipping in the GWA reports the performance, complete with her singing of the "Marseillaise." Presumably, after this opening, she presented a more conventional song program. Blanche Aral (p. 324; repeated by Alda, p. 289) erroneously indicates that the operetta ran for only one night. In reality, the leading lady changed, and the show went on with its intermission of songs perhaps as late as August. Press clipping, May 8, 1915 (GWA): "Mme. Walska, noted for her beauty, has a new repertory of songs." *New York Tribune* (May 7, 1915); *New York*

Tribune (June 13, 1915): B8: *Hands Up* to open. "Mme. Ganna Walska, the Russian beauty," will sing the part of a prima donna. The musical opened on July 22 (https://www.ibdb.com/ broadway-show/hands-up-4177).

29 The Biographical Document 1915 provides a valuable summary noteworthy for the ennoblement of both Eingorn, here called *baron* for the first time, and Walska, who is displaced from Brest-Litovsk to Warsaw and attached to the Leszcynska royal family, a lofty origin that (she said) had to be concealed while she was on the stage in Russia. She made her debut in Kiev (it says) as the lead in *The Merry Widow* and after Kiev played all the large cities in Europe. Further, Eingorn was killed while with the Russian army in Poland, but this had not yet been absolutely confirmed. The pairing of Eingorn's baronage with Walska's definitely fictional royal descent suggests that both were inventions. Cf. Biographical Document 1921: "Instead of being a baron in his own right, he is now said to have been 'the descendant of a baron.'" A brief notice of Walska's engagement to Palmer (with a picture of her) ran in *Musical America* 22 (1915): 2, and the *Detroit Free Press* (August 12, 1915): 7, which reported that Lowell Palmer, Jr., was "a scion of one of the wealthiest families of Brooklyn." Coles Phillips: *St. Louis Post-Dispatch* (August 22, 1915): B14C, refers to "Madame Ganna Walska, prima donna, hailed as peerless for her beauty in Warsaw and Petrograd," and reports that she was one of four beauties seen in Phillips's studio. She is noted again as a Leszcynska. Phillips's portrait (ART, opposite p. 33) came into Walska's possession; it was her favorite (ART, p. 55). When compared with contemporary photographs, it is a poor likeness, but its daintiness may have appealed to Walska.

30 The engagement to Palmer was broken: *Chicago Daily Tribune* (February 14, 1916): 1. The grounds were, "when I announced that I would remain on the stage he objected." Why did

her career become a problem only in the sixth month of the engagement? A pertinent issue is given in the news items announcing the Palmer engagement and its termination (*New York Evening World,* August 2, 1915; and February 14, 1916): it would have been prudent for Palmer, head of his family since his father's September death, not to marry until assured that his wife-to-be was a widow, i.e., that Eingorn's death was officially confirmed, but it wasn't. Singing was a cover story. The news item promotes Mme Walska to prima donna of New York's Metropolitan Opera.

In June, 1916, the Stember portrait of 1912 reemerged and was reproduced in the *New York Sun* (June 18, 1916): Section 4, Pictorial Magazine, image 38, with the caption, "Mme Ganna Walska of the Theatre Francais before her own portrait" (see fig. 2.3). The painting had evidently been in Paris and accompanied Walska to America. About her voice problems, see *Moving Picture World* 29 (July 15, 1916). The film, released on July 24, 1916, does not survive, but a synopsis does. It called for Walska to play the heroine's mother, who kills herself so as to make way for her daughter's happiness. In ART (p. 142), Walska would claim to have been "barely twenty" at the time of this movie when, in fact, she was 29.

Otto Kahn (1867–1934) was a prodigious figure in finance, New York musical theatre, and much else; he liked to consort with singers and other performing artists (see Matz, *Many Lives*). Dr. Fraenkel was not a throat specialist. A colleague, Charles Loomis Dana (pp. 546–47), refers to him as an endocrinologist, but his main practice was in neurology (i.e., he was a psychiatrist). His great reputation may have been as a diagnostician. He suggested that Walska's problem had nothing to do with her throat and would be cured once she changed singing teachers, counsel that appears to have worked (ART, p. 146). For the Fraenkel-Walska marriage, September 7, 1916, see ART (p. 22); Gardner (p. 114); and Adams (p. 46).

31 For Fraenkel's curriculum vitae, see https://mahlerfoundation.org/mahler/personen-2/fraenkel-joseph-1867-1920 (retrieved July 12, 2017). A somewhat romanticized account of his life is in *Mein Leben* by Alma Mahler-Werfel (pp. 50–52); also see Dana's very appreciative obituary letter. He calls Fraenkel a "therapeutic individualist . . . [who] had a commanding practice among the most intelligent and wealthy members of this New York community," and his patients held him "in an almost God-like reverence." Walska says that Fraenkel was an "enemy of stereotyped medicine" (ART, p. 244). Where personal accomplishments, intellect, and distinction are concerned, there is no contest between Fraenkel and Walska's five other husbands. In what language did Walska (who was fluent in Polish and Russian) and Fraenkel (German) converse? Presumably in English. In spite of Walska's evident multilingualism, in ART she never tells how she learned her languages. It was while married to Fraenkel that she became a naturalized U.S. citizen.

32 Gustav Mahler, a great conductor as well as composer, came to New York to conduct the Metropolitan Opera and the New York Philharmonic; for the Mahlers with Fraenkel, see Monson (pp. 85, 90, 92, 99, 125–29, 133–34); for Walska's words see ART (pp. 12–13). Monson (esp. p. 134) delves into Fraenkel's attempt to marry Alma after Mahler's death. Fraenkel traveled to Vienna several times to press his suit, but she believed that they were incompatible. Long after Fraenkel's death, Walska and Alma Mahler met at a Venice music festival and became fast friends well into their old age in California (Adams, p. 207; Monson, p. 285). Walther Straram's "Biographie" (note 3) includes an undated, very complimentary comment by Alma: "Paris without Ganna isn't Paris." In *Mein Leben,* Alma does not favor the idea that she and Walska looked alike. Kahn and Fraenkel were good friends. Kahn took him on his railroad tours of America (Matz, p. 39).

Whenever Walska writes about her marriages in ART, she avers that her suitors were carried away and demanded instant marriage, as though they would expire if she did not yield immediately to their need. For example, ART (p. 53): "Men whose lives I touched always professed love for me. I was the woman of their whole life, the lady of their Destiny—the Only One." Elopement with Eingorn was in harmony with this leitmotiv of precipitate marriages, which needs to be taken with a grain of salt. Fraenkel is the clearest example of this leitmotiv (10-day courtship), but in ART all others except Harold McCormick (husband 4) fit that pattern. She intimates that McCormick fell in love with her as soon as they met in New York, but he could not offer immediate marriage because he had a wife. Only the fable of the clean-shaved Russian millionaire is free of this theme (ART, pp. 6–12).

33 ART: playful with age (p. 188); Fraenkel's age (p. 363); Fraenkel's studies (p. 20); "juvenile heart" (p. 55); "terrible loss" (pp. 59–60); worthy companion (p. 22); sacrifices soul (p. 190); loses personality (p. 55). Alma's comment, Monson (p. 134).

34 Alma's opinion of Fraenkel, Monson (p. 134). Walska's resemblance to Alma, ART (p. 23).

35 Walska tells of her first steps in vocal study in ART (p. 31). Photographs from GWA. Minor concerts, *Musical America* 22 (1918): 2. For the Biographical Document 1917, see Part 2 bibliography.

36 On the Biltmore concert, very fully, Adams (p. 49-50). There is a photograph of the program in ART (opposite p. 40).

37 The Havana débacle is clearly described in ART (pp. 33–34); Schiaparelli (pp. 36–37). About Pavlova in Havana, see Keith Monay, *Anna Pavlova: Her Life and Art* (New York: Knopf, 1982), p. 272. The arrival of the newlywed Cochrans in America (*Washington Post* [October 10, 1920]: 64; *Detroit Free Press*

[October 10, 1920]: E7). Gardner (p. 114) claims that, during the marriage to Fraenkel, Walska "trotted the hemisphere pursuing her 'career'" and was away for long periods. This looks like an inflation of the single Havana episode. Gardner (p. 113) suggests that Fraenkel letters, which he summarizes, support his claim. They don't.

38 ART (pp. 25–26, 31, 33): audition; (pp. 25–28): meeting with McCormick. Walska prided herself on how, by persistence, she succeeded in getting a McCormick interview. When describing the initial meetings with McCormick, she leaves little doubt that he was smitten. He came to her house fearing a seduction and bringing his young son Fowler as protector, but was reassured by the presence of Dr. Fraenkel. *Chicago Tribune* (December 10, 1920): 1, specifies that she was engaged for *Zaza* in the autumn of 1919.

39 Quotation, ART (p. 56). In ART (pp. 56–57, 62), Walska gives details about his affliction and the circumstances of his death. He died in hospital, not at home. At this time, she was already in continual touch with McCormick, whom she thanks for his support. She gave Fraenkel little recognition or gratitude for the large part he had in raising her from an unemployed, so-called diva to a lady of fashion and an opera singer. About her inheriting Fraenkel's 94th Street house, see *New York Times* (November 29, 1921): 11; *New York Tribune* (same date, n.p.). The very substantial four-story row house at Park Avenue was not far from the Central Park reservoir. Walska maintained it as her New York base for many decades. The only photograph of it I have found is in a feature newspaper article by James Aswell in the *Atlanta Constitution* (June 10, 1934): SM5. The house site, with neighbors, is now occupied by an apartment block. In summer 1916, Walska's first consultation and meeting with Fraenkel was at a house on East 66th Street that was fitted out both for his medical practice and as a residence containing his library (ART, p. 19).

She describes a dark, impressive library again when McCormick visits Fraenkel's Park Avenue residence in 1919 (ART, p. 27). Veenhof (p. 302) says that the Fraenkels acquired the Park Avenue house during their marriage, which is plausible in timing.

40 Walska did not come into this inheritance as soon as she was widowed. It's hard to tell to what extent she could draw on it in the 19 months until it was settled. Gardner (p. 114) and other sources inflate its amount, mentioning values as high as $500,000. In 1920, before her marriage to Cochran and while the Fraenkel inheritance had yet to be sorted out, Walska's financial situation was very uncertain.

41 Fraenkel clearly had a flourishing, lucrative practice. While dropping resplendent names, Walska writes that "the most important New York and Newport homes were open to me" (ART, p. 55). She received guests at a place in the Catskills she rented for the summer months (ART, pp. 40, 62, 63). According to *Music Magazine–Musical Courier* 75 ([1917]: 149), in another summer, "Ganna Walska, Russian soprano, recently entertained at her summer home at Great Neck, Long Island, Eugène Ysaÿe, celebrated Belgian violinist, and Mr. and Mrs. Pierre Monteux."

42 On Walska's interest in Cochran before meeting him, see the summary by Adams (pp. 52–53); also note 3, above.

43 In ART (p. 92), Walska notes: "I was given headlines *hors concours* after marrying 'the richest bachelor in America' and after the mysterious way I had left Chicago." These headlines are examples: "Romance of America's $100,000,000 Bachelor ... [Marries] Lovely, Lively, Twice Widowed Mysterious Polish Singer" (syndicated article, October 10, 1920); "Prima Donna to Fight Husband's Divorce Move," *San Francisco Chronicle* (October 2, 1921): D1; "Malone from Paris to Act for Walska" (*New York Times* [October 2, 1921]: 9); Marjorie Wilson, "How Psychoanalysis and

Rockefeller Millions Failed in Strange Trial of Hearts, Money and Ambitions" (syndicated; *Atlanta Constitution* [October 16, 1921]: F6); "Diva Increases Divorce Price" (*San Francisco Chronicle* [October 17, 1921]: 1). Her Cochran marriage and divorce combined with the *Zaza* failure mark the moment when Walska became a celebrity. Helped by continual publicity, until her divorce from her sixth and last husband, she never ceased to be one. In ART (p. 417), she quotes Will Rogers intimating (in the 1930s) that "Ganna" was heard of weekly. A similar story had been told long before in the *Music Magazine–Musical Courier* 83 (1921): 21: "A man aged 122 died the other day in Alabama. The last thing he said was: 'What's the Walska news today?' "

44 Cyrus McCormick's reaper invention generated a huge fortune shared by Harold with Cyrus's other children. Harold was president of IH at the time he met Walska. Adams (p. 61) calls him "one of the richest men in America." Although Harold continued to have widespread philanthropic interests (Hafstad, p. 40-42), the scale of his generosity toward Walska far exceeded Cochran's. His association with the Chicago Opera ended near the time of his marriage to Walska, perhaps with that money going to sustain Walska's Paris theatre.

45 For biographical background on McCormick, see "Harold Fowler McCormick" (https://en.wikipedia.org/wiki/Harold_Fowler_McCormick) and "Edith Rockefeller McCormick" (https://en.wikipedia.org/wiki/Edith_Rockefeller_McCormick); also see "McCormick, Harold Fowler," in *National Cyclopedia of American Biography* 35 (pp. 9–10). Birmingham (pp. 137–38) offers glimpses of Harold and Edith McCormick's relationship. Harold had been a popular athlete at Princeton, and was a stylish dresser and enthusiastic aviator. Edith lived with their three surviving children in Zurich for eight years, although more to be near Jung than to retaliate for

Harold's womanizing. McCormick was in Switzerland in 1915 (see H. F. McCormick), and in 1917–1918, when he was a purchasing agent for the American Expeditionary Force in World War I. On his Villa Turicum blog, Todd Protzman-Davis mentions Harold's affability: "This was a fellow that everyone loved, the peacemaker and someone who just wanted everyone to get along" (https://villaturicum.blogspot.com/2011/02/divorce-edith-style.html). McCormick's nephew describes him as having "the most winning of personalities" (C. McCormick, p. 232). Harold and Edith had five children, two of whom died very young. The three who survived all married persons markedly older than they: *New York Times* (October 11, 1931): 24 (in connection with the Walska divorce). On McCormick's whistling talent, Dedmon (p. 316) confirms what a *Time* magazine article of January 30, 1933 (p. 34) says: "In Chicago, Harold Fowler McCormick, able amateur whistler, radio-whistled Mozart's 'Wiegenlied' in a campaign for a temple of music at the Century of Progress." Walska concurs (ART, p. 196) referring to him as "whistling as only he knew how." Adams (p. 195) tells of virtuoso whistling recitals, and John Murray Anderson recalls Harold's saving the day aboard a ship: "Ganna Walska, the opera star, was supposed to sing, but didn't do so, and her then husband, Harold F. McCormick, filled in for her with his whistling 'specialty,' … which brought thunderous applause" (*Out Without My Rubbers: The Memoirs of John Murray Anderson* [New York: Library Publishers, 1954], p. 116).

46 A further explanation for Edith's going to Dr. Jung was deep depression after the death of her second son (Marsh, p. 61).

47 On McCormick's opera patronage, Marjorie Wilson, "How Psychoanalysis and Rockefeller Millions Failed in Strange Trial of Hearts, Money and Ambitions" (syndicated; *Atlanta Constitution* [October 16, 1921]: F6); "Chief among [Campanini's] backers [in creating the Chicago Opera Company] was Harold McCormick of the Harvester Trust, then the husband of John D. Rockefeller's daughter" (*Time* [November 5, 1923]:17). He was president of the Chicago Opera until 1921.

48 Harold thought she had agreed in September 1920, but she delayed leaving Zurich for a year, and on her return to America the press denied there were any divorce proceedings (*St. Louis Post-Dispatch* [August 11, 1921]: 1). For preliminaries to the divorce, see Protzman-Davis, "Divorce—Edith Style," Villa Turicum blog. The McCormicks' separation was only announced in October (*New York Times* [October 3, 1921], reproduced without page number by Protzman-Davis). At issue in the Cochran divorce was the property settlement, which was decided on May 1, 1922 (*New York Times* [May 2, 1922]: 4). McCormick's sister Anita Blaine thought Walska had done well, receiving "a sizable settlement, a car, a house, and the jewels and furs he had lavished on her" (Harrison, p. 190). Walska had grander expectations (see Appendix 2.2). Although the divorce took place on May 1, 1922, it only became final on August 7 and was followed immediately by Walska's marriage to McCormick.

49 Karlsbad, now called Karlovy Vari, is a celebrated watering place in the Bohemian mountains (now part of the Czech Republic). Once frequented by royalty and high society, it lost much of its luster after World War I. Still, the fashionable McCormicks visited. Its specialty was slimming, and Walska was concerned with precisely that; she lost 12 pounds (*The Music Magazine–Musical Courier* 85 [1922]: 23).

50 They originally met in 1919. Walska maintained that they became great friends and that McCormick sustained her during Fraenkel's final illness (ART, pp. 27–28). Although he mostly remained in Chicago, they were certainly in close contact during

the Cochran-divorce period (1921 to 1922), when McCormick made his lavish prenuptial undertaking. Walska describes McCormick's visit to her family (ca. 1924) in ART (p. 404). McCormick's "blue eyes" (ART, p. 26). The French musician was Walther Straram (ART, p. 239). Walska all but ignores her family in the memoirs, but was more solicitous in real life.

51 Harold worked out and kept fit, and his search for youth was front-page news: "Gland Expert Operates on McCormick ... Now 51. He Seeks to Restore Youth. ... The operation was performed by Dr. Victor D. Lespinasse ... famous for operations by which he grafted glands of lower animals upon human beings ... the object of which is ... rejuvenation. ... This often includes grafting glands from a younger man or from a monkey .... Mr. McCormick is said to have decided in favor of human glands purchased from a youth in need of money. ... Fear that excitement of the patient through undue publicity might be detrimental was given as the reason for the unusual efforts to keep the operation secret" (*New York Tribune* [June 18, 1922]: 1). Someone must have had fun writing all this deadpan. Around Chicago, they loved the story, complemented by a poem celebrating the blacksmith who had lost his "glands" to the millionaire (Adams, p. 99; Deadmon, p. 314). Adams (p. 163) says there was no consummation; Walska's declaration is in ART (pp. 200–201). Adams (p. 112) says of her upbringing and early life that they had made her "a woman for whom the ideal of romantic love was paramount .... Walska developed an almost manic indifference to the physical side of relationships." Rather than about her unknown upbringing, one thinks of her early life in Russian and Parisian music halls and her breaking from it. Neither of her later marriages was consummated either. For more on Harold's operation and his Paris arrival, see "McCormick's Surgeon Silent on Gland Story. Millionaire Is Recovering from Operation" (*Chicago Tribune* [June 18, 1922]:

22); "McCormick Silent on His Operation" (*New York Times* [June 19, 1922]: 13); McCormicks' departure, *St. Louis Post-Dispatch* (July 16, 1922): 2.

52 There is no systematic record of McCormick's visits to Paris; a thorough study of his letters in GWA would be needed. According to a piece about their divorce in the *New York Times* (October 11, 1931): 24, Harold visited Walska "at frequent intervals." At IH, McCormick held a string of executive positions beginning with vice president (1902) and moving up to president and CEO (1919–22). "The publicity generated by Harold's courtship of Madame Walska sent shock waves through the executive offices of the International Harvester Company" (Harrison, p. 190). He resigned the presidency. In his Walska period, he was chairman of the executive committee, with undefined duties. He became more active in 1932 after divorcing Walska. He soon withdrew to California for his health and was long an invalid, but still held positions at IH. McCormick could have spent considerable time in France between 1922 and 1929, when their separation preparatory to divorce began, but apparently he did not. (I thank Rose Thomas, my informant about GWA, for this information.) The long, puzzling transatlantic marriage of Walska and McCormick needs investigation in GWA. See "McCormick, Harold Fowler" in the Part 2 bibliography.

53 According to Harrison (p. 192), Anita Blaine (Harold's sister) claimed that "the marriage was in ruins" two years after it began, omitting that quite a few more years passed before its final breakdown. Elsewhere, newspapers trace a possibly rocky road: signs of danger in 1924—"Ganna Walska Silent on Divorce Report" (*New York Times* [Jan 25, 1924]: 1); talk of divorce in 1927 ("M'Cormick to Sue Diva for Divorce, Is Report" [*Washington Post* (November 14, 1927): 1])—but both his daughter Muriel and his lawyer immediately denied this. The *Atlanta Constitution* (September 25,

1928: 4) included vigorous denial of reports of the couple's plans to divorce. But see "Report Ganna Asks $4,000,000," in the *Boston Daily Globe* (February 2, 1928): 1, which includes information that a settlement was being negotiated in Paris. The talks must have been suspended.

54 On the purchase of the Théâtre des Champs-Élysées, see Walther Straram's biography: http://straram.fr/biographie.htm (retrieved July 12, 2017). Walska started voice lessons with him on May 4, 1921, when still married to Cochran. The TCE was a great architectural and artistic success at its opening in 1913; it was the site of the famous, tumultuous première of Stravinsky's *Rite of Spring*. But within six months it was in financial trouble. It remains a prominent landmark today. For its recent past, see Fred Plotkin, "Paris's Théâtre des Champs-Élysées Stays Cutting Edge," https://www.wqxr.org/story/255909-pariss-theatre-des-champs-elysees-stays-stayed-cutting-edge/ (retrieved July 13, 2019): "In 1953, it was one of the first 20th-century edifices in Paris to be awarded landmark status, becoming a *monument historique* not only for the notoriety that attended its beginnings but for its particular beauty," as well as for much else, but its long ownership by Walska has been forgotten more than commemorated. In 1921, the TCE was on the verge of bankruptcy. Walska's relationship with the theatre began as early as July 29, 1921, when, according to the Straram "Biographie," she bought its *concordat*. This purchase suggests that, in July 1921, even before the Cochran divorce proceedings had begun, Walska (or her sponsor) envisioned that she would play a central role at the TCE. "Mme. Walska Buys Paris Theatre" headlined a December 1922 dispatch from Paris (*Music Magazine–Musical Courier* 85 [1922]: 49), which also stated that Walska had purchased a majority of the "privileged" (or preferred) shares in the TCE. The article went on to explain that, because preferred shares carried with them voting power, unlike common stock, she now held controlling interest in the TCE. The total investment was stated as "upward of 5,000,000 francs," prewar value. Walska said that her purchase of the TCE was merely an investment and she had no intention of singing in operas there with her own company. (Note that her purchase was of the fabric [i.e., walls, floor, and roof] of the theatre only. The performing spaces were controlled by long-term leaseholders.) Walska's wedding to McCormick was in August 1922, and four months later the *New York Times* reported: "Walska Buys Theatre" ([December 15, 1922]): 8). The article continues: "She gave [the *Chicago*] *Tribune* to understand that the purchase was simply an investment of her own funds, and not the gift of her wealthy husband." An interview cited by Gardner (p. 112) claims Walska said the TCE was "the gift of my husband," but Gardner is not a reliable source. Even though by then she had "funds" from two former spouses and one new one, it is improbable that she could have made the purchase by herself. Blumenthal (p. 259) claims that McCormick's contribution toward the purchase was only $100,000. Walska bought all 17,000 privileged shares that had been floated to rescue the TCE, making her its owner until 1970. She was generally inactive after Straram's death in 1933, when Enrich Straram, Walther's son, took over; she became an absentee owner after World War II began. See also *Washington Post* (December 16, 1922): 9, which includes names of other stock owners. Enrich Straram, in chapter 3 of his *Histoire croisée* (see Part 2 bibliography), says that Walska was elected president of the TCE company on April 23, 1923, and she then appointed Walther Straram administrator. According to chapter 9 of the *Histoire,* when Walska became the theatre's owner, Harold undertook "*à soutenir financièrement le théâtre,*" so in 1931, when the McCormicks were divorced, it was feared that the TCE would be deprived of Harold's support. The implication seems to be that

Harold's money had been in the background for eight or nine years. The story must be more complicated in view of the not entirely smooth marriage of Walska and Harold (see note 53, above). Walska was the indispensable angel of the excellent Orchestre des Concerts Straram, organized by Straram in 1925. (Arturo Toscanini chose it for his performances on Paris visits.) It is hard to exaggerate the importance of the TCE in Walska's Paris life. However disappointing her singing was, through Walther Straram she maintained a central place in Paris musical as well as social activities. Her "studio" at the theatre could accommodate a seated dinner for 40. The TCE stood out as a desirable concert venue in the city, and it also included an opera stage (ART, pp. 156, 158, 168). In his *Histoire croisée* (ch. 10), Enrich Straram evokes Walska in her box surrounded by resplendent society. Walska's eventual sale of the theatre is dated variously to 1970 or 1973, probably explained by the complicated nature of such a transaction. The buyer was an organ of the French government. The theatre might be considered a significant part of Walska's fortune, but it is unlikely to have made money for her.

Walther Straram had changed his name from Marrast. He was a central figure in this part of Walska's life from 1921 until 1933, when he died. The Yale Music Library has a recording by his orchestra entitled "Concerts Straram (1928–1930)," only very few parts of which are conducted by the maestro himself. These are the only traces of him. (The recording has more tracks of his orchestra being led by other conductors.) Straram's share in 1920s musical life in Paris was large and beneficial. His orchestra was his central concern, but he also did all he could to give Walska a musical career. On Straram, see Patrice Imbaud, "Le centenaire du Théâtre des Champs-Élysées: l'histoire d'une fabuleuse aventure," *L'éducation musicale* (October 2013) https://www.leducation-musicale.com/index.php/

paroles-d-auteur/5834-le-centenaire-du-
theatre-des-champs-elysees-l-histoire-d-
une-fabuleuse-aventure (retrieved August
15, 2019). The section headed "1928–1934: 'Les
saisons Straram' " tells that "*Walther Straram
fut l'une des figures parisiennes les plus en vue
pendant plus de dix ans. . . . Il créa son orchestre
et devient directeur artistique du Théâtre des
Champs-Élysées en 1928, sur la demande de
son amie et élève, la soprano Ganna Walska,
propriétaire du théâtre.*" Straram recognized
Walska's value to both the TCE and his own
musical career: "Freed from concerns of
breaking even by being backed by Mme. Ganna
Walska's money, [Straram] could allow himself
to deviate from the normal repertory and put
his talent and that of his instrumentalists at
the service of contemporary composers. He
had no need to worry about the number of
rehearsals or their duration as long as [the
performers'] fees quieted any protests. . . . [H]e
took the . . . initiative of departing from the
sacrosanct weekend concerts and organizing
his concerts for Thursday evenings, . . . a good
idea at a time when Parisians were beginning
to taste the country on weekends." Ravel's
Bolero was among the new works premiered
by this orchestra and, under Stravinsky's
direction, it performed the composer's *Rite
of Spring* on its first recording. Walska relied
wholly on Straram to run the TCE. After he
sickened in 1931, probably from lung cancer, she
did much to keep him alive; see ART (pp. 151–52,
239, 315–16). Intimate relations between them
were rumored (e.g., see "*amie*" above), but not
credited: "Tuning in on Ganna Walska's Billion-
Dollar Operamania" (*Atlanta Constitution*
[December 6, 1931]: SM5).

55 Walska's supposed plans to use the TCE
for personal performances are reported in
several places, notably by Erté in *Things I
Remember* (p. 55): "As a wedding present
McCormack [*sic*] had given her the [TCE],
where she could sing whatever she liked." The
idea is also espoused in E. Straram, *Histoire*

croisée. Further, the *Chicago Tribune* of August
27, 1922 (part 7, p. 8) reported that Walska was
rumored to be having a season of opera in Paris
the next winter (see note 54, above, about
the stages being controlled by other hands
until 1928); see also W. Straram "Biographie."
Owing to these leases (see ART, p.112, where
she mistakenly says the stages held 11-year
terms), Walska averred: "I had nothing at
all to do with the management. I was in the
same position as anyone else—I could rent the
theatre from the lessee for a day, a week or a
month." Well aware of public opinion, Walska
is reported as saying, "I will never appear in my
own theatre until I have gained recognition
based only on my merits as an artist" (*New
York Times* [December 15, 1922]: 8). Also
see E. Straram, *Histoire croisée* (ch. 5) and
W. Straram "Biographie" (for September 1930);
ART (pp. 117–20); and Erté, *Things I Remember*
(p. 55). For Walska on the Paris social scene,
see ART (pp. 408–413).

56 Although Walska's memoirs are entitled
Always Room at the Top, she says nothing in
them to suggest that, in 1923, her theatre and
$120,000 annual income might have placed her
at the top. About the memoir's title, see Adams
(p. 253). To her, probably, "the top" would have
involved singing, which clearly remained out
of reach. A curious relic of these years is a five-
column article published in November 1924 in
the monthly *Revue internationale des questions
politiques, diplomatiques, économiques* (see
"Raffestin-Nadaud" in the Part 2 bibliography).
The magazine published rather short issues,
and today copies are found nowhere except
the Bibliothèque nationale de France, which
warns that its holdings have gaps. It is almost
wholly concerned with foreign affairs, so the
Walska article departs from its normal diet.
Signed "Raffestin-Nadaud" and entitled "Les
Femmes d'Aujourd'hui dans la Vie et dans
l'Art: Mme. Ganna Walska," it constitutes an
unrelieved panegyric, as these extracts (in
my translations) suggest: "With a ceaselessly

increasing and always appreciated talent, she sang Mozart's operas all over America.... In 1923, she sang *Rigoletto* successfully at the Paris Opera." Although he talks about "the Théâtre des Champs-Élysées, which she has bought" (the purchase seems unremarkable), he makes no reference to Harold McCormick or any of her previous husbands, but Straram is mentioned twice. Raffestin-Nadaud calls her, "a world-class artist, known and acclaimed everywhere, her triumphs are no longer counted, and the high artistic reputation that she has won by her efforts, perseverance, and fine talent may no longer be disputed.... The woman with whom we are concerned has been able, besides—and it does her honor—to sustain the legitimate ambition that destiny marked in her with an inexhaustible taste, a genuine passion, for work and effort." The writer addressed her philosophy vis à vis fashion: "She refuses to bend to new fashions when they are unaesthetic. She reproves short hair, short skirts, everything tending to limit the imagination, to strip woman of her natural harmony, of her mystery, that is, of the invincible and sacred attraction for which she has been created." Something in all this, especially about Walska's outlook and hard work and her cultural preparation for operas, anticipates the sound of ART. The article looks like planted publicity. Raffestin-Nadaud claims (in error), that Walska's serious voice training began in Paris in 1914 with Édouard de Reszke. This reversion from the prevailing inclination toward her teacher having been his brother Jean probably stemmed from its being dangerous to claim the still living Jean as her teacher in Paris. Édouard had taught in London, not Paris, and died in Poland during the war. The cover page that Crawford reproduces (p. 10) of the *Revue internationale* showing a portrait of Walska is not authentic. That issue's true cover showed the president of Chile, and the Walska article was not illustrated.

57 Erté, *Things I Remember* (p. 56): "She had bought many splendid gems from Russian refugees who had managed to bring them out of Russia at the time of the Revolution. Since she was extremely mean with her money, she always concealed her identity in these negotiations. Posing as a poor Polish refugee she would pretend to be representing (for a tiny commission) some rich patron. On these occasions she would dress for the part."

58 Walska bought the Fabergé egg, known to have been the Duchess of Marlborough's, at a Paris benefit auction in 1926 and sold it at Parke-Bernet Galleries in New York on May 15, 1965, along with items of important jewelry. Erté, *Things I Remember* (pp. 55–56) writes eloquently about her jewels, for which he assumes McCormick paid, but Walska must have also bought jewelry using her own resources. A later sale at Parke-Bernet New York was held on April 1, 1971; see Gardner (p. 97); Degen Peren, "The Cone Heads," *New York Times* (August 17, 2003): 138.

59 Barbara Hutton (1912–1979), whose troubled life was much chronicled, was the heiress to the Woolworth fortune. "Countess Barbara Buys Gem Fortune" (*Washington Post* [June 17, 1936]: 1). The rumor was denied in *Time* (June 29, 1936): 68; and ART (pp. 184–85), but it did not go away: Helen Welshimer, "Special Correspondent Tells Story of Barbara Hutton," *Atlanta Constitution* (July 11, 1938): 10.

60 Walska's niece, Hania Puacz Tallmadge, gave a number of her aunt's Erté costumes to LACMA, and others were bought by the museum. LACMA's web site used to show these costumes, along with many other clothing items as well as Erté's design sketches for costumes. Presumably they may be seen by special arrangement. Abundant pictures of opera costumes may be found through Google by searching "Ganna Walska Operatic Costumes"; they are interspersed among other Walska pictures, but are easy to detect.

61   Walska's wardrobe is widely chronicled. See, for example, James J. Conway, "Dress-down Friday: Ganna Walska" at Strange Flowers (https://strangeflowers.wordpress.com/2012/03/02/dress-down-friday-ganna-walska; retrieved March 2, 2012): "Key to the Polish soprano's protracted campaign to conquer a reluctant public was fashion. A noted beauty, she was also a modish dresser and collector of baubles. Her war chest brimming with conjugal contributions, Walska raided boutiques in Europe and America, returning with pieces by Adrian, Boulanger, Madame Grès, Schiaparelli and Lanvin." The *Washington Post* (June 2, 1929): M10, described her as an actor playing the Countess Castiglione at the TCE (June 1, 1929), during which she changed costumes at each of the eight acts, always ablaze in jewelry. The March 18, 1929 issue of *Time* (p. 16), told of her travel entourage of trunks, and in its January 29, 1934 issue (p. 25) the magazine describes the clothing she wore at a Philadelphia concert. For Walska on clothes, see ART (pp. 75–81).

62   The rear of the passenger compartment in the Rolls Royce was convertible—known as a landaulet body. She turned the Cochran-bought 1920 Silver Ghost into a pickup truck for her chateau. Both cars were discovered on blocks and without tires at Galluis in 1967; collectors bought them. See note 93, below.

63   The Paris store at 2, rue de la Paix, was just off the Place Vendôme and steps from the Ritz, and her perfumes were sold at the TCE as well. Walska was ambivalent about the business. In ART (pp. 404–405), she claims a snobbish revulsion at going into commerce, but that may have been pretense and a way to assert her claim to an aristocratic past. Her expectation of great profits turned into a reality of substantial loss, and the business folded in 1931 (ART, p. 425). As my wife has kindly pointed out, the name "Divorçons" for a perfume needs careful handling. What woman would display a bottle to her husband? Even less, what husband would give a bottle to his wife? Still, Divorçons was not considered problematic and perhaps was taken as just a joke. It was conspicuously advertised and seems to have sold. Other Walska fragrances had less provocative names.

64   The Chateau de Galluis had to have been acquired in 1928. Walska indicated her ownership in connection with a U.S. customs dispute (*New York Times* [January 23, 1929]: 17). The building dated from 1704 and was torn down in 1983. (This information was on the internet in 2017, but has since vanished.) Walska's quotations are from ART (pp. 315, 405). In 1930 Walska would have turned 43, if based on her actual birth date, or 40 if based on her purported birth in 1890. McCormick could order the farm machinery from one or all of the three IH factories in France, and it was probably cost-free to him. Since, as full-size agricultural machines, they could hardly be used in the modest gardens of Galluis, what became of them is an unanswerable question. For the divorce to proceed, McCormick and Walska had to remain separate for two years, precluding Harold from personally accompanying the machinery. The last he saw of Walska prior to the divorce was in March 1929, when she returned to Paris after her quarrel with U.S. Customs in New York (*Los Angeles Times* [October 11, 1931]: 3).

65   ART (p. 425). The income was generated by a million-dollar principal, as detailed below. A false claim made by the press at the time of Walska's divorce from McCormick was that she obtained "her independent fortune" from Cochran (*Los Angeles Times* [October 11, 1931]: 3); the statement was widely circulated. Absurd estimates of her wealth were sometimes bruited about. For example, in 1926 a Polish composer said she had an annual income of $500,000 (see July 24, 1926, entry in W. Straram "Biographie"); actually, it was $120,000. Another almost certainly wrong report was in the *Washington Post* (November 14, 1927): 1: "It was understood at the time of her marriage to Mr. McCormick he settled $10,000,000 in her name." The accurate sum was more modest, but not contemptible; see Adams (p. 121), the invaluable, but unverifiable, source: in 1923, Harold reorganized Walska's holdings of IH stock—27,771 shares of common stock and 1,286 shares of preferred—amounting to a total value in excess of $2 million. Walska had Harold's wealth to back her up from 1922 until at least 1929 and perhaps to 1931, but, in view of her capital worth, her standard of living did not plummet after the divorce. Twice she entered into enterprises she hoped would rapidly make a killing (the perfume business and marriage to Grindell Matthews in 1938), but both failed. She handily survived these setbacks. Beginning in the 1960s, her finances were helped by selling her stake in the TCE, her New York house, and her jewels. (She also sold to MMA the rich collection she had amassed of the photographic portraits of Countess Castiglione). But Gardner (p. 130) assures us that such sales were unnecessary. Even with spending much on her California garden, her wealth held out for the rest of her life, and she left a large legacy, including the Paris house, to the Ganna Walska Lotusland Foundation as the cornerstone of the garden endowment. A detailed account of Walska's finances is unattainable, however, without study of GWA, if then. Finances are a mysterious aspect of Walska's life. It will not do to say, airily, that she had six rich husbands. Only two were really rich, and one of those successfully defended his millions against her. The last two were drains on her fortune. As far as one may tell from published sources, McCormick was the donor of much the largest part of her riches. Fraenkel was small change, and Cochran's settlement in 1922 was a fraction of McCormick's contribution.

66 In *Things I Remember* (p. 56), Erté mentions tradespeople waiting to be paid and refers to her as being "extremely mean with her money." Adams's account of the Lotusland years (pp. 373–425) also suggests that, rich as she was, she could be difficult when money was involved.

67 Adams, p. 405, "Madame tended to swing wildly between generosity and stinginess.... Attorneys and housekeeper alike were victims of her mean streak, while less worthy recipients often benefited from Ganna's munificence."

While both Downes and the anonymous *Boston Globe* writer were appreciative, they each concluded that a good voice was not enough for the starring role she assumed. (The writer for *Le Ménestrel* 84 [1922]: 487, also is unknown.) Wagner, pp. 329–30.

Harold's sister in Harrison (p. 193). Scathing comments from the press are easily found. One of the most telling accounts of Walska's inconsistent singing is in Blumenthal. The chapter entitled "Ganna Walska's Wagnerian Opera Company" (pp. 247–60), is filled with tales of money worries, with both Walska and McCormick disbursing tens of thousands, although McCormick eventually closed his purse and left the tour. But Blumenthal also writes of Walska the singer. The opera company Blumenthal organized in her behalf took *The Marriage of Figaro* into its repertory for her sake, although it was unpopular; another soprano in the troupe was expected to fill in when Walska dropped out. Blumenthal recalls the problem: "[Walska] kept insisting that she would be able to sing the role. [In Louisville] she was determined, come what may, she would sing the part that afternoon.... Walska went on ... [and within Blumenthal's earshot a spectator said] 'the one singing the part of the Countess is very poor,' Ganna had sung the role charmingly at rehearsals, but a severe nervousness overtook her before and during the presentation. Her vocal cords were so affected that it was very hard for her to even finish the performance." That was not the whole story, however. In Buffalo, "Walska had assured us that this time she positively would sing. She did, and really gave a good performance." But a few days later, in New London, "at the last minute [Walska] refused to sing" (pp. 253–55).

68 Walska's reputation for nonappearance (Bernays, pp. 169–70) might be regarded as a continuation of the *Zaza* syndrome. Large portions of ART are devoted to her experience with both vocal studies and spiritualism. She continually moved from teacher to teacher, guru to guru; see Appendix 2.4. Her stage fright was no secret to herself or to audiences. Erté tells in *Things I Remember* (p. 55) of his attempt to help relieve her nervousness by providing her with a mink bracelet that she might tear to bits with her nails during the performance to relieve her nervousness.

69 The best source of information about her various government decorations is the biographical note about Walska in the Walther Straram "Biographie." The Polish decoration is well documented (e.g., *Baltimore Sun* [July 24, 1931]: 13); she refers to her Légion d'honneur award in ART (p. 279). Adams (p. 477) lists the signatories who recommended her for the award, all of whom were musicians, including four composers. Many dozen awards of this decoration are made each year; the Légion d'honneur is not an exclusive club. The French government also gave her the Ordre national des Arts et des Lettres in 1972, when she sold the TCE. For color photographs of the medals, see *Lotusland: Newsletter for Members* 23, no. 2 (2014): 4.

70 Walska in esteemed company, see *Chicago Tribune* (May 1, 1930): 19; *Chicago Tribune* (February 7, 1932): D2. Walska prided herself on keeping distinguished company (see ART, pp. 169–70). She and Straram brought the

Bayreuth company to Paris, a musical coup that made a great splash on the Paris musical scene. Among the noted guests were a former president of France, the president of the French Supreme Court, the French attorney general, "and their wives—great friends of mine—[who] were constant guests in my box at all musical events." Walska's stature as a figure in Paris society was a crucial aspect of her life, too little mentioned in ART, where spiritual quests predominate.

71 Walska's sole pre-McCormick operatic performance was in Giordano's *Fedora* in Havana; Leoncavallo's *Zaza* was scheduled for December 1920, but it did not take place. In ART (opposite p. 136), Walska is shown costumed as Massenet's Manon, but though she mentions it later (p. 305), she did not sing the part. Using material in the GWA, a list of Walska's roles could be developed; Reese (p. 284 n. 6) provides a rundown that I think may include some for which Walska commissioned costumes only. The partial roster of performances (derived in part from ART, pp. 122, 125) includes *Fedora* (Havana); *Tosca* (Linz, Belgrade, and perhaps other venues in central Europe [ART, pp. 122, 130–32]); *Madama Butterfly* (Nice, Vienna, Bratislava, Linz, and others [ART, pp. 122, 125, 128–29]); Countess Almaviva in *Marriage of Figaro* (Paris Mozart Festival, 1924; Buffalo, New York [Blumenthal, p. 255]; *Time* (February 4, 1924): 16]); Donna Elvira in *Don Giovanni*, venue unknown (Erté, *Things I Remember*, p. 55); Gilda in *Rigoletto* (Paris, 1923); and Mélisande in *Pelléas et Mélisande* (Paris, TCE, 1933 [ART, pp. 461–62; W. Straram "Biographie," June 20, 1933]). ART (pp. 130–32) adds Mimi (*La Bohème*) in central Europe. Another role, the tiny comprimaria part of Xenia in *Boris Godunov*, was performed at TCE. This list is almost certainly incomplete. Walska sometimes received good press, e.g., "Walska Triumphs in Tosca in Belgrade" (*Time* [January 10, 1927]: 30). A circular anticipating her U.S. tour in 1923 (GWA) includes positive notices from three recitals, and an advertising page from the *Musical Courier* (October 22, 1925) celebrates her performances in *Madama Butterfly* in central Europe and France, but it is discreet about her singing as distinct from her costumes and acting.

72 The benefit performance announcement (*Le Temps* [June 20, 1923]: 5, col. 1 emphasized the other singers and treated Walska as an also-ran.) The June 26, 1923, edition of the *New York Times*, (p. 14) announced, "Mme. Walska in Paris Opera Debut Tonight," and quotes her saying, "I am preparing myself for this performance as for a religious ceremony." For a good, detailed report of the evening, see *New York Times* (June 27, 1923): 29: "Audience Titters at Walska's Gilda . . . Opera Hopes Are Dimmed." In a long, devastating review, *Time* (July 9, 1923) announced in its headline: "Beautiful, Wealthy, She Has No Voice." The conductor was Gabriel Grovlez (https://en.wikipedia.org/wiki/gabriel_grovlez). For Walska's response, see ART (p. 105). Erté (*Things I Remember,* pp. 54–55) recalled that the audience laughed, and that Walska, who blamed personal enemies, held a celebratory supper nevertheless. Adams (pp. 115–17) relies heavily on Erté's account and alludes to a blackmail attempt by some Russians, crediting Walska's claim that the noise came from personal enemies. Except for Straram's Mozart festival and the minor role of Xenia in *Boris Godunov,* Walska did not sing opera again in Paris until the self-financed production of *Pelléas et Mélisande* at the TCE in 1933.

73 Her trial run performances in minor French opera houses with less discerning audiences were sung under the name Anna Navarre (Adams, p. 131); they apparently went well. The most serious and developed assessment of Walska's voice and singing is a review by Olin Downes of her Carnegie Hall concert of February 12, 1929, "Mme. Ganna Walska Sings for New York. Analysis of a Serious Effort by an Artist Who Has Striven Long and

Ardently. . . . A Pleasing, Natural Voice Marred by Deficiencies" (*New York Times* [February 13, 1929]: 21). He mentions a "brilliant" audience made up of a "curious assortment of people, many of them distinguished in other affairs, who have nothing to do with music and who seldom or never attend a song recital." Final lines, "Long and strict apprenticeship is usually indispensable for [artistic interpretation], which is the tale and the moral of yesterday's recital." A thoughtful earlier appraisal was "Walska in First Boston Concert" (*Boston Daily Globe* [February 26, 1923]: 3), which refers to her voice as "naturally of unusual power and beauty. . . . For such a voice as hers a concert career and an operatic career in non-coloratura roles that do not demand heroic singing is possible."

74 That Edith McCormick created trouble for Walska is unconfirmed; see ART (p. 133). Adams (p. 134) says that she sang "Butterfly" all over Europe. Performances in Bratislava and Vienna are confirmed (*New York Times* [January 29, 1925]:13, and [February 29, 1925]: 13). Her performances were not met with unrelieved praise, however. As reported by the *Atlanta Constitution* (November 6, 1932): SM6, one critic in Vienna called a Walska performance "the most painful evening in the history of the Volksoper." The account of her performance in Nice (Adams, pp. 131–33) suggests that it was such a disaster the mayor forbade her to repeat the performance (confirmed in *Le Petit Parisien* [February 24, 1925]: 4, col. 6). For a more favorable response, see the *Washington Post* (January 29, 1925): 4. I am advised by Judith Malafronte, of the music faculty of Indiana University and member of the Elizabethan Club, that Mélisande is not a demanding role. Concerning McCormick's enthusiastic response, see India Moffet, "Walska Charms with Costumes and Her Beauty" (*Chicago Tribune* [June 25, 1924]: 13): "The applause after each song was led by Harold F. McCormick. . . . It seemed to us that his applause was louder and longer when the soloist appeared for her last group of songs." McCormick's response comes closest here—after the divorce—to suggesting a brief, memorable scene of the Orson Welles film *Citizen Kane,* in which Kane leads the applause for his wife's deplorable singing (see Appendix 2.3, "Ganna Walska and Orson Welles's Susan Alexander").

75 Walska referred to as a "famous opera star" (*Los Angeles Times* [December 15, 1928]: 8). *Stella della lirica* (star of the lyric theatre) is in Speranza Cavenago-Bignami Moneta, *Gemmologia: pietre preziose ed ornamentali naturali* (Milan: Hoepli, 1980), p. 443, in connection with a 95-carat diamond.

76 "'Met' Opening to Find New Faces in Circle. . . . Mme Ganna Walska, whose life ambition was to sing at the Met, will get there this season. But her activities will be confined to Box 4 on Monday nights, not the stage" (*Washington Post* [December 1, 1940]: S4). Descriptions of singing lessons and teachers receive much space in ART, where her quest for an ideal teacher parallels the one for metaphysical help for her singing. Walska also calls attention to the extraordinary number of hours she devotes to practicing (ART, pp. 165–66), writing that her daily schedule allows at least five hours for singing; elsewhere (pp. 347, 361, 382), a minimum of four hours singing per day is mentioned. Alda's (pp. 290-91) description of Walska's day allows no time for singing practice.

77 *New York Times* (September 20, 1928): 26; *Chicago Tribune* (same date): 3. Greeted by McCormick: *Atlanta Constitution* (September 25, 1928): 4. The SS *Paris* was the flagship of the French Line; reportedly, its "living spaces were divinely comfortable and luxurious" https://en.wikipedia.org/wiki/SS_Paris_(1916).

78 News reports emphasized that Walska's possessions were properly declared; no attempt at evasion of duty had taken place. About the principle at issue, see *New York*

Times (September 21, 1928): 26. Press coverage names her able lawyer. For the duty rate charged, see *Chicago Tribune* (September 21, 1928): 4; *New York Times* (September 27, 1928): 43. The Customs impounded 15 trunks: *New York Times* (September 22, 1928): 28. Estimated values, *New York Times* (September 27, 1928): 43.

79 For Customs ruling, see *Manchester Guardian* (September 26, 1928): 9. "Rights of the modern woman form the basis of the appeal of Mme Walska" (*Washington Post* [September 26, 1928]: 4). During marriage, Walska was never resident in the U.S., and she had visited only twice before. Affidavit filed by McCormick stating that he consented to her living abroad (*New York Times* [September 27, 1928]: 43). No Customs problem on visits in 1923 and 1925–26 (*Chicago Tribune* [January 23, 1929]: 3). The lack of difficulties on the two previous visits is intriguing.

Walska proved by listing them in detail that certain jewels had been acquired in the U.S. and she was allowed to reclaim them (*New York Times* [October 9, 1928]: 15).

80 *New York Times* (October 9, 1928): 26; *Boston Globe* (October 11, 1928): 2. Mellon is famous for his great wealth, art collecting, and philanthropy, but he had grave shortcomings as treasury secretary, which he was for eleven years, including at the start of the Great Depression.

81 Customs court appeal: *New York Times* (October 12, 1928): 27; *Boston Globe* (October 30, 1928): 17. In 1922 Walska became a life member of the National Women's Party (*Chicago Tribune* [July 2, 1922]), to which she sent a check for $1,000 (a large amount at the time). The first woman appointee to a Federal bench sat on the Court of Customs Appeal: "Woman Federal Judge to Hear Walska Women's Rights Case" (*New York Times* [October 31, 1928]: 7). Walska before the Customs Court: "The fight was not for money, but to establish the legal equality of women" (*Chicago Tribune* [January 23, 1929]: 3). About half of her effects were proven to be U.S.-bought, and they were released (*New York Times* [January 23, 1929]: 17). This is surprising, as one would expect her clothes to have been bought mainly in Paris. Walska's reference during her testimony to "a country home" near Paris is the first trace of her possession of Galluis, which suggests she must have acquired it later than September 24, 1928 (*Chicago Tribune* [January 23, 1929]: 17). The case was being tried as a test, and only a piece of old lace that required $40 duty was at issue (*Chicago Tribune* [January 23, 1929]: 3). *Time* (January 27, 1930): 17: alleged (in error) that all of Walska's possessions except this lace had been shown as U.S.-bought.

82 *New York Times* (February 7, 1929): 20; *Washington Post* (February 21, 1929): 12. Governor Roosevelt signs the bill into law: *Chicago Tribune* (April 11, 1929): 33. In ART (pp. 143–44), Walska's rather generalized account of the events since September 1928 unduly emphasizes the New York State part, and the more important Customs court proceedings go unmentioned. Walska returns to Paris with her possessions: *Washington Post* (March 21, 1929): 12. In ART (pp. 194–95), Walska tells a story illustrating how her sorry marriage to Cochran "finished in beauty." According to her, while she was still in New York in 1929, she learned that Cochran was "dangerously ill at the Savoy Plaza," so every day she sent him roses, taking precautions to maintain anonymity. He died after she was back in Paris. This story (except for Cochran's death) is fiction. Walska was in Paris at the end of March, and the dying Cochran was not brought back from California to New York until early April.

83 *Time* (January 27, 1930): xv. Other coverage included *New York Times* (January 18, 1930): 8; *Hartford Courant* (same date): 12. *Chicago Tribune* (January 18, 1930: 16) headed an article "Walska Ruling to Affect Few, Lawyer Says," but

the case was noticed in legal circles. See S.P. Breckenridge, "Separate Domicile for Married Women," *Social Service Review* 4 (1930): 50. The *University of Pennsylvania Law Review and American Law Register* 78 (April 1930): 780–81, deemed it "thoroughly in accord … with the modern tendency toward complete emancipation of women, which it helps decidedly to confirm."

84 Crawford (p. 15) and the entry for 1931 in "Lotusland History" (https://www.lotusland.org/learn/lotusland-history/), allege that Harold divorced Walska when he finally realized that she would not live with him in Chicago. This is unconvincing. One would have to think that he was in Chicago for close to a decade waiting for her to make up her mind to join him or for him to determine he would move to Paris. In seven years, the couple would have established a tolerable modus vivendi that accommodated McCormick's spending time with her in Paris and Walska's coming to America in connection with singing dates. Besides, with the divorced Edith still leading Chicago society, among other reasons, the idea of Walska's settling in Chicago is unlikely. There had to be other reasons for their separation, which may be revealed in the McCormick letters in GWA. Was Harold pressured by business associates and/or family? At the time, Cyrus McCormick, Jr., Harold's brother, was considered the family's head. Harold's divorce from Edith and marriage to Walska had definitely been scandalous, and nothing had happened since to let the scandal be forgotten. Perhaps it was agreed that a leader of American industry should not spend long periods in France, lavishing IH money on his wife's causes, such as the TCE and the Straram orchestra or jewels. The *New York Times* report of the divorce (October 11, 1931): 24, said of Harold's concerns: "His business interests were here, all his friends were here and he preferred not to desert them." By 1929, there may have been more than a grain of truth in his remark: after ten years (1919–29) McCormick's passion for Walska may have abated; he was content with the company of his friends and business associates in Chicago. He was linked with a few women after Walska.

85 A Paris gossip columnist was cited by the *Atlanta Constitution* (December 6, 1931): SM5: "Tuning in on Ganna Walska's Billion-Dollar Operamania." Signs of continued marital attachment included the purchase of Galluis (although probably paid for by Walska herself), and the lavish 1930 birthday gift of farm machinery for Galluis. In September 1928, Harold met her boat and was involved in her concert tour that extended into 1929. He may also have financed the legal talent for her Customs dispute. Flowers in 1934: ART (p. 282). Walska wondered how the marriage could have lasted so long (Adams, pp. 186–87). Walska and Harold were apart from 1929 to 1931 to establish desertion.

86 Harold's press release announcing the divorce, possibly written by Thomas H. Fisher, his attorney, is a small masterpiece of blandness and concealment. It shies away from mentioning any property settlement by Harold and manages to shift issues of monetary interest to the late Alex Cochran: "Mme. Walska received no property settlement or alimony [from McCormick]. . . . It was from Cochrane [*sic*] that she received her independent fortune" (*Boston Globe* [October 11, 1931]: A8; *Los Angeles Times* [same date]: 3). The fountainhead of this allegation is an article in the *New York Times*, ([October 11, 1931]: 24): "Harold M'Cormick Divorces Walska," a long news item based on the divorce press release but adding many false statements. The $3 million legacy is treated as though accurate by Gardner (p. 115); *Time* (January 29, 1934): 25; Veenhof (p. 305); as well as many other sources. Even without receiving millions from Cochran, Walska's financial condition remained rosy. See Adams (p. 182): Her New York lawyer assured her that her $100,000 per

year remained. Her trust fund from McCormick had swelled to $7 million. This may be because the divorce settlement gave her one quarter of his holdings of IH stock, worth many millions (Adams, p. 187). How she could have won a settlement on this scale defies belief, but it is hard to contest because her riches definitely grew.

87 The musical high point of the period following her divorce from McCormick was Walska's performance as Debussy's Mélisande. The production at the TCE in July 1933 was a special occasion, financed by Walska and conducted by the dying Straram. The divorce, and perhaps even more, Straram's death, may have diminished Walska's social life. The perfume business folded during the Depression. She divided her life between Paris and New York. For the brief New York visit for house repairs, see Adams (pp. 194–95). She also reduced her involvement with the TCE, now under the able management of Straram's son, Enrich. What association she continued to have with it is hard to determine. She continued as its owner until 1970. That she no longer had Harold's money behind her was balanced by now having major capital. This aspect of her life, the possibility that she had become wealthy in capital (not just income), is not mentioned in ART. She had Galluis, town houses in Paris and New York, and two Rolls Royces. She paid for expensive singing lessons, notably with the distinguished teacher Cécile Gilly. See Marjorie Lawrence (chapter 10, and especially pp. 73–74), who calls Walska very rich and without talent; for the situation from Walska's standpoint, see ART (pp. 347–48, 360, 381–82, 465). Alda (p. 291) reports that Walska paid her $10,000 for the lessons, too much to refuse during the Depression. For a very positive account of Galluis, see Adams (pp. 229–30).

88 Grindell Matthews is interesting enough to have two biographies, Barwell's and Foster's. Barwell, who had friendly communications with Walska, is credulous about Grindell's achievements. Foster proceeds on the premise that where there was smoke, there must have been fire, but retains some critical distance. Neither has much use for Walska. (Barwell said that he left her out so as to focus on Grindell.) See also https://en.wikipedia.org/wiki/Harry_ Grindell_Matthews (uninterested in Walska). Grindell Matthews comes across as a perhaps deluded confidence man, who succeeded in living off his wives and gullible or greedy investors. When he met Walska, he had an elaborate, fenced laboratory with landing strip in Wales, the financing for which is mysterious. Foster (pp. 173–74) tells that Grindell declared bankruptcy in 1931, with debts of £11,500, virtually no assets, and owing his London hotel £311 for room and board,.

89 See ART (pp. 435–50). Grindell Matthews's appearance: tall (6 foot 4), good looking, and well turned out (Foster, p. 188). He was "a magnetic personality with very tidy habits" (Foster, p. 189) and "immaculately dressed" (p. 217); photographs bear out some of this. He spoke fluent French (Foster, p. 190). Walska wrote much more positively about him than she did about Fraenkel, let alone Cochran; for "poor human wreckage," see ART (p. 442). She also mentions that he shaved his forehead to push back his hair line, smoked incessantly, had trembling hands and a patch over a bad eye (pp. 409–410). As usual in Walska's storytelling, Grindell expresses his instant love and total need of her. She is horrified by the idea of marriage: "I no longer expect a personal expression of love" (p. 439); her need for "enormous returns" (p. 443). As it happened, the TCE owed a tax bill of 700,000 francs (Le Figaro [October 27, 1936]: 5, col. 3), and she had a share of responsibility in this, the newspaper suggests. Grindell's major sonar experiment failed and could not be attempted again until the following year (ART, pp. 444–45). Grindell occasioned one of the more absurd comments about Walska's fortune: "Along the way,

[Walska] inherited much of her ex-husbands' vast fortunes, totaling $125 million (that's about two billion dollars today)": Becky Ferreira, "Humanity's Endless Quest to Invent a Death Ray: A History," The Awl (February 2, 2011) www.theawl.com/2011/02/humanitys-endless-quest-to-invent-a-death-ray-a-history/. The only husband she inherited from was Fraenkel—a share of $160,000.

90 ART (p. 446): the success of the eye operation disposed Walska to marry Grindell Matthews. Foster (p. 191) claims, improbably, that Walska felt herself falling in love with him. Grindell came to Galluis, where they found common interests in cats and knocking dead branches from trees (ART, pp. 447–49). But the mood changed. Anticipating a great fortune and peerage from his invention, "Already he was calling me Lady Grindell." She responded testily that, if she had wanted, she could have married royalty, ancient nobility, etc. (ART, pp. 449–50). He stayed little more than a week (Adams, p. 250). The ART narrative about Grindell ends suddenly, before the marriage, which is not atypical of Walska's manner (or perhaps that of her editor). The car for Grindell was nothing fancy (Adams, p. 253).

91 Walska wedded Grindell Matthews in a London registry office on January 22, 1938. This would be another nonsexual union. Because each member of the couple had her or his own reputation—failed singer or failed inventor—the engagement and wedding were much noted in the press. Marriage notice in Time (February 7, 1938): 43: "Ganna Walska d'Eighnhorn [sic] Fraenkel Cochran McCormick, 45 [more accurately, 51], Polish-American opera singer, perfumer, feminist … to Harry Grindell Matthews, 57 … in London. The bride went on her honeymoon alone, while the inventor rushed to his Clydach, Wales, laboratory (fenced with electrified wire) to perfect an aerial torpedo." Foster (p. 189) claims they honeymooned in St. Moritz, but is wrong. Barwell (p. 163) says Grindell "refused a marriage settlement, and took little from her."

92 Foster (p. 192) gives the laboratory site its Welsh name, Tor Clawdd. Walska's automobile visit mentioned by Foster is not confirmed elsewhere and may be imaginary. Adams (pp. 252–53) implies that Walska and Grindell never saw each other after the marriage, although she sent him periodic remittances.

93 Although Walska claims to have read six dailies in as many languages every morning (ART, p. 165), current affairs rarely figure in her memoirs. In ART, she gives little notice to either world war, and what she does write is better overlooked. For example, she was well disposed toward Mussolini, who accorded her a much longer audience than he did to others (pp. 250, 420–21); and approved of Portugal's Salazar (p. 427). She favored a united Europe (p.144) and instant peace (on Grindell Matthews making war impossible, pp. 444, 446). She seems unaware of the Great Depression (p. 480). On the Rolls Royces, see Jess Pourret, "32AE: The McCormick Silver Ghost (1920 Kellner tourer)," *Rolls Royce Enthusiasts' Club Bulletin* 166 (January– February 1988): 55–56; for crating of valuables, see Adams (p. 257–58), who also describes the generally favorable condition of her houses and possessions through the war (pp. 338–39). Enrich Straram, manager of the TCE, had a part in their preservation. After the war, many of the movables were shipped to America.

94 According to Crawford (p. 16), "she escaped France on the last commercial passenger ship before the German occupation in 1940." Similarly, Adams (p. 478) evokes a hair-raising escape from Europe. The reality was less dramatic: "13 U.S. Citizens Arrive on Clipper. [Gen. Reilly] and Ganna Walska Are Aboard American Flying Boat" (*New York Times* [October 10, 1939]: 48). The story specifies that the plane left from Lisbon (which Walska probably reached undramatically from Paris by rail). For her transatlantic flight see ART (p. 482). The flight from Lisbon to New York with one (refueling) stop took a little more than one full day. "The standard of luxury on Pan American's Boeing 314s has rarely been matched by heavier-than-air transport since then; they were a form of travel for the super-rich" (https://en.wikipedia.org/wiki/ Boeing_314_Clipper). Perhaps because of the high cost of the flight, her plane carried fewer passengers than its capacity for overnight accommodation allowed. Adams (p. 258) says that the ticket cost was $375 one way (2017 equivalent is $6,600), which is confirmed (www.clipperflyingboats.com/ transatlantic-airline-service).

95 The life of Theos Casimir Bernard up to meeting Walska and their relations afterwards are chronicled in detail in two biographies, one by Paul Hackett and the other by Douglas Veenhof. These accounts also explain why and how he has had an enduring influence, through his books, among persons interested in Eastern spirituality and New Age themes. WorldCat lists German, French, Spanish, and Vietnamese translations of his books. Influenced by his exploitative relationship with Walska, my encapsulation of his career and character is more negative than the assessments by his biographers. An unsympathetic British account of Bernard's time in Tibet is in Hackett's *Theos Bernard, The White Lama* (pp. 296–98). All Bernard's wives were accomplished women (besides Walska, they were Viola Wertheim, a psychiatrist, and Helen Park, an interior decorator, who never married him). None remarried after him, and all lived to their nineties or close. Unlike his other relationships, Bernard's with Walska was tumultuous, at least in the closing years. For his doctoral thesis, Bernard first submitted a warmed-over version of his master's thesis. The examiners at Columbia rejected it as too thin and laid down necessary revisions. It was agreed at the second submission that an acceptable minimum of the revisions had been made and that, because the work was an account of personal experiences, scientific documentation could be dispensed with. One guesses that, as sometimes happens in academic life, the examiners wanted to be rid of Bernard, standards be damned. 1947 was a bad year for a journey to India; the division of India into Hindu and Muslim parts took place amidst hideous sectarian strife. Helen Park had remained with Bernard until his ill-fated excursion; helped by the authorities and the American embassy, she made every effort to find him. Once enough years passed for him to be declared dead, it became possible to begin the dispersion of his vast legacy of Tibetiana.

96   Walska tells that her "admiration for the people of India was great and has remained so ever since" in ART (p. 36). The parts of ART most relevant to her attraction to Eastern wisdom concern Paul Brunton (a noted mediator between East and West) and Meher Baba (pp. 254–65, 373–80). For more on Brunton, see https://en.wikipedia.org/wiki/Paul_Brunton. The Hotel Pierre is at Fifth Avenue and 61st Street. It continues to be an especially luxurious establishment. On Walska's relations with Bernard, see Crawford (pp. 17–18); Veenhof (p. 307); Hackett (pp. 313–15); also ART (pp. 487–94). Bernard came to her at her summer rental in Yonkers (Adams, p. 265).

97   ART (p. 488) "prodigy"; "American boy" (p. 492); "physical body" (p. 494).

98   Where Walska's past is concerned, neither of the Bernard biographies is reliable. Veenhof spreads mistakes right and left; Hackett is sparer, but his very loose reading of ART is supplemented with unacknowledged other sources. Both biographers give detailed accounts of the Walska-Bernard relationship, much of which was derived from the Bernard papers in the Bancroft Library. Walska's "My Life with Yogi" is unpublished, but Crawford seems to quote very brief fragments of it

without acknowledgment. It was amply used by Adams (pp. 260–334), whose account of the Bernard marriage is longer and more detailed than those of the more important husbands.

99   Death notice for Grindell Matthews (*Time* [September 22, 1941]: 44): "Died. Harry Grindell Matthews, 61, inventor of a highly publicized 'death ray,' fifth husband of Singer Ganna Walska; in his lonely, electrically guarded bungalow laboratory near Swansea, Wales." He died penniless. A solicitor wrote to Walska asking for £50 for burial expenses, but received no response (Veenhof, p. 308).

100   Walska's final wedding took place in Las Vegas on July 27, 1942 (Veenhof, p. 317), or almost a year into her recent widowhood. Walska willed the properties to Bernard, but retained them in life. The secret of their union was well kept; its revelation when divorce proceedings began made a stir in the newspapers. Walska was sensitive to the age difference between herself and Bernard, and she was not eager for marriage. Bernard had designs on her money, and he spent it freely, sending bills for payment to those in charge of Tibetland (Veenhof, p. 314). Walska claimed that $20,000 went for books. Bernard was building a reference library with purchases from the Gateway Bookshop in New York; see Alan Watts, *In My Own Way: An Autobiography 1915–1965* (NY: Pantheon, 1973, p. 169), which includes a list of Bernard's purchases. Non-consummation of last marriage: Adams (p. 324).

101   On the purchase of Cuesta Linda (later Tibetland, then Lotusland), Veenhof (pp. 310–11), while indispensable, is perhaps too brief to encompass such a complicated transaction; the details he supplies are unverifiable; also see Adams (pp. 273–81). Hackett, *White Lama* (p. 317), is uninterested and focuses instead on Bernard's religious ideas. Crawford (p. 18) comments on Walska's thinking on the subject with a date in September 1941. As well as Cuesta Linda, Walska bought a large estate in the mountains—El Capitan—to be Bernard's study refuge, which he renamed Penthouse of the Gods, i.e., Tibet, as in the title of one of his books. Both properties included extensive buildings (especially Penthouse). Cuesta Linda, the future Lotusland, is in the district of Santa Barbara called Montecito, one of the wealthiest areas in the United States. Veenhof suggests that Walska bought the property at a low price. Maintenance would be costly, but Bernard later complained that she neglected it (Veenhof, pp. 320–21).

102 The plan to install Tibetan scholars at Tibetland focused on Gedun Chöpel, known to Bernard from his Indian voyage. Walska paid Chöpel a small retainer and had her lawyers work hard to get him into the U.S., but in vain (Veenhof, pp. 312–14; Hackett, *White Lama,* pp. 319, 321–22). This is hardly surprising in view of the world situation at the time.

103 In the autumn of 1941, once Walska had taken possession of the now-renamed Tibetland (without Tibetans), her thoughts moved away from the Academy of Literature and lemon trees and toward landscaping: Veenhof (pp. 315 [quotation], 320). Earlier owners had already taken Cuesta Linda in this direction: Gardner (pp. 16–20); Adams (pp. 282–83). Walska had had experience with garden development at Galluis (ART, pp. 447–48). Lockwood de Forest III (or, more usually, "Jr.," 1896–1949) is a celebrated American landscape architect. His homonymous father is better known (https://en.wikipedia.org/wiki/Lockwood_de_Forest).

104 About Walska and Bernard in New York (1941–45), see Hackett, *White Lama* (pp. 324–25); Veenhof (pp. 317–23); Adams (pp. 301–305). They spent time in New York both before and during their marriage. Bernard had a floor of the house, where he held classes (Veenhof, p. 317). He and Walska

continued together in the winter of 1944–45, then Bernard went to his Penthouse in March 1945 and she to Tibetland in April, returning to New York in October. Throughout the 1940s, Walska was a conspicuous figure at the opera. In an article headlined "Opera First Night a Brilliant Event" (*New York Times* [November 25, 1941]: 30) we learn that, on that night, Walska's guests in Box 4 were the ambassador of Poland and his wife, and the financial attaché to the Polish embassy. Later, "At the Opera" (*Time* [December 10, 1945]: 67) informs us that "Ex-singer Ganna Walska generously exposed her midriff in a Lakmé sort of gown and stole the show, so far as the tabloid cameramen were concerned, from Mrs. George Washington Kavanaugh." Referring to the Met years earlier, Bill Cunningham recalled that: "Not to be outdone in Box 4 [on Monday], directly across from Mrs. Vanderbilt, was the opulent Ganna Walska, wearing three enormous emerald necklaces, swathed in sable and sprouting a feathered headdress" ("Nights at the Opera," *New York Times* [September 4, 1985]: SM36). Cochran had given her a sable coat 20 years before. Was this the same coat? See Veenhof (pp. 321–22) on Walska showing off her young lover; he quotes from unflattering yellow-press articles from 1943 that were more damaging to Bernard, who had received good notices for his Tibetan exploits, than to Walska. This was also the year when *Always Room at the Top* was published, so not a bad time for publicity, no matter how derogatory. For a later Met opening, see Adams (pp. 323–24).

105 Hackett, *White Lama* (pp. 329–39) and Veenhof (pp. 323, 334–37) discuss Bernard's cheating. His paramour was Helen Park. The secret relationship was revealed when Bernard inadvertently switched letters, sending Walska the one meant for Park (Hackett, pp. 338–39; Veenhof, pp. 323–24); but Walska could not tell from the contents of the letter that another woman was intended. Immediately afterward, assuming that the truth was out, Bernard started to prepare for divorce by removing property not just from his refuge, but from all the houses. Veenhof (p. 336) says the relationship with Park was chaste until the divorce. Hackett, however, documents trysts in various places, east and west. (Curiously, Adams never mentions the switched letters.) Despite the indiscretion, Walska remained sufficiently in the dark that Bernard initiated the divorce, and her voluminous countersuit never named Park or mentioned adultery. The ongoing quarrel with Bernard came about because she, refusing money from outside donors (Veenhof, p. 310), had undertaken to finance all of his ambitious projects (real estate, the academy, Tibetan-language publications, etc.) but, pleading poverty, was not doing so but rather developing her garden (Veenhof, pp. 315, 320, 327). She complained to Bernard that her income was only $3,000 per month and that she had gone deeply into debt to sustain her expenditures, including those for him (Veenhof, p. 321). Adams (pp. 336–37) is somewhat more believable in his mention of an income of about $250,000 per year during the period from 1942 to 1945, and he paints a rosy picture: "her total assets at this time were estimated by [her lawyer] at between three and five million dollars." (Adams does nothing to justify the high income figures, however, making them hard to credit.) Gardner (p. 130) affirms that she was very wealthy in her later years, and did not need to auction off her jewels in 1971 to finance her cycad garden: "By then, [the almost $1 million proceeds of the jewel sale] was a small portion of her wealth." But he doesn't explain. Adams (p. 404) claims the opposite because the value of her IH stock was sinking, making the sale of her superfluous jewels appropriate. Gardner (pp. 110–11) calls Walska "an astute businesswoman.... She died a multimillionaire." An interesting comment, and apparently true, but it leaves us asking how her finances were sustained. Along these lines, "When the income from her stock in the International Harvester Company declined precipitously, she stubbornly refused to sell her shares in the company, which had been the source of much of her wealth" (Chiacos, p. 62); instead she sold jewels. Wikipedia, "International Harvester" (https://en.wikipedia.org/wiki/International_Harvester) suggests that the company went into a precipitous decline from 1979 on, seemingly too near Walska's death to be relevant to the quotation. Walska's finances are best reported by Adams, but how she managed to leave almost $10 million to the Lotusland Foundation, as she is said to have done, is hard to understand (Adams, p. 444). Our knowledge of Walska's finances rests on Adams's say-so rather than on documentary evidence; it's very imperfect.

106 Bernard's father, Glen, was the family's original adept of Oriental philosophy and had had a long, beneficial relationship with his son. Bernard brought him to share the Penthouse in 1944. Calling him LaVarnie, he did not initially reveal their relationship to Walska, who did not take to Glen.

107 Walska's arrival at Burbank is related dramatically by Adams (pp. 325–27); presumably he got his material from "My Life with Yogi." Served with the divorce papers, but without her Cadillac, Walska had to take a taxi from the Burbank airport to Montecito. Bernard and his father plotted a major raid on Walska's wealth. On the personal side, Bernard's ostensible poverty, poor health, and rich tastes acquired in married life—Hackett (p. 342) quotes him saying he was "spoiled by the life she provided him"—were presented as justifying high alimony. On the property side, the more ambitious part of the suit, Walska's failure to fulfill any of her many undertakings for Bernard's enterprises was argued to justify the transfer to Bernard of the two West Coast properties along with the wherewithal to carry out needed maintenance and repairs. Walska's lawyer had little trouble driving off Bernard, especially by extracting the admission that his claim of poverty was false (outright perjury) and that he had considerable resources, notably a trust fund given him by his first wife when they divorced. Bernard's alleged ill health was discredited by forcing the admission that he stood on his head for three hours at a time. Since none of Walska's undertakings for Bernard's projects occasioned written contracts, that part of the suit was disregarded; see the accounts by Hackett (pp. 340–46), Veenhof (pp. 331–33), and Adams (pp. 328–34); also newspaper stories: "Suit Discloses Fifth Ganna Walska Marriage" (*Los Angeles Times* [May 26, 1946]: A3); "He Can't Work but Stands on His Head for 3 Hours" (*Gettysburg Times*, July 6, 1946: google search, retrieved March 13, 2013); "Madame Walska Fights Her Yogi Husband's Suit" (*Chicago Tribune* [July 9, 1946]: 6); "Ganna Walska Fights Mate's Support Suit" (*Los Angeles Times* [July 9, 1946]: A-1); "Ganna Walska Is Freed" (*New York Times* [July 14, 1946]: 31). I am very grateful to my friend William Summers, professor emeritus of medical history at Yale (and a member of the Elizabethan Club), for supplying me with a number of documents, including a copy of Bernard's complaint and, especially, Walska's countersuit to Bernard's charges and demands, which he obtained from the Bancroft Library at Berkeley. They include colorful allegations and accusations.

108 "Leasing a house in town, Theos and Glen began grabbing everything they could carry from the Tibetland estate" (Hackett, p. 339). This was in the wake of sending the Helen Park letter to Walska. When she arrived from Burbank, Walska found her house stripped of its furnishings (Adams, p. 327). Perhaps the most interesting part of the Bernard story is what happened and will happen to the great hoard he brought out of Tibet in 1937, much of which has been distributed among various units of the University of California at Berkeley. About books at Yale, see *Hartford Courant* (November 28, 1963): 75C; and *New*

York Times (November 26, 1964): 30. Some books are almost unique, often printed from carved wooden blocks that today are burned for fuel by the Chinese. Other books from Bernard's hoard are at the University of Vienna. The Yale volumes appear to be unused and remain virtually uncatalogued. Hackett, who prepared a valuable study guide to Bernard's papers at Berkeley, disregards this part of the story. Veenhof (pp. 385–90) takes serious interest without exhausting the subject. The uncovering of the secreted Bernard treasures in 1999 moves one's imagination.

109 Walska's prophetic remark, "forces in me," was written in 1941 at the latest (ART, p. 54). A party for the distinguished tenor Lauritz Melchior, August 19, 1952, is an example of her entertaining at Lotusland (Adams, p. 371).

110 Anne Pavord, "Lotusland in California," in *The Independent* (London) (November 24, 2001): 14.

111 For the nursery visit to Los Angeles, see Chiacos (p. 33). Walska's inspiration and labor in designing and laying out the garden needed to be supplemented. Kirst, "Landmarks" (pp. 48–54) provides a list of the many persons involved in bringing the Lotusland gardens to their current perfected state.

112 Lehmann obituary: *New York Times* (August 27, 1976): A1. No sign of Walska's ever having sung with Lehmann has come my way. The two of them were paired in a photograph in the *Los Angeles Times* (June 11, 1954): part III (GWA), captioned: "Opera Greats: Mme. Ganna Walska, at left, and Mme. Lotte Lehman, at right," in the context of encouraging a group of young singers. Walska could hardly do better than being presented as an "opera great" on a par with Lotte Lehman. GWA contains a telegram of thanks from "Lotte" to Madame Ganna Walska, August 8, 1960. Clearly, they were on friendly terms.

Appendix 2.1

THE STEMBER PORTRAIT

The central piece of evidence documenting Walska's life among high nobility (e.g., consorting with the czar of Russia's family) and great wealth (enjoying rich clothing and extensive travels) is a portrait of her by the Russian artist Victor Stember (d. 1921), painted in 1912 and now at Lotusland. The explanation of this portrait favored at Lotusland tells that, at an imperial ball, the czar singled out Walska as the most beautiful woman present and had her portrait painted by a court artist for display at the Hermitage Museum in St. Petersburg (Crawford, p. 8; there are minor variations elsewhere). In the caption of the portrait reproduction at the Stember website (www.victorstember.com/stember_gallery.aspx; retrieved February 26, 2017), Hania Tallmadge, Walska's niece, adds "Shtember painted her in 1912 and held the painting in his possession until his death in 1921. Walska left Russia before the painting was complete.... Walska told her that she did not know the whereabouts of the painting until she received it from Shtember's wife in her home in Paris in 1922." There are two faults in the Tallmadge version: according to Stember's wife, in the account reproduced below, the finished portrait was exhibited twice in Russia, in 1912 and 1913; and a photograph of Walska and the Stember portrait was published in the *New York Sun* on June 18, 1916. In *Always Room at the Top* (ART), Walska's 1943 memoirs, she tells a story similar to the Lotusland version giving different but still "imperial" circumstances; she claims to have bought the finished portrait from the needy artist after the Russian Revolution (p. 398). This version is repeated and filled out by Adams (pp. 32–33), who identifies the painter as Victor Stemberg.

In that same website caption, a completely different story begins below the one by Tallmadge. Here, the speaker is Stember's widow, Nadejda. She calls Walska by her professional name, Ganna Valska, not Hannah Puacz or

Baroness Eingorn or Madame Ganna Walska. The Stembers saw her at the theatre and, finding her to be "exceptionally beautiful," invited her to sit for a portrait. The artist believed that, although there was no commission, the portrait would sell for a good price. For the portrait, the artist dressed Walska in rich clothes, and the finished canvas was exhibited twice in Russia (1912, 1913), where it was admired but not bought. Walska moved to Paris in 1913. She invited Stember to send her the portrait so as to exhibit it at the Paris Salon. Tempted, Stember sent it to her in 1914. War broke out, interrupting relations. Stember, still in St. Petersburg, now renamed Petrograd, heard in 1918 that Walska, by then in New York, had married a rich man, Cochran. (The rumor could have reached Stember only after September 1920.) Stember wrote to her to request that she send $5,000 to his daughter, who was in the U.S. and in need. Walska replied that Stember had been misinformed about her wealth.

Nadejda continues: Stember died in 1921. Years passed. A photograph of Walska (then Mrs. Harold McCormick) with her portrait appeared in a mass-market magazine in February 1929. (The newspaper photo of Walska with her portrait that was published on June 18, 1916, is unlikely to be the one discussed here.) Stember's daughter saw the magazine picture. (The next information, complementing Nadejda's account, was reported in both the *New York Times* and the *Chicago Tribune,* which are transcribed below.) In February 1929, Stember's daughter sued Walska for $10,000, her stated owed price for the portrait in Walska's possession. The suit came to trial in 1932 with Walska winning complete victory because the claimant had no valid proof.

THE STEMBER PORTRAIT:
NADEJDA STEMBER'S STORY

(Copied from Stember "Gallery" webpage)

The following excerpt is from "Story of My Life," by Victor Stember's widow Nadejda, as dictated in Russian to her sister-in-law Olga Fuhrman and translated by Nadejda's daughter Natalie Warren in 1935.

Once Victor was severely punished for his overly trusting character. Once we both saw in a theater an exceptionally beautiful young woman! Victor said to me "If only I could get her in my studio…. I would paint her portrait that would create an ecstasy! Will you try to talk to her about it?" But I said: "You cannot paint a portrait if she does not order it, what will you do with a portrait on your hands?" "Never mind, when she will see herself painted, she will buy it or make somebody to buy it for her…. Anyway it will bring me more orders—the portrait I'll paint of her will be something extraordinary! Please get acquainted with her and present me to her. I'll make the offer myself!" So I approached her during the intermission when she stopped in front of the mirror to powder her face, saying "Excuse me Madam, permit me to present myself—I am the wife of the portrait painter Stember. He noticed your beauty and asks the permission to be presented to you—if you don't mind." She exclaimed: "Stember? Is he here in the theater? … Yes, yes let him come," but Victor was already approaching and the acquaintance was made.

Next day she appeared at the studio. Her name was Ganna Valska (Polish origin). She was a performer (singer) at one of the dashing night clubs. She would gladly pose for a portrait…. It was decided that she would appear on the portrait wearing [an] ermine coat (half off), electro-blue brocade gown and a paradisean feather in her hair! Then Victor took several photo-shots in different poses to chose for the portrait and made an appointment for the first sitting.

When in a few days the canvas for the portrait was delivered (ready on the stretcher), I was astounded by the size of it. It definitely was much larger than any of Victor's paintings of a single person was ever before....[1]

When sittings began she was always late for the appointment and since the daylight during the winter is very short—sittings were short too, and the progress was slow. She could never be earlier than 2 p.m. (possibly directly from the cabaret) always tired, sleepy, and sometimes not too sober.... Nevertheless the portrait was finished in time for the Spring Exhibition. When set in the beautiful golden frame, it really was something extraordinary! It is hard to describe the reaction of Ganna when she saw the finished portrait (Victor did not let her see it until it was complete): She was actually beside herself with rapture and could not tear her eyes from it! Of course she wanted to have it and swore that she will find someone who will get it for her.

At the exhibition (it was 1912) it attracted big crowds and was no doubt the most outstanding piece of art among the exhibits that spring! Victor was the center of the "talks." There was an article in the paper full of praise.... People were congratulating him.... Yes, he received several orders for the portraits, but ... Ganna Valska's portrait came from the exhibition back to the studio.... Just what I was afraid of and was warning Victor about....

In the winter of 1913 the unfortunate portrait was adorning one of the walls of Victor's Jubilee exhibition and again came home at the end of it. In the spring of 1914 Victor received a letter from Ganna

1 The Gallery of the Stember website (www.victorstember.com/stember_gallery.aspx) reproduces ca. 208 paintings, only two of which are head-to-toe portraits—those of Walska and of Anna Pavlova, the great ballerina. See *New York Times* ([March 15, 2018]: C1, C5) for a report on a New York exhibition of full-length portraits from the sixteenth to the twentieth century. The story is headlined, "Self-Promotion from Head to Toe: When the full-length portrait was the most expensive form of representation." (The Stember Gallery includes about 15 three-quarter-length portraits, but none of that size was included in the New York exhibition.) Clearly the Walska painting was not just any old portrait, but a notable, self-promoting image.

Valska, she wrote from Paris saying that if Victor would send her portrait to Paris, it would be exhibited at the "*Salon*"—no doubt Mr. Stember would not want to miss a chance of such a honorable offer to have his work admitted to the "*world famous Salon*"! So much the more she is sure that one of her new friends (or admirers) will certainly purchase it for her!... Victor was very excited—his work—in the "*Salon*"! Who could resist it? Of course he will send the portrait to Paris....

I did not agree.... Yes the "honor" was great but there is no guarantee that the portrait will be paid for! Victor would not hear any objections—and the portrait was sent to Ganna Valska... (I said goodbye to it)....

In July of the same 1914 the war with Germany started and communications with abroad became unreliable.... The destiny of the portrait became unknown! The big drastic events followed one another: war expanded to become World War and protracted until the revolution of 1917 and soon after the Bolshevik revolution and endless dreadful civil war....

About in 1918 Victor heard a rumor that Ganna Valska is in New York and is married to a millionaire—Cochran—and that her portrait is also in New York![2]

He immediately wrote two letters: one to Ganna—congratulating her with the happy turn in her life [and] giving her feasibility to compensate him at last for the portrait. Adding that since Russia is now in a turmoil, she would render him a favor by forwarding five thousand dollars to his daughter, Natasha Voinova, who finds herself in New York with her husband and three-year-old son in difficult financial situation. The second letter was for

2 The rumor of Walska's marriage to Cochran would have had to come no earlier than September 1920, when it took place, and Stember's letters would have had to be sent between September 1920 and his death the next year—a narrow window. Walska's marriage from 1916 to 1920 to Dr. Fraenkel, who was rich but not a millionaire, would better suit the circumstances. Confusion is possible.

Natasha—enclosing the copy of the letter to Ganna, he advised her to also write to her with the same idea. Natasha did it and received an answer where Ganna said that unfortunately the rumors about her wealth are very much exaggerated, that she also has relatives in Poland to whom she sends all she can spare … that she is sorry … and so on.… Not a word about the fact that she owes money for the portrait!

Meanwhile, in 1929 Natasha happened to see in a magazine [*Time,* February 25, 1929] a large-sized photo of Ganna—standing by her portrait, and the printing line under saying that "Mrs. Ganna McCormick (formerly Cochran) near her portrait painted by a distinguished European artist."[3] That gave Natasha hope that *now* Ganna cannot say that her wealth is exaggerated.… She was advised to bring the case to court, [and] she did. But Ganna … instead of offering Natasha five thousand—she paid her attorneys and they won the case declaring that Stember *gave* the portrait to Mme Valska! All the proof Natasha had that it was not so … was her Father's letter—asking to be at last compensated for his work! It was not enough!

---

3 When I examined the February 25, 1929, issue of *Time,* I did not find the photograph in question. (Besides, the lawsuit was filed on February 22, three days before the indicated date for the photograph's being first seen.) Further search in issues of *Time* from 1928 and 1929 was also unsuccessful.

THE LAWSUIT

New York Times (February 22, 1929): 1
Sues Ganna Walska for $10,000
A suit against Mme. Ganna Walska to recover $10,000 for an oil portrait
of the singer, was disclosed in Supreme Court yesterday when Justice Bijur
signed an order allowing her until March 12 to answer the complaint. The
action was brought by Mrs. Natalie Warren, administratrix of the estate of
her father, Victor Stember, who is said to have painted the picture in Russia
in 1913.

Chicago Daily Tribune (January 20, 1932): 13
Ganna Walska Wins Suit Over Portrait of Herself
A swift victory was won by Ganna Walska, singer, today when Supreme
Court Justice Isidor Wasservogel dismissed a $10,000 action against her
without Mme. Walska having appeared in court or having put on a single
defense witness. The suit was brought to recover the price of her portrait
in oils. The Judge held Mrs. Natalie Warren was unable to prove a contract
existed between her father, the late Victor Stemper [*sic*], Russian artist, and
Mme Walska.
(A briefer version ran in the *Los Angeles Times* [January 20, 1932]: 1)

Appendix 2.2

ARCADIE EINGORN AND THE COCHRAN DIVORCE

> Mme Walska is said to have been greatly disappointed at the
> amount of money she receives. She is said to have wanted $500,000.
> At one time it was reported that she would get $1,500,000.
> (*New York Evening World* [June 7, 1922]: 16)

When Cochran separated from Ganna Walska in April 1921, he had no
legally admissible grounds for divorce. Her lawyer, Dudley Field Malone,
emphasized this fact when interviewed by the press that October. Cochran
must learn, Malone added, that his wife was not like the houses, horses, and
yachts he discarded at pleasure. But Cochran did discard his blameless wife
for a very small part of his wealth. He succeeded in limiting his alimony
to Walska to the "greatly disappointing" sum of $20,000 per year—the
proceeds of a $300,000 trust fund that was topped up annually to yield the
promised income. How was this result achieved in a divorce suit that had
no basis in Walska's conduct?

As it turned out, what mattered was Walska's history: the Cochran
divorce hinged on Walska's divorce from her first husband, Arcadie Eingorn.
Cochran's approach was to prove that Mme Walska had not been free to
remarry and so the union of Cochran and Walska had been null and void.
Also central to the suit was the question whether Eingorn was alive or dead
when Walska and Cochran were married.

Walska wedded Cochran on September 15, 1920, after an engagement
that dated from July, soon after her introduction to Cochran aboard
the *Aquitania*. (Contrary to what she writes in ART, a newspaper article
contemporary with Walska's marriage to Harold McCormick reports that
she was engaged to Cochran by the time they disembarked in Europe

[*New York Evening World* (August 12, 1922): 3]. Her recent past had been respectable and decorous: she was the widow of Dr. Joseph Fraenkel, whom she married in 1916 and who died in April 1920. Fraenkel, a prosperous doctor with a New York town house and a comfortable income, had not only encouraged Walska's singing but also arranged fashionable summer rentals on Long Island and made possible a social life among distinguished persons, such as the noted Belgian violinist Eugène Ysaÿe (*Music Magazine–Musical Courier* 75 [1917]: 149). When introduced to Cochran on shipboard Walska was the protégée of none other than Harold McCormick, president of International Harvester and also president of the Chicago Opera. (Cochran and McCormick knew each other.) McCormick had accepted Walska's avowal that she was an established operatic soprano, and he engaged her to sing the title role in Leoncavallo's *Zaza* in Chicago the following December. It is hard to tell what more about her Cochran learned between their July shipboard romance and September wedding, but quite a few details of her earlier life were in circulation in New York. A long, unsigned, syndicated feature article that appeared in American newspapers on October 10, 1920—one day after the newly wed Cochran and Walska landed in New York from Paris—rehearsed these details (e.g., *Philadelphia Inquirer* [October 10, 1920]: 73; *Washington Post* [October 10, 1920]: 64). A trail of stories in the press had followed Walska ever since her arrival in America in 1915.

Several incidents in her past would have a future in the Cochran divorce. The press noted that, in 1915, during her first month in New York, on the eve of a planned debut, she learned that her husband, a captain in the Russian army, had been killed in the war. Her debut was postponed. This heroic end of her spouse assured Walska status as a war widow, but it was not confirmed by official notification of his death. Finally making her New York debut, she appeared in a French operetta that opened in April. More facts became available in the announcement of an August engagement to the very rich Lowell Palmer, Jr., when it was reported that she was Polish, of royal blood (a Leszsynska), and that her late husband Arcadie Eingorn had been a baron. Although Eingorn's death had still not been officially certified, several newspapers from early 1915 reported him as deceased

(*Chicago Daily Tribune* [February 14, 1916]: 1; in GWA: *Morning Telegraph* (January or February 27, 1915); Biographical Documents 1915 and 1917; *New York Tribune* [April 25, 1915]: n.p.). After the Palmer engagement ended, the scene shifts to September 1916, the eve of Walska's marriage to Dr. Fraenkel. According to Adams's biography (p. 46), "she had now received a document from the Russian Orthodox Church granting an ecclesiastical divorce from Arcadie Eingorn before his demise on the Prussian battlefield, which provided sufficient evidence for the New York authorities, in lieu of a death certificate, for [Walska and Fraenkel] to be married." (Adams's book lacks documentation, and it is uncertain whether what he relates has a source basis or is merely his surmise.) So, at the time of the Fraenkel marriage (September 1916), there still was no official notice of Eingorn's death. In lieu of such notice, to prove that Walska was free to marry again, a document was produced certifying a Russian church-sanctioned divorce. With that document in hand, the marriage could proceed. The Fraenkel union was when the story of a divorce from Eingorn first entered the narrative of Walska's marriages.

The account of Walska's early history that circulated generally at the time can be summarized as follows: she began as a lady of royal blood, resident in Warsaw; Eingorn was a baron; he and Walska had eloped to St. Petersburg, and they later divorced; she came to Paris, then to America; he was killed while fighting in the war, but his death had not been officially certified. On the strength of her divorce from Eingorn, Walska married Dr. Fraenkel, only to be widowed again four years later.

In seeking his divorce, Cochran obtained the services of Samuel Untermyer, one of the most famous New York lawyers of his day and a Yonkers neighbor of Cochran. (For more on Untermyer, see *Who Was Who in America* vol. 1, *1897–1942* [Chicago: Marquis, 1942], p. 1254; Gil Troy, "Samuel Untermyer: The Superlawyer Who Took on Hitler," *Daily Beast* (November 19, 2017) https://www.thedailybeast.com/samuel-untermyer-the-superlawyer-turned-superlandscaper [retrieved April 19, 2019]; Bill Cary, "Samuel Untermyer: A Man for All Seasons," *Westchester* (May 24, 2017) https://westchestermagazine.com/publications/samuel-untermyer-a-man-for-all-seasons/ [retrieved April 19, 2019]; Richard Hawkins,

"Samuel Untermyer (1858–1940)," *Immigrant Entrepreneurship: German-American Business Biographies,* https://www.immigrantentrepreneurship.org/entry.php?rec=181 [retrieved April 19, 2019]). The Cochran and Untermeyer properties had adjoined each other until Cochran sold his portion to Untermeyer a few years earlier. Celebrated mainly as a corporation lawyer, Untermeyer did not normally do divorces. Cochran was fortunate to secure this exceptional legal talent.

It seems as though, in the early months of the separation, Cochran tried to avoid legal complications and to end the marriage quickly, with a minimum of bad feelings. He offered Walska an annual payment of $10,000 in return for a speedy, uncontested divorce. In October 1921, Walska's lawyer, Malone, was aware of this paltry offer (*New York Herald* [October 4, 1921]: 6). Cochran, who harbored no ill will toward his wife, must have thought that an annual $10,000 plus the rich presents he had given her were adequate compensation for what had been, in effect, a six-month marriage. This offer was rejected as derisory, especially from a man suing for divorce with no grounds. When speaking to the press, Malone empha-sized Cochran's weakness in this regard. Untermyer's task was to undermine Walska's resistance to Cochran's substantial but, in her view, inadequate offer.

In the summer of 1921, someone working for Cochran or his lawyer investigated Walska's early history, probably traveling to Poland for that purpose. The results of the European research were summed up in a newspaper article published on September 27, 1921, headlined "Cochran's Marriage to Polish Actress Illegal" (*New York Herald,* image 1; datelined from Paris, September 26). This dispatch—identified in the bibliography as Biographical Document 1921—is a comprehensive challenge to the account of Walska's life outlined above. (The three paragraphs from this document quoted below have been reversed sequentially from the published order so as to clarify the chronology.)

> The story is that Mme. Walska at the time of her first marriage was none other than plain Hannah Puaoz, member of an obscure and humble family of Sieldec [Siedlce]. She is said to have one brother, Leon Puaoz. Capt. d'Eingorn, instead of being a baron in his own right, is now said to have been "the descendant of a baron."

The legal action between Mr. Cochran and his wife … will revolve
around Mme. Walska's first marriage and subsequent separation
from Capt. d'Eingorn, to whom she was married in Poland when
she was 17. Her argument, it is said, will be that she obtained
an ecclesiastical divorce on the grounds of drunkenness in April,
1914, through the Synod of the Holy Russian church. No such
grounds for a decree exist, the only grounds that do exist for a [*sic*]
ecclesiastical divorce in the Russian church are the same as the
statutory grounds for divorce in New York State.…

It is Mr. Cochran's intention to challenge the legality of his
marriage to the Polish singer on the ground that she was never
legally divorced from her first husband, Capt. Archadie d'Eingorn
of the Russian army, that he was still alive at the time of her
marriage to Mr. Cochran. Friends of Cochran have said that the
Russian officer is alive yet.

The document setting out Cochran's side of the suit begins by sweeping
away the trappings of nobility from Walska's biography. She was neither
of royal blood nor from Warsaw; and Eingorn, though somehow related
to a baron, was not one himself. Siedlce is a small town between Warsaw
and Brest-Litovsk; that it was Walska's birthplace is contradicted by a birth
certificate (in GWA) issued in Brest-Litovsk. Then there is her brother Leon.
In 1921, when the investigation took place, Leon presumably was found in
Siedlce and invited the conclusion that his sister Hannah came from there
too. (A unique detail: the presence of Leon's name helps to authenticate
the European investigation by Cochran's counsel. Besides the 1921 document, the only place where Leon's name is given is Adams's biography of
2015 [p. 342]! In ART [p. 185] he is alluded to but never named.) In Siedlce
or Brest, Walska had humble origins at the time of her marriage to the
non-noble Captain Eingorn, and the document gives no indication that
Eingorn was a casualty of World War I. To make up for this fact, Walska
in 1916 had shown proof of a Russian divorce so as to clear the way for
marriage to Fraenkel. It was now explained that the Holy Synod of the
Russian Orthodox Church had granted an ecclesiastical divorce from

Eingorn in April 1914 on the grounds of his drunkenness. If Walska was not liberated by Eingorn's death, her marriage to him had ended by divorce nevertheless. Untermyer rejected the validity of this divorce, maintaining that the alleged grounds were baseless, since the Russian church only accepted the same grounds for divorce as those established by New York State (namely, at the time, only adultery). Cochran's lawyer took it as fact that no valid divorce from Eingorn could be documented, but even more startling was the claim that Eingorn was still alive at the time of the Cochran wedding in September 1920. Doubly illegal, the Cochran marriage was null, and there could be no question of a financial settlement beyond what had been offered, which was not revoked.

The evidence for illegality was strong if the contestable parts could be proved. To underscore the nullity of the union with Walska, Cochran obtained a writ of replevin to remove from the Fraenkel-Walska house on 94th Street the new furnishings he had supplied for it in their first weeks of marriage. The removal was carried out with legal formality within days of the claim that the marriage had been illegal ("Cochran Gets Writ for $25,000 of Art Pieces Taken from Home of Mme Walska, His Wife," *New York Times* [September 29, 1921]: 2; the *Philadelphia Inquirer* edition of the same day [p. 4], gives a fuller account). Another early Cochran move—to lock Walska out of the Paris house—had been thwarted by her lawyer, and she retained possession. (Cochran continued to be its owner, and he later sold the house to Harold McCormick: *New York Times* [May 2, 1922]: 1; *New York Evening World* [May 4, 1922]: 4). Some of the objects seized from the Fraenkel house were itemized when, after the divorce, Walska and Cochran reached an agreement about the removal during their separation (*New York Herald* [September 1, 1922]: 20).

In early October 1921, a few days after the Cochran side laid out its case, Malone reached New York from Paris and was interviewed by reporters. What did he have to say to the contention that the Cochran-Walska marriage had been "irregular"? "Mr. Malone ... [replied] that not only was the divorce obtained in Russia strictly legal, but that the singer's first husband died a year before the marriage to Mr. Cochran" (*New York Herald*

[October 4, 1921]: 6). Walska's spokesman admitted a sensational fact: after years of being a war fatality, Captain (no-longer baron) Eingorn turned out to have outlived the World War at least until 1919, in any case uncomfortably close to the time when his survival would make the Cochran marriage bigamous. But the case had not been lost. Malone demanded $500,000, whether as a lump sum or annually is not wholly clear. His decisive asset was the point of departure: that Cochran lacked grounds for divorce (*Minneapolis Tribune* [October 17, 1921]: 11); "Diva Increases Divorce Price. Wants $500,000 if Millionaire is to Have Freedom," *San Francisco Chronicle* (October 17, 1921): 1; also in the *New York Tribune* of that date (p. 6). Although disquieting facts had been brought to light, Cochran seemed not to be in a position to corroborate them decisively.

Contemporary press reports did not endorse the claims made by Cochran's side, and they disregarded Eingorn's being alive. They sympathized with Walska by fastening on her Russian divorce and trying to improve her version of it included in Biographical Document 1921. But Eingorn is no longer referred to as a baron, nor is Walska said to be of royal blood. "[Walska married at seventeen] …. The couple separated and the wife went to Paris…. Soon she secured, through the efforts of a Russian priest in Paris, a writ of divorce from the dashing captain" (Jane Dixon, *New York Evening Telegram* [October 4, 1921]: 3).

Dixon corrected a flaw in Walska's version by taking into account that in April 1914 she resided in Paris, not Russia. Accordingly, Dixon introduced for the first time a Russian priest in Paris, perhaps invented by Malone. (This priest remained in the story as recently as 2015 in Adams's biography [p. 34]). The priest turned up again 12 days later in a syndicated article by Marjorie Wilson: "In 1915 she sought New York. With her she brought a writ of divorce from d'Eingorn that she had received from a Russian priest in Paris. It was granted on the grounds of drunkenness." A few lines later, Wilson reports Captain d'Eingorn's death in battle (*Atlanta Constitution* [October 16, 1921]: 23). Wilson lent much support to Walska's side. Walska was correctly traced to New York. She had received a writ of divorce from the Paris priest, and the ridiculed grounds of drunkenness had a new outing. Most valuable of all, Eingorn was again said to have been killed in the war. If these circumstances were correct, Walska had been doubly free to marry Cochran legally.

After this, the progress of the Cochran divorce slowed down. Fall and winter passed, and it was only in March of the next year, after a two-month postponement reluctantly granted by Untermyer (*New York Times* [March 31, 1922]: 13), that the case reappeared in the press. Cochran's argument was again presented:

> Investigation, it was learned, indicates that Cpt d'Eingorn died at Roskow [possibly Rostov-on-the-Don], Russia, in October 1920, a month after Mme Walska's marriage to Mr. Cochran. Mr. Cochran's lawyers believe that the legality of the marriage may be successfully attacked regardless of Mme Walska's intervening marriage to Dr. Joseph Fraenkel. (*New York Herald* [March 31, 1922]: 8)

The previous October, Malone had contended that Eingorn had died in 1919, not at war in 1915. As was typical of Untermyer's methods, an investigation had been carried out that established both the date and even the place of Eingorn's demise. But, there was an important omission: the Eingorn divorce was not contested or even mentioned. In the same month, Cochran doubled his offer of monetary compensation: it was now $20,000 per year.

The preliminary decree of the Cochran-Walska divorce was granted on May 1, 1922, with the amount of the settlement set at the annual stipend most recently offered. The press was given to understand that the long delay was occasioned by negotiations about finance. Where that was concerned, Walska remained disappointed, but Cochran had not been vindictive: in addition to the doubled yearly stipend, Walska was allowed to keep all the wedding presents he had given her. Walska's lawyer repeated his arguments of the previous year, but conditionally: "Ganna Walska's first husband was Archadie d'Eingorn, a captain in the Russian Army, to whom she is said to have been **married when she was 17**. She alleged that she obtained an ecclesiastical divorce from Eingorn in April 1914, through the Synod of the Holy Russian Church" (*New York Times* [May 2, 1922]: 4). (Notice the abandoned contentions: Eingorn does not die at war, and the Russian priest in Paris vanishes.)

The Cochran side of the case was set out alongside: "Had the settlement not been made at an early date it is believed Mr. Cochran would have gone into the courts and presented affidavits containing sensational charges against his Polish wife" (*Chicago Daily Tribune* [May 2, 1922]: 2). Since adultery was not in question, the sensational charges against Walska would have been bigamy.

For a biographer, the problem overhanging the Cochran-Walska divorce is how Cochran, a very rich man starting from a very weak position, managed to limit his financial settlement to as modest a sum as he did. The probable answer is that he was magnanimous. Having had his lawyer thoroughly debunk Walska's life story, he did not push his advantage to the limit by wholly discrediting the Eingorn divorce and by producing incontrovertible proof—if it was to be had—that Eingorn was alive in September 1920. He was generous enough to allow Walska a respectable pension and call it quits.

The divorce from Cochran was a sad chapter of Walska's life. It is little wonder that this disappointment and most of the circumstances surrounding it were left out of ART and may have colored Walska's emphatically negative assessment of Cochran. Eingorn was banished to a first appearance more than 300 pages into the memoirs, and then not as a dashing cavalry captain and baron, but as a tubercular scapegrace saved from an early death by his 17-year-old spouse—just as imaginative a fable as the noble baronage (ART, pp. 312–14, 320–27). As for Walska, the royal blood was forgotten, but in its place the Stember portrait, in royal robes and surrounded by its legend, was put to work as the document of her early history as a star at the czar's court. One imagined past, not wholly lacking in factual elements, was superseded by another one that was even more imaginary. For Walska, "real life" began with Dr. Fraenkel.

Appendix 2.3

GANNA WALSKA AND ORSON WELLES'S SUSAN ALEXANDER

It is often said that Ganna Walska served as model for the lamentable singer named Susan Alexander, the title character's second wife in Orson Welles's film *Citizen Kane*. One opinion—for example, Conway (https://strangeflowers.wordpress.com/2009/11/02/mrs-kane/ [retrieved March 21, 2017])—is that the then living Ganna Walska was "reborn" in the Susan character, a contemporary celebrity transposed to fiction. Now, Walska may well be associated with the movie character. Writers have multiple inspirations, including living people, and Walska as a poor singer was certainly notorious when the screenplay was written. But to properly understand Walska as well as Susan Alexander, the two women definitely should not be considered interchangeable.

The congruence of Walska and Susan Alexander is this: a soprano with a poor voice is financed by her rich husband and makes repeated, deplorable opera appearances. The way this plot works out for the fictional Susan is wholly unlike the reality of the experience of Walska.

According to the movie's plot, Kane was the Svengali behind Susan Alexander's sad career. She was reluctant to perform, constantly bullied by Kane, and humiliated on the stage. She had no illusions about her voice and no desire to sing publicly, but Kane drove her to do so. Essential to the story is the cause of Kane's bullying. Discovery of his affair with Susan, announced by the newspapers in headlines such as: "Kane Found in Love Nest with 'Singer,'" ruined his run for governor. In order to erase the scornful quotation marks from around the word *singer,* Kane opened his purse and forced poor Susan into a humiliating operatic career she did not want.

With Ganna Walska, the driving force was Walska herself. She was determined, from early in her life, long before she had a rich backer, to be

Madame Ganna Walska, the celebrated operatic soprano. In her twenties she assumed the honorific "Madame" as an enhancement of her stage name; she claimed to be a diva and prima donna, took voice lessons, secured singing dates, and eventually had the very rich Harold McCormick, her fourth husband, finance her appearances in recitals and operas. Even though her singing ability was generally dismissed, continual (often negative) publicity resulted in her being accepted everywhere as a "noted Polish soprano." McCormick's support and her own persistence made her one of the recognized singers of her era. He loved her and paid the bills, but was far from assuming a Kane-like role. On one occasion, in fact, he may have tried half-heartedly to keep her off the stage; this was a condition, evidently not enforced, of her grand prenuptial settlement (*Washington Post* [August 17, 1922]: 1).

Appendix 2.4

THE SORROWS OF MADAME WALSKA: A REVIEW OF *ALWAYS ROOM AT THE TOP* (1943)

Madame Ganna Walska (1887–1984) was a Polish interwar celebrity, widely known in America and Europe as an opera singer with a poor voice and rich husbands. Living deep into her nineties, she spent the later part of her life at Lotusland, her Santa Barbara estate, whose gardens she turned into a superb showplace, now open to the public. Her memoirs, *Always Room at the Top* (here abbreviated "ART"), end before she began her masterly garden development. They are the celebrity's view of herself in her operatic and married years, extending from beginnings in Poland (1887) until 1941, in America, on the eve of her sixth and last marriage. Although this review is mainly written as if of a book recently published, it is an assessment made seven decades after the appearance of ART.

A gossip columnist, upon learning in 1939 that Walska's memoirs were in preparation, commented, "Ought to make very snappy reading" (*Chicago Tribune* [January 7, 1939]: 13). This is not the case. ART is sometimes vague and often boring; it is wholly humorless; and many pages are concerned with describing metaphysical and spiritual quests. A recent commentator outlines a negative reaction: "[The book] is an admittedly tough read by any standard. The frustratingly vague, almost stream of consciousness style loses most readers within the first few pages" (Kirst). Anyone in search of entertainment may well respond this way. Enjoyment of the book calls for interest in the author and attentiveness to details. Conventional narrative should not be expected in ART, despite its progressing in approximate chronological order. The memoirs are not about Walska's history, acquaintances, and times; even Hitler's rape of Poland in 1939 goes unnoticed. The subject is the author's inner self.

"Ganna Walska's Calvary," the unsigned *Newsweek* review of ART, accurately indicates the direction Walska's account follows. To hear her tell it, she had suffered much, carrying two crosses—her dismal singing career and her quest for inner clarity and peace. Yet, "I could not have lived a single day in tranquility if I had left anything undone in my search either for the spiritual truth or for the realization of my life's work—my singing" (ART, p. 335; all parenthetical numbers in this appendix refer to pages in ART). There were also the men in her life. "[B]ad luck has persisted in each of my romances as well as in every one of my marriages" (208). At least three of her husbands were disappointments, and the tuberculosis of the first heavily burdened his teenage bride. In her spiritual quests, Walska had gone from guru to guru and, although she initially believed in each of them, all had failed to supply enduring help for her singing and inner serenity for herself; she had a "sorrow impregnated life" (231).

This portrait is very selective. It tells of a brave, forceful Walska who sustained herself in pre-World War I Paris and, again, without fluency in English, in late-1910s New York. Though ill-equipped in vocal training, she pushed herself into opera; acquired one of the finest theatres in Paris; amassed a "luxurious" fortune; covered herself in jewels; sold perfumes; promoted women's rights in America; glittered in 1920s and 1930s Paris society as well as in her box at New York's Metropolitan Opera; won medals from governments; and built a horticultural monument in California. These notably successful Walskas appear in ART, but they are not the person whom the book is about. Her memoirs convey her as a self-made woman whose existence was full of disappointment and little pleasure.

Her appeals for sympathy can be contested. ART unhesitatingly displays the affluence in Walska's life. For a start, the second richest man in Russia fell in love with her (6–17). Later, the three houses, the theatre, the copious income, the famous jewelry, the Rolls Royces, the stays at luxury hotels, the Atlantic crossings on fabled liners, the celebrities and titled men and women with whom she consorted—these and other prizes do not suggest the paving stones of a "road of suffering." At one moment she drops the standpoint of victim to describe herself as a "practical, cold-minded woman" (385); she writes, "Whatever I have got I have got by hard work, unshakable tenacity and a very strong will" (24). She makes it clear, however, that these trappings brought neither delight nor contentment. It is as though readers, forgetting her upbeat book title, were intended to mourn the fame that escaped her as a singer rather than to marvel at the riches and ease that came her way.

A *via dolorosa* has no room for joy. Walska's memoirs omit many topics, especially those that include cheerful times. She wholly conceals the sources of her fortune. One learns fleetingly that once past the first, boylike husband, whom she loved, the only males she found lovable were Harold McCormick (husband no. 4) and the French conductor and singing coach Walther Straram. Neither of them is featured in ART. Husband no. 3—Alex Cochran—whom she loathed and lived with for a mere six months, appears again and again, whereas her family and friends are virtually unmentioned or even identified. A "brother who adores me" (185) is the sole family member noted, but not by name, and she cannot find anyone to whom she can leave her money (179). Because ART is for an American audience (471–75), her life in Paris—she was based there from 1920 to 1939, and was prominent in society—is underplayed. The key role that her ownership of the Théâtre des Champs-Élysées must have had for her, socially and professionally, is largely concealed. How this Pole became fluent in French, English, and other languages is wholly ignored. Although the convertible top of her limousine was open "winter and summer, sun or snow" (166), her robust constitution and excellent health earn no comment; we learn only that she was near-sighted and hated glasses (402). The medals she received from the Polish and French governments are downplayed. She misunderstands the details of her blow for women's rights. Among the houses she owned, the chateau outside Paris is alone in gaining her special notice, "the only place in which I feel ... less unhappy" (315). She recalls hardly any of the servants and assistants she employed over the years (400–401). Her chronology is loose, though approximately implied.

Often, Walska turns her attention from singing and husbands to provide long accounts of the "spiritual" personages and writings that she sampled with little profit. These pages contain "some of the most disorganized philosophical ramblings ever set down" ("Ganna Walska's Calvary"). They are crucial for one's appreciation of the book, however. Only a reader who welcomes these metaphysical meditations and debates and gladly retraces Walska's dealings with a sheaf of spiritual guides will be able to like

ART. She emphasizes that she neither smoked, drank, nor fancied black coffee (89, 178, 413), and she recoiled from dancing (207–208). The pleasures she avoided were, one fears, offset by the many (often sham) probers of the ultimate whom she cultivated in person or through their books, sometimes for long periods, until she became disillusioned. Near the end of ART, though recognizing that all these mentors ultimately failed to satisfy her needs, she expresses thanks to them (271, 456). There was no end to her search for a serenity she could not attain. A high degree of daring was required for her to pose as "Madame, the prima donna" before she ever sang on an operatic stage and afterward to perform rarely and without praise. Her insecurity was beyond help, until she turned to gardening, for which she received wide and deserved acclaim.

An ART in which achievements are subordinated to failures and disappointments is a long lament and a plea for sympathy: "I have only put down the most minute part of my sufferings as it would require volumes to tell all the trials I have experienced" (450). She maintains that she has opened her heart "in spite of my great reserve" (451). These remembrances, far from dwelling on victories, are rich in defeats. At their center, Walska has no illusions about her singing. Disasters are admitted, although excused. Several voice teachers are named; they seem miraculous at first, then eventually fade from sight without having durably improved a frail voice that was unable to do what young aspirants achieved with ease (459). The various gurus were equally impotent—except, perhaps, Theos Bernard, the young, California-born god with whom she was involved as the memoirs close. (An unpublished supplement to ART, "My Life with Yogi," fills in her subsequent disillusionment.) Luxury and comfort aside, the celebrity she attained exacted a heavy personal cost.

Always Room at the Top, a cheerful title, is wholly out of keeping with Walska's customary tone. Her normal, grieving voice is better displayed in her dedication—"Dedicated to all those who are seeking their place in the sun"—as though to say that winning just a little success is as much as one might expect. Her own lesson was that a long masquerade as a singing artist had proved lucrative especially in her fourth marriage, and had assured her an arresting social ascent, but was not much fun. Her later years, a protracted aging devoted to developing the magnificent Lotusland gardens, may not have been fun either; to go by her memoirs, Walska had little taste for pleasure of any kind. Nevertheless, this second life gave a grandiose, lasting, and deserved foundation to her fame.

NOTE: Was Walska the author of ART? Adams's biography indicates that the making and publication of ART involved an appreciable amount of editing and "Englishing" her manuscript. Walska cannot have been educated beyond high school (in her native Polish, or perhaps in Russian, with Polish only at home). Later, she added English and French—both learned without formal instruction. She claims in ART to have read newspapers in six languages daily, which may be only a slight exaggeration. In any case, she had noteworthy linguistic achievements, but they may not have extended to prose composition, even though she wrote much.

The biographer of Anita Blaine, Harold McCormick's sister, used a letter from Walska in the 1920s to offer a sample of what Anita called Walska's "idiosyncratic English":

> People made about me quite wrong impression, and they imagine that I am foolish, vane, consited personne who imagines that she can sing because she is pretty and through her husband's money tries to push herself. As a matter of fact I am entirely, not consited, but wrongly or rightly, (to be seen some day!) quite sure that something is in me and that I should deliver a message and leave something behind me as an example. I want other people to know that Harold did not marry a foolish woman, but a person who wants to give at cost of terrible suffering and undiscrable misery. (Harrison, p. 191)

This is the authentic voice of ART—Walska affirming that she had a destiny and that she would suffer much to fulfill it. The language is intelligible and would not take great effort for an editor to "English." It is very creditable for an uneducated woman. Instead of having to labor over Walska's language, the editor's main task may have been to trim what must have been a long manuscript. According to Adams (p. 270), Walska's principal editor was Jere Knight (1907–1996), a writer of some distinction.

Appendix 2.5

SUMMARY CATALOGUE OF THE GANNA WALSKA ARCHIVES AT LOTUSLAND

By the kindness of Rose Thomas, who has long worked with GWA, I have been supplied with selected material from the archives, for which I am very grateful. Brian Adams, Walska's biographer, had access to more, but because he did not annotate his book it is impossible to identify archival information. The first file of the archives, with letters from her husbands, would cast much needed light on her marriages. Some files, notably the one on Walska's Tibetan Collection, document a part of her life about which I cannot speak for lack of any information outside GWA. The most valuable comprehensive component of GWA may be one (or more) clipping book(s) that were commissioned by Walska herself; they contain all articles from newspapers and other publications about herself and were collected by a clipping firm. Regrettably, I have not seen it because it can be consulted only in the original, owing to the fragility of the contents. A final observation: any researcher at the GWA will find that Walska's handwriting is challenging.

The following list is quoted from a letter from Rose Thomas to the author (January 28, 2017).

Organized primarily by subject, the archives include files on:

Information and correspondence on her husbands.

Her jewelry collection, including letters and invoices from Cartier in Paris, London and New York

Her perfume business

Her music career, repertoire, song recitals, etc.

Her Tibetan Art Collection

Legal files

Correspondence in French, Italian, Polish, Russian, German, English

Philanthropic donations

Several drawers of written pages in her hand (this may be what Adams is referring to when he speaks about a diary), most of which went into ART. I have not found a journal or diary as such. There is the *My Life with Yogi* manuscript that we will be publishing in the future.

Copious files on the garden

Clipping books that GW had compiled by the Romeike agency. They begin around the time she first arrived in the US in 1918 through the 60s. These large books have every newspaper article written about her, and while they contain a lot of misinformation, they are an important source of 'who, what, when, & where.' They are very fragile as you can imagine and impossible to scan or copy.

Files containing hundreds of calling cards that read like the who's who of the Belle Époque. Additionally there is correspondence from musicians, artists, diplomats, royalty, writers and many other significant and historical figures of the time. I found a seating chart for a dinner party that included the names of Chanel and Sert.

This is just a partial listing of what we have here at Lotusland.

Bibliography

Adams, Brian. *Ganna: Diva of Lotusland* (N.p.: CreateSpace Independent Publishing Platform, 2015) Print-on-demand. Biography, with use of GWA. Frequent references to Walska diaries and papers, presumably the raw material for ART, which itself is also much used. Adams is my sole source for much information, notably about Walska's finances, and it supersedes Crawford and Gardner, but its references to sources are rare and uncritical, offering no weighing of the evidence, and therefore open to unverified allegations.

Alda, Frances. *Men, Women and Tenors* (Boston: Houghton Mifflin, 1937). Glimpse of life at Walska's Chateau de Galluis by a noted Australian soprano.

"Another Opera Singer Comes to the Screen," in *Moving Picture World* 29 (July 15, 1916): 464. Yale, Sterling Memorial Library, Film (microfilm) Coll. S2214.

Apraxine, P., and X. Demange. *La Divine Comtesse: Photographs of the Countess de Castiglione* (New Haven: Yale UP, 2000). In connection with an MMA exhibition. Translation of the catalogue prepared for a Musée d'Orsay exhibition. Many photographs are from Walska's outstanding collection, which was sold to MMA.

Aral, Blanche. *The Extraordinary Operatic Adventures of Blanche Aral,* tr. Ira Glackens (Portland, Ore.: Amadeus Press, 2002).

Barwell, E. H. G. *The Death Ray Man: The Biography of Grindell Matthews, Inventor and Pioneer* (London: Hutchinson, 1943). Virtually disregards personal life. Short paragraph about Walska.

Bernays, Edward L. *Biography of an Idea: Memoirs of a Public Relations Counsel* (New York: Simon and Schuster, 1965). The Walska section has errors, but also shrewd comments.

Biographical Document 1915. "Brooklyn Man to Marry Mme. Walska, Singer," *New York Evening Telegram* (August 12, 1915; clipping without page number, from GWA). This short announcement contains a capsule account of Walska's life evidently supplied by her. The first Walska "autobiography."

Biographical Document 1917. "Manager's Circular" (R. E. Johnston), reproduced almost entirely in *Musical America,* July 7, 1917 (both from GWA). A second capsule biography, designed to introduce Walska as a singer to prospective employers; summarized, p. 152, above.

Biographical Document 1921. "Cochran's Marriage to Polish Actress Illegal," clipping from an unidentified newspaper, September 27, [1921]; in MSSA, box 3, folder 179; *New York Herald,* image 1, datelined from Paris, September 26. Arising from the Cochran-Walska divorce. Full summary in Appendix 2.2, "Arcadie Eingorn and the Cochran Divorce."

Birmingham, Stephen. *The Grandes Dames* (New York: Simon and Schuster, 1982). Walska incidental to Edith McCormick. Many errors.

Blumenthal, George, as told to Arthur H. Menkin. *My Sixty Years in Show Business: A Chronicle of the American Theater, 1874–1934* (New York: Osberg, 1936). "Everything was dictated to me from memory" (p. xiv). Although Blumenthal had an astonishing memory, it is evident that the dates are unreliable. But the memories are *sine ira et studio,* and I could not resist appropriating some.

Chiacos, Elias, "Madame of Lotusland: Ganna Walska," in *Montecito Magazine* 11, no. 2 (1991): 28–33, 61–63. Good, impressionistic account of the Lotusland years.

Conway, James J. "Dress-down Friday: Ganna Walska." https://strangeflowers.wordpress.com/2012/03/02/dress-down-friday-ganna-walska/

———. "Stranger Than Fiction" (April 10, 2012). https://strangeflowers.wordpress.com/2012/04/10/stranger-than-fiction/ (accessed June 4, 2013).

Crawford, Sharon. *Ganna Walska Lotusland: The Garden and Its Creators* (Santa Barbara, Cal.: Ganna Walska Lotusland Foundation, 1996). Excellent on Lotusland. As the publisher's name suggests, this is at least the semiofficial biography of Walska; it is short and lacks details. Crawford had access to Lotusland materials (e.g., the unpublished continuation of Walska's memoirs). In view of its origins and intermittent inaccuracy, the book should be read with great caution. It was the source for Gardner, who sometimes differs from Crawford.

Dana, Charles L. "Obituary: Dr. Joseph Fraenkel," in *Journal of Nervous and Mental Disease* 56 (November 1922): 546-47.

Dedmon, Emmet. *Fabulous Chicago* (New York: Random House, 1953).

Erté [Romain de Tirtoff]. *My Life, My Art: An Autobiography* (New York: Dutton, 1989). Erté was a celebrated twentieth-century artist, who sometimes has been called the "father" of Art décoratif. This book from 1989 adds little to the 1975 autobiography (below), much of which is reprinted.

—————. *Things I Remember: An Autobiography* (New York: Quadrangle, 1975). Valuable pages on Walska by a well-informed observer, who also was a gossip and liked a good story.

Foster, Jonathan. *The Death Ray: The Secret Life of Harry Grindell Matthews* (N.p.: Inventive Publishing, 2008). Informative about the Walska marriage.

"Ganna Walska's Calvary," in *Newsweek* (September 6, 1943: 92, 94). The only review of ART listed in *Readers' Guide to Periodical Literature* for 1943–1945. (See also, Leighton, "Marriages and Opera Make Interesting Memoirs.") Some comments are included with newspaper reviews that accompanied notice of the book's publication: *Hartford Courant* (October 31, 1943): SM14; *Chicago Tribune* (August 29, 1943): E19. Other newspaper notices offer little praise.

Gardner, Theodore Roosevelt. *Lotusland: A Photographic Odyssey* (Santa Barbara, Cal.: Allan A. Knoll, 1995). Primarily a picture book with biographical material perhaps drawn from Lotusland archives; indicates that research was by Crawford, but Gardner is richer in information and differs about important details. It needs to be used with caution.

"Granger, Hartley" (pseud.). "First Complete Story of Fascinating Ganna Walska," in *Minneapolis Morning (Sunday) Tribune* (1928): December 9 (pp. 64–65); December 16 (pp. 68–69); December 23 (pp. 50–51); (1929): January 6 (pp. 62–63); January 13 (pp. 58–59); January 27 (pp. 58–59); February 3 (pp. 90–91); February 10 (pp. 58–59); February 17 (pp. 68–69); and February 24 (pp. 62–63). A sensation-inclined, ten-installment "biography" of Walska to the eve of her divorce by McCormick. Includes material about the first four husbands. Unreliable but worth reading as it sums up Walska journalism to that date. The theme, not far from mine, is that Walska gained wealth and comfort, but not what she really wanted—fame as an opera diva. Not unsympathetic about her singing.

Hackett, Paul G. "Barbarian Lands: Theos Bernard, Tibet, and the American Religious Life." Ph.D. diss. Columbia Univ., 2008.

———. *Theos Bernard, The White Lama: Tibet, Yoga, and American Religious Life* (New York: Columbia UP, 2012). A published version of Hackett's dissertation. Based in part on Bernard archives, which Hackett indexed at the Bancroft Library, University of California, Berkeley.

Hafstad, Margaret R., ed. *Guide to the McCormick Collection of the State Historical Society of Wisconsin* (Madison: Wisconsin Historical Society, 1973).

Harrison, Gilbert A. *A Timeless Affair: The Life of Anita McCormick Blaine* (Chicago: University of Chicago Press, 1979). Anita was Harold McCormick's sister and not a Walska fan. Harrison was her grandson-in-law.

Hayes, Virginia. "*Enemy of the Average Exhibition,*" in *Lotusland: Newsletter for Members* 23, no. 2 (spring 2014): 1–3.

Jeffers, H. Paul. *Diamond Jim Brady: Prince of the Gilded Age* (New York: Wiley, 2001). Refutes Brady's alleged infatuation with Walska.

Johnson, Susan. "Lotusland," in *Word Worth: On Line Magazine of Ideas and the Arts* 2, no. 3 (March 2002). https://www.wordworth.org/

Archives/2002i.3WordWorthvIIMar.pdf. Excellent on the garden today and Lotusland's endowment.

Lawrence, Marjorie. *Interrupted Memory: The Story of My Life* (New York: Appleton Century Croft, 1949).

Kirst, Lynn P. "Fashion Game: Ganna Walska, Diva of Her Time," in *Montecito Journal* (Glossy Edition, Summer–Fall 2010): 28–32, 34, 36. http://themjmag.com/4/files/assets/basic-html/page28.html (accessed July 12, 2017). Stunning photographs of young Walska.

———. "Landmarks: A New Era for Lotusland," in *Montecito Journal* 2 (2009–2010): 48–54. Important information on how and by whom Lotusland was developed into a garden showplace.

Leighton, Mary. "Marriages and Opera Make Interesting Memoirs," in *Cincinnati Inquirer* (September 5, 1943): 38.

MacPherson, Sean K. "Enemy of the Average," in *New York Times* (April 14, 2002). Mainly about Lotusland.

Mahler-Werfel, Alma. *Mein Leben* (Frankfurt a/M: Fischer, 1960), pp. 50–52. Important but somewhat fanciful about Dr. Fraenkel.

Marsh, Barbara. *A Corporate Tragedy: The Agony of International Harvester Company* (Garden City, N.Y.: Doubleday, 1985). Informative in view of the large block of IH shares in Walska's fortune.

Matz, Mary Jane. *The Many Lives of Otto Kahn* (New York: Pendragon Press, 1963). Important for the Fraenkel marriage.

McCormick, Cyrus. *The Century of the Reaper* (Boston: Houghton Mifflin, 1931).

McCormick, Harold F. *Via Pacis: How Terms of Peace Can Be Automatically Prepared While the War Is Still Going on* (Chicago: A.C. McClurg, 1917). Written in Zurich in 1915. In McCormick's plan for moving toward peace, he seems to be applying the methods of business negotiation to ending World War I. The Yale copy had been presented to Yale President Hadley.

"McCormick, Harold Fowler," in *Marquis Who Was Who in America 1607–1984* (New Providence, N.J.: Marquis Who's Who, 2009).

"McCormick, Harold Fowler," in *National Cyclopedia of American Biography* 35 (New York: J. T. White, 1948), pp. 9–10. Very full.

Mintzer, Charles. *Rosa Raisa: A Biography of a Diva with Selections from Her Memoirs* (Boston: Northeastern UP, 2001).

Monson, Karen. *Alma Mahler, Muse to Genius: From Fin-de-siècle Vienna to Hollywood's Heyday* (Boston: Houghton Mifflin, 1983). About the Fraenkel courtship of Alma.

Moore, Edward C. *Forty Years of Opera in Chicago* (New York: Liveright, 1930), pp. 214–15.

Nash, Jay Robert. *People to See: An Anecdotal History of Chicago's Makers and Breakers* (Piscataway, N.J.: New Century, 1981). Sensationalist; marginally reliable.

Needham, Wesley E. "Edna Bryner Schwab: Tibetan Scholar and Yale Benefactor," in *Yale University Library Gazette* 44, no. 1 (July 1969): 21–29. Notes Beinecke 1957 acquisition of 395-volume Tibetan collection from the Theos Bernard estate (p. 27). Unfortunately thin. There appear to have also been acquisitions in 1963 and 1964.

———. "The Tibetan Collection at Yale," in *Yale University Library Gazette* 34, no. 3 (January 1960): 127–33. Names the benefactor who paid for the acquisition of the Bernard collection.

Owens, Mitchell. "Garden of the Slightly Macabre," in *New York Times* (August 22, 1996): C1. https://www.nytimes.com/1996/08/22/garden/garden-of-the-slightly-macabre.html?searchResultPosition=1. Brief but good, especially on Lotusland.

Pener, Degen. "The Cone Heads," in *New York Times Magazine* (August 17, 2003): Sec. 6, 138. https://www.nytimes.com/2003/08/17/magazine/the-cone-heads.html?searchResultPosition=1. Important article on cycads and Lotusland. A little on Ganna Walska, including a 1971 sale of jewels.

Protzman-Davis, Todd. "Divorce—Edith Style," at The Villa Turicum Blog: https://villaturicum.blogspot.com/2011/02/divorce-edith-style.html. About McCormick's first divorce.

Raffestin-Nadaud, Charles. "Les femmes d'aujourd'hui dans la vie et dans l'art: Mme Ganna Walska," in *Revue internationale des questions politiques, diplomatiques, économiques*, 14e année (November 30, 1924): 3–5.

Reese, Kirsten. "Ganna Walska—*Lotusland*—*Lotussound*. Eine (Ex-) Sängerin, eine Garten, eine Klanginstallation," in *Musikgeschichten— Vermittlungsformen: Festschrift für Beatrix Borchard zum 60. Geburtstag*, ed. Martina Bick et al. (Cologne: Böhlau, 2010), pp. 281–94. A careful article arising from Reese's sound installation at Lotusland. Contains a careful but not definitive inventory of Walska's singing performances.

Schiaparelli, Elsa. *Shocking Life* (London: Dent, 1954).

Stember, Nadejda. "Story of My Life," as dictated to Olga Fuhrman in 1935; tr. Natalie Warren. "Victor Karlovich Stember, 1863–1921." www.victorstember.com/stember_gallery.aspx (To read the text, click on the small reproduction of "Ganna Walska-McCormick: Artwork ID: 122"— the center image in row 2.) See Appendix 2.1.

Straram, Enrich. *Histoire croisée d'une institution et d'une famille: Le Théâtre des Champs-Élysées et les Straram,* at www.musimem.com/champs-elysees_ straram.htm (retrieved August 15, 2019). This and the next item are relevant to the 1920s and early 1930s, especially musical life in Paris. Both Walther and Enrich Straram were very important to Walska in connection with the TCE.

Straram, Walther. "Biographie: Violiniste, pianiste et chef de chant," at Walther Straram (1876–1933). http://straram.fr/biographie.htm (retrieved October 20, 2019).

Swartley, Ariel. "A Diva Who Loved High Drama," in *Los Angeles Times* (March 10, 2005). http://articles.latimes.com/2005/mar/10/home/ hm-lotusland10. Impressions of a visit to Lotusland.

Tentler, Courtney, and Virginia Hayes. "Romancing the Garden," in *Lotusland: Newsletter for Members* 22, no.3 (summer 2013): 1–3. A rundown of Walska's marriages that endorses the "authorized" narrative of her origins.

Towers, Dolores Delargo. "A Remarkable Madame," at blog of Dolores Delargo Towers Museum of Camp. https://doloresdelargotowers .blogspot.com/2011/02/remarkable-madame.html (retrieved July 12, 2017). Unsympathetic. Filled with inaccuracies.

Veenhof, Douglas. *White Lama: The Life of Tantric Yogi Theos Bernard, Tibet's Lost Emissary to the New World* (New York: Doubleday Religion, 2011). Detailed on Bernard and his marriage to Walska, but provides little pertinent to Walska's life before 1940.

Wagner, Charles L. *Seeing Stars* (New York: Putnam, 1940), pp. 329–31.

Walska, Ganna. *Always Room at the Top* (New York: R.R. Smith, 1943); 2d ed. (reprint), 2015. A necessarily one-sided but indispensable source for her life. Not boastful. Smith, a vanity publisher, charged Walska $4,000 to publish her manuscript. Adams has much on the publication. The book is weighted toward spiritual quests, regrettably. See my review, Appendix 2.4, "The Sorrows of Madame Walska." For other reviews, see "Ganna Walska's Calvary," above.

———. "My Life with Yogi." Unpublished memoir that supplements ART. The MS is at Lotusland. After a delay of 30-odd years since Walska's death without publication, it seems possible that Lotusland has tacitly decided that this complement to ART will be kept from general view. Not seen by me. Adams's disproportionate account of the Bernard marriage (pp. 260–334) must derive from it.

Woon, Basil. *The Paris That's Not in the Guide Books* (New York: R.M. McBride, 1931).

Digital and Audio Resources

Internet. Google searches have been of continual assistance. Wikipedia has been a constant resource for the instant identification and introduction of secondary persons and places. ProQuest, HathiTrust, and JStor have supplied newspapers and books, many of which would have remained unknown without the search capabilities of the Internet. I have done my best in citations to provide enough guidance to permit access. The Library of Congress database "Chronicling America: Historic American Newspapers" (https://chroniclingamerica.loc.gov) is very rich but, in my experience, challenging to use. During editing of my manuscript, I came upon "Gallica BnF," an extraordinary collection of French sources, including files of all major Paris dailies. They were invaluable to me for documenting Walska's time in Paris in 1913–14, but regrettably for nothing else. The newspaper database of the Bibliothèque nationale de France is very hard to access.

Recordings of Walska. YouTube, at "Ganna Walska," plays a recording of Georges Thill singing a duet from Massenet's *Manon.* The soprano Mary McCormic, once confused with Walska (McCormick), no longer is. (With thanks for the help of Thomas Murray, Yale University Organist.)

Adams (p. 478), supplies a list of thirteen discs at Lotusland of Walska's voice. The discs have not been professionally appraised and badly need to be transferred to more up-to-date media. This is an important inaccessible source, which Lotusland needs to be encouraged to make available.

Lotusland. The articles listed above concerning Lotusland are a selection, because that part of Walska's life is not examined here. YouTube includes many entries under the heading "Ganna Walska." Most of them concern Lotusland and supply photographic surveys of the gardens. The one biographical podcast, entitled "The Many Husbands of Ganna Walska," is a poor excuse for biography.

Postscript

Ganna Walska is thinly disguised as "Hanna Mazurka" in the novel *Enemy of the Average* (Santa Barbara, CA: Knoll, 1998) by Margaret Nicol. This character lacks any redeeming feature. She is bent single-mindedly on enrichment by fraud, and is one of the most repellent heroines ever fashioned. Mazurka also lives amid impossibilities: oceanliners dock in Paris; trains run from Paris to Estonia during World War I; Hanna reads music, plays the piano, and drives a car despite never having learned how to do these things. Nicol, a Santa Barbara resident and gardener, is a neighbor to Lotusland. It is hard to imagine why one would write this slipshod novel except to cause damage to Lotusland by traducing the life of its founder.

When *The Industrialist and the Diva* was in production, there appeared *Ganna Walska: Portraits of an Era* (Santa Barbara, CA: Hania Tallmadge, 2019). Hania Tallmadge, the book's author-compiler and publisher, is Ganna Walska's niece. Her book is an album of portraits of Ganna Walska drawn from the trove of photographs at Lotusland. The text comments on the illustrations without intending to be biographical, but the pictures illuminate Walska's life. Although the group photo on page 34 is said to show Walska beside Alexander Smith Cochran, it is very hard to find a resemblance between the man shown and any other known picture of Cochran. (It also is the only photograph of him in the book.)

INDEX

INDEX